GW00391539

highSurf

the world's most inspiring surfers
waveriding as a way of life
the ocean as teacher

by tim baker

HarperSports
An imprint of HarperCollinsPublishers

Harper*Sports*
An imprint of HarperCollins*Publishers*

First published in Australia in 2007
by HarperCollins*Publishers* Australia Pty Limited
ABN 36 009 913 517
www.harpercollins.com.au

Copyright © Froth Productions Pty Ltd 2007

The right of Tim Baker to be identified as the author of this
work has been asserted by him under the *Copyright Amendment
(Moral Rights) Act 2000.*

This work is copyright. Apart from any use as permitted under the
Copyright Act 1968, no part may be reproduced, copied, scanned, stored
in a retrieval system, recorded, or transmitted, in any form or by any
means, without the prior written permission of the publisher.

HarperCollins*Publishers*
25 Ryde Road, Pymble, Sydney, NSW 2073, Australia
31 View Road, Glenfield, Auckland 10, New Zealand
77–85 Fulham Palace Road, London, W6 8JB, United Kingdom
2 Bloor Street East, 20th floor, Toronto, Ontario M4W 1A8, Canada
10 East 53rd Street, New York NY 10022, USA

National Library of Australia Cataloguing-in-Publication data:

Baker, Tim.
  High surf
  ISBN 978 0 7322 8486 2 (pbk.).
  1. Surfing. 2. Life skills. I. Title.
797.32

Cover design by Gra Murdoch at Aqualuna Design
Front cover images:
Top Ross Clarke-Jones tackles a monster wave at Todos Santos in Baja Mexico. (Photo by Rob Brown)
Bottom Sometimes getting there is half the fun — coastal rock walk. (Photo by Stuart Gibson)
Back cover image: Waiting for the day's first wave. (Photo by Hilton Dawe)
Illustrations and internal design by Matt Stanton, HarperCollins Design Studio
Typeset in 11.5pt/18pt Bembo by Helen Beard, ECJ Australia Pty Limited
Printed and bound in Australia by Griffin Press
79gsm Bulky Paperback White used by HarperCollins*Publishers* is a natural, recyclable product made
from wood grown in a combination of sustainable plantation and regrowth forests. It also contains up to
a 20% portion of recycled fibre. The manufacturing processes conform to the environmental regulations
in Tasmania, the place of manufacture.

5 4 3 2   08 09 10

To Kirsten,

for sharing the ride

and

in honour of Duke Kahanamoku,

who pushed us all into our first wave.

contents

'There is a
wisdom
in the wave . . .'
DORIAN 'DOC' PASKOWITZ

foreword

The central question posed throughout this collection of surfing profiles, anecdotes and quotes is: 'What have I learnt from surfing?' If I were to ask myself that question, the short answer is 'a lot'. But that hasn't always been the case.

Like the undulations of a wave itself, it has varied; at some stages in life the answer has been, 'everything', and at others, 'very little'. However, this question has been at the core of almost every surf story I've ever written over many, many years, seventeen of which make up my 2006 published collection *Wind on the Water*. There are 40,000 words in that book; a figure which would seem to indicate (as do the reflections here in *High Surf*) that there's more to surfing than surfing, and that the question about what has been learnt is quite profound!

From the moment you become aware of undulatory vibrations and wave energy, whether through surfing, awareness of the ocean, or repeated, detached observations of life around you, strange understandings enter the realm of your consciousness. The wash of words such as ebb and flow, rise and fall, high times and low times, night and day, rich and poor, male and female, black and white, yin and yang, life and death, and so on, come to assume some special significance.

These are things you have to discover in your own way, alone, and in your own time. As far as surfing itself is concerned, not one of them has anything to do with media and surf industry clichés.

The line of our lives may appear to be straight, from a drop of semen and a tiny egg, to a pile of ashes, but in reality we are forever rising and falling, riding waves. One of them is something we call time, and which we measure in seconds, minutes, hours, days, years, and so on.

What we perceive as a linear phenomenon is in fact a circulatory one, and something that is beyond measurement. Our little world is actually part of a wave that is endlessly circulating up and down, over and around, cycling and recycling this way and that way. Sometimes it feels the bottom and feathers or breaks on a sandbar or reef in the form of a setback or a hiccup in our lives. It then re-forms to roll on and on, its energy emanating from who knows where?

This is the wave that is closest to us, it's the one we call life, and sometimes think we understand. But in fact it is only a component part of a bigger wave, which in turn carries us onto other waves beyond our comprehension, reaching out forever into the cosmos.

At the end of our lives we pull off our little wave, and stand utterly alone, staring into infinity. That's where our ultimate wave stands waiting to be ridden, and it's not a tow-in, it has to be paddled into alone and unaided!

That's one of the things I've learnt from surfing, along with being free. The two are in fact part of the same wave. The challenge at my age is to stay with it. In fact the challenge of every age is to stay with it!

As the reflections here in *High Surf* make abundantly clear, that is exactly what millions of surfers are doing every day — hanging in there! It's what we've always done.

The publication of this book is a long overdue recognition of another piece in the complex jigsaw of just what surfing is, and what it means to be a surfer. The fact that writers like Tim Baker and others are now addressing questions such as 'What have I learnt from surfing?' is a cause for optimism. It means that so long as the earth has oceans, the indefinable wave of nature that is surfing will continue to roll, and somewhere, somebody will be riding it!

JACK FINLAY, WRITER, SURFER

introduction

{ why surfing? why now? }

*Surfers are the 'throw-aheads' of mankind,
not the dregs; they aren't the black sheep of
humanity, but the futurists and they are
leading the way to where man ultimately
wants to be. The act of the ride is the epitome
of 'be here now', and the tube ride is the most
acute form of that. Which is: your future is
right ahead of you, the past is exploding
behind you, your wake is disappearing, your
footprints are washed from the sand. It's a
non-productive, non-depletive act that's done
purely for the value of the dance itself. And
that is the destiny of man . . . It's perfectly
logical to me that surfing is the spiritual
aesthetic style of the liberated self and that's
the model for the future.*

TIMOTHY LEARY, *SURFER* MAGAZINE,
JANUARY 1978

In a boardroom in Bangkok, several hundred miles from the nearest surf beach, big wave rider Ross Clarke-Jones lectures a group of advertising industry directors. Their conference is titled 'The Year of Living Dangerously', and Ross is their impeccably qualified guest speaker. His topic: risk taking, trusting instincts, jumping through windows of opportunity — the tenets of surfing huge waves neatly mirroring the latest business school doctrine.

In New York, eminent scientist and biotechnician Vezen Wu, after discovering a new form of antibiotic in carnivorous plants and developing cutting-edge medical software, has his world of computers, petri dishes and microscopes abruptly turned upside down when he discovers surfing. He finds himself thinking about waves all day long, doodling them in his notepads between dedicated surf sessions in New York's grey and chilly waters. So smitten is Wu by the sense of euphoria surfing gives him, he devises a new research project — running clinical trials using surfing to treat depression. Wu becomes convinced that the negative ions generated by breaking waves could provide a natural alternative to anti-depressant drugs.

In California, professional longboarder Israel Paskowitz, of the legendary Paskowitz surfing family, discovers that taking his young autistic son surfing dramatically helps his condition. Israel and his wife Danielle soon launch Surfers Healing, a charitable foundation dedicated to introducing autistic children to the calming powers of the waves.

In Indonesia, New Zealand born doctor Dave Jenkins takes time out for a surfing holiday in the remote Mentawai Islands. The oppressive health problems of the local people provokes an epiphany that sees Dr Dave throw in his well-paid medical career in Singapore, mortgage his house, and launch a humanitarian aid agency. Surf Aid International soon attracts the support of the world-wide surfing community, drastically reduces rampant malaria in the Mentawais, and comes to the aid of remote island communities devastated by the 2004 tsunami. In so doing, this tiny group of surfers earns the praise of the World Health Organization, the US Navy, the UN, and established aid agencies like AusAID and NZAID.

In south-west France, wealthy English industrialist Greville Mitchell takes his wife Lisa and surfing son for a seaside holiday, to coincide with the French leg of the pro-surfing tour. He wanders down the beach one afternoon in Lacanau and becomes entranced by the spectacle of pro surfers Luke Egan and Jeff Booth surfing a heat. So mesmerised is Greville by the surfers' unearthly grace on the waves, he wades waist deep into the ocean to get a closer look. He returns to his family's holiday apartment wearing soaking trousers and a glazed expression. His wife Lisa claims he has never been the same. Greville soon diverts large chunks of his personal fortune into funding a full-time medical team on tour for the surfers, and propping up the sport's cash-strapped world governing body. A chronic workaholic, Greville takes up longboarding and credits surfing with literally saving his life.

In Australia, surfwear label Billabong, launched on Gold Coast surfer Gordon Merchant's kitchen table in 1973, debuts on the stock exchange at $2.30 a share after a massively oversubscribed public float. Five years later, its shares top $15 and are prized blue-ribbon stock, while the company founder retires to go surfing at his favourite wave havens around the world, his personal worth estimated at over $500 million. And he's not alone. A quick scan of the BRW rich list reveals no fewer than nine of the top 200 wealthiest people in Australia made their fortunes from surfing-related enterprises. That's nearly five per cent of the country's mega-rich.

As a 'millionaire factory', surfing holds its own with almost any other business sector.

What is going on here? Weren't surfers once reviled and despised as drop-outs, drug addicts and threats to public morality? Weren't parents once aghast at the onset of the dreaded waveriding disease — that rendered the stricken victims useless for all gainful employment, with no hope of a cure?

Today, surfers are respected and admired as highly skilled and well-paid elite athletes, visionary business leaders, creative artists, bold adventurers, all somehow tapped into a seemingly bottomless well-spring of inspiration, good health and vitality.

Surfing, it seems, is suddenly everywhere. About 2.8 million Australians claim to surf, according to the latest Sweeney Report, the nation's most comprehensive sports survey. The booming surf school industry introduces another 250,000 newcomers (and rising) to the waves each year, more than half of them female.

Top pro surfers earn more than our leading cricketers and footballers. Boys barely out of their teens — no doubt told they'd never amount to anything if they surfed their lives away — are multi-millionaires with global reach, revered throughout Australia, North and South America, coastal Europe, Japan, Africa and beyond.

Big-wave rider Laird Hamilton advertises American Express and his film *Riding Giants* opens the Sundance Film Festival to rave reviews. Every Hollywood actor and rock star worth their sea salt seems to cite surfing as their chosen recreation. Even if they don't actually surf, they try to look as if they do. 'Seventy-five per cent of the hours I'm in one pair of camouflage swim trunks — no shirt, no shoes. General surfer vibe. I don't surf, but I hang out and look like one,' perennial rock and roll survivor Iggy Pop reported recently.

A new hair product promises 'surf hair . . . for that "just off the beach" look'. A business article on share market predictions for 2006 uses an image of a surfer riding a huge wave, with the headline: 'Few people saw this year's market gains coming. Who's to say the next wave won't be just as big?' Our two most pervasive forms of technology rely on surfing metaphors: we 'surf the net' and 'channel surf'. Itinerant travellers are said to be 'couch surfing'. Surfing seems to be the image, metaphor and recreation of choice for our times. Why surfing? Why now?

I'd argue that the social shift surfing has undergone over the last forty years is as dramatic as feminism, the Civil Rights movement, or the rise of Indigenous cultures world-wide. The claims of acid guru Timothy Leary in 1978 don't seem quite so far-fetched nearly thirty years later: 'Surfers are the "throw-aheads" of mankind, not the dregs; they aren't the black sheep of humanity, but the futurists and they are leading the way to where man ultimately wants to be.'

Leary's notion that life is a dance, and that surfers had been awoken to this great truth, might seem less like acid-soaked hippy idealism in these increasingly uncertain times, when living in the moment seems an eminently sensible response to the horrors of the nightly news, the threats of global warming and terrorism. This dance, Leary theorised, was the real point of our existence, rather than the grim accumulation of material wealth. And he hoped surfers might awaken wider society to this message — he saw this as their mission on the planet.

Surfing provides instant meditation. It absolutely requires you remain clear and present, in the moment, in the state yogis call 'no mind', undistracted by thoughts of the past or future. Leary hoped surfers might apply and spread this way of being to life on land. Admittedly, old Timothy consumed vast quantities of lysergic acid before he had his earthly remains catapulted into outer space. But, presumably, you don't spend that much time in an altered state without gaining a few insights.

Today, surfing's influence on mainstream society has never been greater. This acceptance is something surfers have both dreaded and craved

— threatening its once maverick counter-culture mystique, while providing career paths and business opportunities once inconceivable. Thirty years ago, the Australian Tax Office was incredulous when they received tax returns with 'professional surfer' optimistically entered under 'occupation', sending them back with a curt note that there was no such vocation. Today, surfing significantly improves our country's balance of payments.

Yet, as surfing's stocks have risen, it seems its essential teachings are in danger of being lost. As surfing's influence has grown, we have begun to miss the point. Rather than the mainstream moving towards us — to embrace surfing's lessons of flow, balance, spontaneity, connection to nature — surfing has moved towards the mainstream. Surfers have become more materialistic, scheming, opportunistic, competitive, ruthless — in business, sport and their simple recreation. Surfing is finally getting its message across, but it is the wrong message, contrived to sell clothing to the masses — a youth fixation, greed, ego, mindless hero worship, and the nonsense that a lifestyle can be acquired through the right arrangement of logos.

The popularity of surfing, growing crowds, and the material rewards it increasingly offers, seem to have drowned out the gentle, soothing, guiding lessons of the sea. It is a very different thing — almost a different pastime altogether — to sit out at a remote surf break, happily trading waves with friends, than to take part in the hassling, squabbling and jockeying for waves that go on at the teeming city beachbreaks most of us surf. It once seemed possible that the joy, ease and spontaneity of surfing might begin to inform and overflow into our lives on land. 'By simply surfing, we are supporting the revolution,' '66 world champion Nat Young once famously declared. Increasingly, it seems the 'dog eat dog' madness of a work–earn–spend capitalist society has spilled over into the waves.

Many lifelong surfers around the world share a sense of mourning, at a loss of innocence, a corruption of our once pure pastime, co-opted by business interests more concerned with their bottom line than their bottom turn.

Imagine for example if yoga existed purely to sell yoga clothing and products to the masses, and to anoint yoga 'champions' in heated competition. Some yogis claim this is precisely what has happened with the corporatisation of yoga in the USA, and they lament the resultant loss or dilution of much of its ancient wisdom. Eminent yogi Swami Rama wrote in 1991: 'Like many profound, beautiful, and powerful arts and sciences, yoga has suffered from the spiritual poverty of the modern world — it has been trivialised, watered down, or reduced to clichés. The deep and eternal essence of yoga has been misrepresented and packaged for personal profit by clever people.'

Surfing, in the hands of big business and the competitive machine, seems to have suffered a similar fate. When competition is the model held up for young surfers to aspire to, every surf session becomes a heat drill. Hassling and jockeying for position become more important than the joy of the ride and sharing the stoke. Brilliantly talented young surfers swear and punch their boards when they fall off, and walk away bitter and broken when lofty dreams of a professional career fail to manifest. The tide of beginners who have entered surfing in the age of crowds, competition and commercialism believe this is what surfing is about — and earnestly emulate the grim exertions of their heroes.

For some, surfing is about dedicated, disciplined, competitive athleticism, and there is nothing wrong with that. But for many others, the great bulk of the surfing population I'd argue, riding waves would be best seen as something else altogether — sanctuary, therapy, creative self-expression, meditation and health tonic all rolled into a blissful watery release from life on land.

I believe surfing can provide a road map, or at least a guiding star, to one of the most healthy, fulfilling and joyful existences it is possible for a human being to lead on planet Earth. This seems especially true in the early stages of the twenty-first century when so much of our adventure, freedom and interaction with the natural world is under threat. The practice of waveriding teaches balance, flow, connection with nature and acceptance of the whimsical play of the elements. It tunes us into the cyclical patterns of the planet: seasons and weather systems, swells and tides — what we might consider the Earth's natural pulse. And when we are in touch with the pulse of the planet, perhaps we are less likely to trash the place. Surfers may be among the first to register the planet's ill-health firsthand, the proverbial canaries in the coal mine. Perhaps, too, surfing teaches us something about life's wave-like nature — its peaks and troughs, its sets and lulls, the tide's ebb and flow.

'It's easy to learn in the ocean. I learnt there because you're very close to nature. You're in it! You're immersed in it! You learn to wait patiently. There's a time for everything to happen. You've got to learn to wait for your wave. You can't make it come to you. It teaches you about life,' Californian surf pioneer Tom Blake once observed.

Modern quantum physics and ancient mysticism alike tell us that all life is made up of waves — light waves, sound waves, radio waves. Even physical matter, that which appears solid, is little more than a field of energy, vibrating at a certain frequency. Waves. The ocean surf we ride is the only form in which wave energy can be experienced on a human scale. The waves most of us surf are, on average, around head high. They move about as fast as we can run or paddle a surfboard. In many ways, they can push us close to, or beyond, the limits of our endurance, taking us to our edge, in an intensely physical, spontaneous, non-negotiable exchange. Perhaps, through our interaction with them, we can come to understand much about the nature of wave energy, how to use it to propel us forwards, how to dance amid its awesome power, and how to avoid its potentially destructive force. The ocean, I've come to believe, is simply life made visible, a convenient parallel reality where the nature of wave energy is easily observable, its lessons immediate, tangible and powerful.

I'm reminded of a favourite Michael Leunig cartoon. A simple wavy line bisects the page horizontally, forming a series of peaks and troughs. Atop every peak, a little man strides out confidently, smiling, chest puffed out. At the bottom of each trough a disconsolate stooped figure trudges dejectedly along. Oblivious to the wave-like nature of existence, each of these characters believes this instant is their whole life — this giddy high or crushing low, this wild descent or daunting climb. When we step back and observe the big picture we realise life consists of hills and valleys, peaks and troughs. Waves. And the surfer of life knows waves are there to be ridden, to propel us onward. Without this broad vision, life's ups and downs can feel like a bumpy road rather than a potential fun park.

I've often marvelled at those charmed surfers who always seem to turn up where and when the surf is best, or who paddle out at the precise place and time to catch the day's biggest and best wave. It is as if their sonar is more finely tuned to the unseen signals sent by these pulses of energy. I eventually figured, too, that the canny business person who buys and sells at the right time, forecasts trends or recognises cycles, is surfing their life, instinctively adjusting to ever-changing circumstances, riding the waves of pitching market forces. What is the successful day trader doing other than recognising peaks and troughs?

I began to suspect that this understanding of wave energy could apply to many areas of life, and that surfers were intuitively in touch with a kind of wisdom that much of the rest of society was trying to learn, that surfers knew things they didn't even know they knew. And that maybe Timothy Leary was on to something after all.

Staff writer for the *New Yorker* Malcom Gladwell, also a leading business consultant, recently published a book entitled *Blink: the power of thinking without thinking*. In it, he argues for the power of snap, instinctive judgements over analytical, reasoned decision making — the very stuff Ross Clarke-Jones preaches to his business clients. Gladwell prescribes getting back in touch with our instincts and intuition and trusting our snap decisions. His ideas are revolutionising the business world, and he consults for major American corporations wanting to integrate his theories.

Psychologist Mihaly Csikszentmihalyi (pronounced 'Chicks send me high'!) has helped pioneer the study of positive psychology for the past twenty years. His book *Flow: the psychology of optimal experience* describes something he calls the 'flow state', which he believes is the ideal condition for human happiness. The characteristics of the flow state are complete involvement, focus and concentration, a feeling of ecstasy, inner clarity, a sense of serenity even as your skills are tested to their limits, obliviousness to the passing of time, and an appreciation of the activity for its own sake. That is, it doesn't need to produce anything other than a sense of well-being. It's a condition that will sound immediately familiar to any surfer.

Csikszentmihalyi based his findings on interviews with thousands of subjects from all walks of life: chess players, rock climbers, musicians, basketball players, doctors — anyone who engaged in an activity that gave them a profound sense of fulfilment. Remarkably, he didn't speak to any surfers, but his description of the flow state seems to apply to surfing more perfectly than almost any other human activity: 'Everyone said that it was like being carried by a current, spontaneous, effortless like a flow. You also forget time and are not afraid of being out of control. You think you can control the situation if you need to. But it's hard because the challenges are hard. It feels effortless and yet it's extremely dependent on concentration and skill . . . In other words, the challenges were in balance with the skills. And when those conditions were present, you began to forget all the things that bothered you in everyday life, forget the self as an entity separate from what was going on — you felt you were a part of something greater and you were just moving along with the logic of the activity.'

This absence of thought, this dissolution of our sense of self, is precisely the state of 'no mind' yogis cultivate. There are growing bodies of evidence — scientific, metaphysical, spiritual — that this state of no mind is really the optimum condition for general well-being. Healing, creativity, judgement, response times, performance levels of all kinds are enhanced when we achieve this state.

Unfortunately for us humans, we have created a world so complex we often feel like we need every ounce of our mental capacities to figure it all out. Our lesson may be that we simply cannot think and reason our way through the complexities of modern life and have no choice but to return to our long dormant instincts. Surfing, I suggest, is one way we can re-learn the art of staying in the moment, trusting our instincts, being present. Waveriding absolutely requires it. It's not the only way — almost any activity can be meditative. My goal is not to inspire the whole world to take up surfing. The waves are crowded enough already. It's tempting to endorse the sentiments of a bumper sticker gaining popularity among surfers in the USA: 'Thank you for not surfing.'

Yet I temper this urge for exclusivity with the thought that, however much grief that floundering beginner or greedy longboarder may cause you in the surf, they are likely to cause you less grief on land for the very fact that they surf.

I'd like to suggest that much of what people might be looking for from surfing, in its current vogue, may be accessible all around them in their everyday lives on land — spontaneity, connection with nature, being present in the moment, trusting instincts and intuition. It is, in fact, possible to surf your life. You can metaphorically paddle into, and take off on, any situation, endeavour, adventure, with the gusto and commitment of the surf rider, take the drop and instinctively read, adapt to, and ride changing circumstances. Poised, senses finely tuned, feeling the shifting terrain under your feet, reacting spontaneously and instinctively to the constant changes.

Waves can rear up and heave and lurch threateningly, or peel away with mechanical precision like rolling liquid drainpipes, or loop and roll invitingly like playground equipment. Surfers never really know what they're in for as they size up a wave, turn and paddle and leap to their feet, poised to react spontaneously to the shifting path ahead. A lot like life.

The ocean may be seen as a laboratory where rules for living can be tested, with swift and immediate feedback. Might not the principles of waveriding offer us all a way of living with greater ease, flow, grace, spontaneity and an embrace of the present moment?

Readers may be relieved to learn I do not propose using the remainder of this book to expand on this theory. This is not another personal development text promising the key to unending wealth, the perfect relationship or dream job — Lord knows, we have enough of those already. I favour the less evangelical approach of allowing real human stories to illustrate the virtues of the surfer's approach to life. What follows is a series of profiles of many of the most inspiring and extraordinary surfing characters I've come across in my work and travels as a surfing writer over the past twenty years, as well as my favourite personal anecdotes and gems of surfing wisdom gathered over that time.

These stories, I hope, help illustrate how life moves on like a series of waves. Or rather, life is the vast ocean, the medium, through which these waves move. And we can learn to ride these peaks and troughs of our daily lives, bringing greater joy, and fulfillment to our everyday existence. I invite you to paddle out and enjoy the ride.

TIM BAKER, CURRUMBIN, AUSTRALIA, 2007

duke kahanamoku

{ the father of modern surfing }

*I think we have to teach a lot of these kids
to first be gentlemen . . . try to help one
another and not hog the doggone waves.*

Call me old-fashioned, but I believe every person who starts surfing should first learn the story of Duke Kahanamoku, rightly revered as the father of modern surfing.

Duke won six Olympic swimming medals, over four Olympic Games from 1912 to 1932, three gold, two silver and a bronze. He was forty-two when he collected his final medal. He strummed his ukulele pool-side to relax before competing, and charmed everyone he met with his easy-going charm and grace. He also introduced surfing to Australia, New Zealand, and many parts of the US mainland, sharing Hawaii's gift of waveriding with the world.

Duke was born in Honolulu in 1890, a full-blooded Hawaiian with royal ancestry on both sides of his family. He grew up in the waves of Waikiki at a time when it was still an unspoilt beachside village. 'My father and uncle just threw me into the water from an outrigger canoe. I had to swim or else,' he once recalled.

At the time, the ancient Hawaiian art of waveriding had all but died out, discouraged by the Christian missionaries who regarded it as a heathen pastime associated with gambling and nudity. Duke was among a generation of young Hawaiians who experimented with surfboard riding again in the early 1900s. In 1908, Duke was a founding member of the Hui Nalu, or 'club of waves', for local Hawaiian surfers. Could this be the origins of the mythical surf god Huey surfers still speak of today?

In 1911, as a virtual unknown and at his first formal swimming competition, Duke smashed the world 100 yard open water record by 4.6 seconds. Officials on the mainland refused to accept that this young unknown Hawaiian could have so eclipsed the world record and his time was disallowed. In 1912, Duke silenced the doubters by winning the gold medal in the 100 yard freestyle at the Stockholm Olympics in world record time. He also won a silver medal for the 4 x 200 yard relay. On his way home Duke stopped over on the east coast of the USA to make good a promise to teach some of his mainland friends to surf. When he eventually returned to Hawaii, thousands greeted him and the Hawaiian *Star-Bulletin* reported that Duke had 'lost none of his modesty that won him hosts of friends everywhere he went. It only dawned on many of his fellow passengers who he was when the boat steamed into harbour'.

Duke wowed crowds in Hawaii and the mainland with a string of world records and first-place finishes in the 50-, 75-, 100-, 220- and 440-yard distances. Between swim meets, he regularly attracted huge crowds to his surfing demonstrations. His much anticipated visit to Australia in the summer of 1914–15 virtually began the sport of surfboard riding in Australia. Duke shaped his own board out of local sugar pine and put on two demonstrations at Freshwater Beach, Sydney, stunning the locals with his expertise. That board still resides at Freshwater Surf Club, a holy relic of surfing's birth in Australia, and Duke's statue still watches over Freshwater from the northern headland.

In 1925, on a visit to California, Duke rescued eight drowning people on his surfboard when a forty-foot pleasure yacht, *Thelma*, capsized in heavy seas at Corona del Mar. The Newport police chief reported: 'The Duke's performance was the most superhuman act . . . Many more would have drowned, but for the quick action of the Hawaiian swimmer.' As a result, paddleboards became standard equipment among lifeguards the world over.

Duke was beloved by the Hawaiian people as the living embodiment of the aloha spirit, served as an unofficial ambassador for Hawaiian tourism for years, and as Sheriff of Honolulu (a largely ceremonial position), for thirteen consecutive two-year terms. He greeted dignitaries and celebrities visiting Hawaii and appeared in numerous Hollywood movies. Despite his fame, and despite lending his name to everything from a surfing contest and sportswear line, a restaurant and nightclub to a music and recording company, Duke lived modestly and remained a dignified and humble figure until his death in 1968 at the age of 77.

In his last interview with a surfing magazine in 1965, Duke had noticed a breakdown in surf etiquette due to increasing crowds. He told *Surfer* magazine: 'I think we have to teach a lot of these kids to first be gentlemen . . . Try to help one another and not hog the doggone waves. You know, there are so many waves coming in all the time, you don't have to worry about that. Just take your time — wave comes. Let the other guys go, catch another one. And that's what we used to do. We'd see some other fella there first, and we'd say, "You're here first, you take the first wave".'

'I think there is something primordial about it. All the great forces in the universe — electromagnetism, heat, light — they all impinge upon the water to make waves. So when you ride a wave, you are tapping into something much bigger, something that is cosmic. It is like skiing down a mountain.

Gravity takes hold, and the skier becomes part of that cosmic force. In surfing, the mountains move themselves . . . But the feeling that I get when I am out on the water, that feeling of being part of something much bigger than myself, is the same feeling that I get when I look at all my children and grandchildren.'

DORIAN 'DOC' PASKOWITZ

ross clarke-jones

{ the big wave business consultant }

*You get out there and the sun's just rising
and you see the swells, just these huge waves
coming in one after another, and you catch
so many waves, the excitement's just
building all day until you're so spent you're
just paralysed physically and mentally from
so much excitement. It's like the aftermath
of great sex — ah, I think I'll have a
cigarette (laughs). You crash out and then
you're just excited about it for days, years
sometimes. You can bring that swell up in
your mind and get excited about it gain.
They're precious times because big swells
don't happen that often.*

It seems an unlikely meeting — big wave surfer Ross Clarke-Jones and business magnate Kerry Packer. But according to Clarke-Jones, 'We got on like a house on fire.'

Packer, the late media mogul and Australia's wealthiest man, spotted a photo of Clarke-Jones riding a huge wave in Hawaii a few years ago and was instantly transfixed.

'He saw the photo at an IMAX movie, and they ran it in one of his magazines,' says Ross. 'He saw it and went, "I want that photo for my office". They got in touch with Quiksilver [Ross's sponsor] and they said, "Ross is in town if he wants to meet him".'

And so Ross, more at home in mountainous waves in Hawaii or southern Australia, trotted off to Packer's PBL head office in Sydney, with a framed photo of his big wave ride under his arm. 'I had a great chat to him for about an hour. He was asking strange questions about the waves, like, "How do you get under that?" I told him the idea is to go around it, not under it. He said, "How does a little bloke like you do that?"'

At one stage, Ross feared he'd offended the great man and their meeting was to be cut short. 'He clicked his little emergency button, and I thought, oh no, he's calling security. But he brought in his secretary and wrote me a nice cheque for my time, which I needed so much at the time. I ended up going to his casino and giving it back to him anyway — I'll just take that in chips, please,' he laughs.

While financial management might not be Ross's strong point, he is making other, unlikely inroads into the business world. At forty-one, after more than twenty years as one of the world's leading big wave riders, he has stumbled into a new, unexpected career as a public speaker to business groups. Ross recently visited Thailand, where he addressed a conference of advertising industry directors. The theme for the conference was 'The Year of Living Dangerously', and Ross was their impeccably qualified guest speaker. He shows a short video of what he does — mind-boggling images of his tiny figure racing down enormous waves as big as six-storey buildings — and talks about his motivations, then answers questions.

'They're just all in shock. They just sit back and go, "Oh my God",' Ross laughs.

What the business types are interested in is Ross's trust in his instincts, his willingness to jump through windows of opportunity as they arise, make sound decisions under pressure and go with his first impulse. This, apparently, is the new business school doctrine, as espoused in influential texts like *Blink: the power of thinking without thinking* by *New Yorker* staff writer Malcolm Gladwell. In *Blink*, Gladwell argues that snap decisions, instinct and intuition often lead to better results than carefully considered, reasoned analysis. It's a philosophy Clarke-Jones stakes his life on time and again — without even thinking about it.

Ross's talks have proven so popular with business groups he has future bookings in London and Cannes, for healthy fees. He describes the slightly surreal scenario of being surrounded by earnest men in suits, pens and notepads at the ready, grilling him with questions about his thought processes as he paddles into a huge wave, and furiously scribbling down his every utterance.

His most recent speaking engagement was to a group of computer-company executives. Ross delivered his usual talk and the next day joined them on a pleasure cruise. His message of living life to the fullest had clearly gotten through to the normally office-bound executives. 'I had all these pissed computer nerds jumping off the top deck of the boat,' laughs

Ross. 'They were all going, "Ross, you can make us do it. Tell us how," and I was just pushing them off.'

This is not a fate anyone would have imagined when Ross quit school at sixteen to chase the dream of professional surfing. Although the contest circuit at the time was generally staged in small waves, Ross found his calling in the booming swells of Hawaii. In the legendary 1986 Billabong Pro, at 25-foot Waimea Bay, a nineteen-year-old Clarke-Jones discovered the bigger it got, the better he did. While others forfeited their heats and cowered on the beach, Ross went head to head with all the giants of big wave riding and forged a reputation for fearless charging that he has maintained to this day. Horribly undergunned on a borrowed 7'11" surfboard, a good foot and a half shorter than many of his competitors' boards, Ross charged all the way to the final, in which four-time world champ Mark Richards staged his second memorable Billabong Pro victory. 'It was like a big day at Terrigal haven,' Ross reckoned at the time, referring to his homebreak on the New South Wales Central Coast. It was a shocking comparison to most surfers — who talk up the danger and challenge of big Hawaiian surf as if it exists in a whole other stratosphere from regular earthly surf.

Since that day, Ross has continued to enhance his reputation as a big wave lunatic of the highest order, with an endless succession of death-defying stunts. In 1992 at Backdoor Pipeline, a notorious reefbreak on Hawaii's North Shore, he endured an almost fatal three-wave wipeout and suffered a fractured vertebra. Most surfers speak with awe of two-wave wipeouts, where the surfer is held underwater so long he doesn't re-surface between successive waves in a set. Survivors of the two-wave wipeout club often speak hauntingly of going to the brink, seeing the white light and making a choice to return to this earthly realm — the full near-death experience. Ross was underwater so long, three waves passed over him. What was it like down there? 'It was really nice and peaceful,' he reflected later. 'Coming up was the scary part.'

Despite the risk of permanent paralysis, Ross defied medical advice to paddle out for his heat in the next event at Sunset Beach just three weeks later — fractured vertebra and all. He needed the few points earned by just turning up to be assured of re-qualifying for the following year's world tour: he rode a couple of smaller waves and returned to the beach.

On the aptly dubbed Biggest Wednesday, one of the largest days ever surfed at an Hawaiian outer reef, Ross and tow partner Tony Ray were mowed down and skittled by a monster wave that sent them tumbling under a mountain of whitewater alongside their jet ski. Tony had been towing Ross into a wave when they both realised they were caught a bit too deep and Tony discovered to his horror that a two-stroke jet ski at full throttle cannot outrun a 40-foot wave.

In 2001, Ross fulfilled his career dream of winning the world's most prestigious big-wave event, the Quiksilver Big Wave Invitational in Memory of Eddie Aikau. The Eddie, as it's known, honours the memory of Hawaiian lifeguard and big wave surfer Eddie Aikau, who disappeared when the traditional Hawaiian outrigger, the *Hokule'a*, capsized in 1978. Eddie paddled for help but was never seen again while the boat and its crew were rescued.

'My devotion to this event has been total for the past twelve years,' Ross said, after his win, collecting a US$50,000 winner's cheque. 'I've wanted it so hard and for so long that I think I've put too much pressure on myself and my past performances have been a bit disappointing. To win has been a dream for so long that I had almost given up on it. It's not even the money. I've spent ten times that amount just staying here every winter waiting for the event to happen. It's purely the prestige. To be able to say you've won the Eddie.'

Ross was born on 6/6/66, and much has been made of his birth date to help explain his devilish, manic, some would say fatalistic approach to almost everything he does — big-wave riding, driving a car, finances, relationships. His recently released biopic video, *The Sixth Element*, was narrated appropriately enough by Hollywood bad boy Dennis Hopper. Ross won the best athlete award at the 2006 X-Dance Film Festival in California, a kind of Sundance for extreme sports, for his role in the film.

How did he get Dennis Hopper to narrate a surfing video? 'My partner in the movie said, "Let's get a Hollywood guy to do it. We'll feel a few out and someone will think it's cool and will do it. They don't need the money, and surfing's cool nowadays".' They drew up a short list, including Mel Gibson, Eric Bana, Flea from the Red Hot Chilli Peppers, and Sean Penn. Ross called on a good friend, eight-time world champ Kelly Slater, to use his Hollywood connections. 'He said, "What about Dennis Hopper?" because he knows his son. I just said, "That's him, let's concentrate on him." So Kelly gave me Dennis's assistant's address, and I sent her an email saying, "Just wondering if Dennis would be interested in narrating a surf video." We sent a video of the rough cut, and apparently in the first ten minutes of watching it he said, "Yes, I'll do it." He spent about eight hours recording it. First take we said, "That's perfect," and he said, "I'll tell you when it's perfect." I've met him a couple of times since and he's been like my dad, like I know him really well.'

Ross's reputation has delivered him into plenty of unlikely scenarios over the years, but none more poignant than his meeting last year with Jessie, a ten-year-old surfer with leukaemia.

'He was in Ronald McDonald House. His dad came along and said, "He's got two weeks to live, can you come and have a talk to him?" I said, "When?" He said, "Now." I said, "Yeah, let's go." I got there, and it was like a funeral. His family were standing around. I went and got a Happy Meal, because he was really frail. He hadn't eaten for two weeks. The doctors couldn't believe I got him to eat. I just went in hard. I said, "I promise you I'll take you surfing if you eat this bit of chicken." He sat up in his chair and started to eat. I thought, "What's he got to lose? Fuck sitting around moping." He watched the movie like a hundred times, kept ringing me up and reciting it to me. A year to the day I took him surfing. Talk about rewarding. If I had anything to do with that . . .' Ross quietly marvels. 'I made him eat chicken nuggets — they could have killed him,' he laughs.

'I took him out near Taree, where he lives, pushed him into a couple of waves. He didn't have the strength to stand up. I put a life-jacket on him,' Ross recalls. 'You should have seen his face — priceless, awesome.'

It's an approach to life, and death, that helped Ross deal with his own father's battle with cancer. 'I did it with my father when he was dying. They wouldn't even let me take him out of the hospital. He said, "Bust me out of here." I took him to the beach, got him in the water, got him a beer. It's the best thing you can do for a cancer patient. You may as well get a bit of sun, have a laugh. He came back to life again just for those couple of hours.'

'I tackled surf-riding and now that I have tackled it, more than ever do I hold it to be a royal sport . . . Ah, that delicious moment when I felt that breaker grip and fling me. On I dashed, a hundred and fifty feet, and subsided with the breaker on the sand. From that moment I was lost.'

JACK LONDON, *THE CRUISE OF THE SNARK*

'It is always easier to ride the wave in the direction it is going.'

GERRY LOPEZ, PIPELINE MASTER

SURF LESSON #14
Go with the flow

I am caught inside by a set of waves while paddling out, pinned in the impact zone, where waves unload on a shallow sandbar. I am duck diving under churning, rolling banks of white water, gasping for air and digging in deep, determined arm strokes. The waves keep coming. Slowly I'm worn down, frustrated and disheartened by the ocean's cruel punishment. I can see others catching and riding waves beyond the breakers. This is worse. I am missing out, being singled out for this harsh treatment, punished while others enjoy themselves. Gradually, I tire and am eventually buffeted out to the side of the break, where I discover to my amazement I am easily, almost effortlessly carried out the back in a current. I have to laugh. The ocean has schooled me again. I was too caught up in my own reaction to the situation to recognise the bigger picture. When I surrender, yield to the greater force and trust in natural laws, I am directed towards the clear path.

jesse billauer

{ the motivator }

I had a lot of burning sensation, pain, in my body, but once I hit the water I have no pain whatsoever. If I'm tight — my limbs are tight — as soon as I hit the water everything's loose. I've got a smile from ear to ear. It's like nothing, nothing, compares to that.

JESSE BILLAUER, FROM THE FILM,
STEP INTO LIQUID

There is something immediately arresting about the images of Jesse Billauer surfing Cloudbreak, the famed shallow reefbreak in Fiji. It is not just the perfect wave barrelling over razor-sharp coral, though that is striking enough. It is the figure of Jesse, in helmet and life-jacket, lying prone on án over-sized surfboard, with his hands clasped firmly in front of him, gaze intent, holding himself in perfect trim in the mouth of the spinning tube.

Jesse is a quadriplegic — a former top-rated junior surfer whose dreams of a life travelling to the world's great waves seemed to have been abruptly dashed in a surfing accident ten years ago.

These days, Jesse gets around in a wheelchair, but to say he's confined to it wouldn't be quite accurate. Jesse continues to surf, travel and pursue his dreams, though those dreams have been modified to suit his circumstances.

'I always knew I would get back in the water,' says Jesse simply.

Surfing was an inevitability for Jesse, growing up on the beach in southern California. 'I grew up at Pacific Palisades, by the ocean, and I always saw people out there, so I wanted to try it. My friend's dad took me out and I just fell in love with it. First I started out on a boogie board, then a longboard, then graduated to a shortboard.'

When he was twelve, Jesse's natural ability earned him sponsorship and contest results. He competed with a stellar generation of surfing talent, including Bruce and Andy Irons and the Hobgood twins, who have gone on to international glory. He was sent on surf trips to Hawaii, Indonesia, Tahiti and Costa Rica. But Jesse's heart was never in competition. 'I thought this was a way to be able to travel and stuff like that,' he says. 'I was more into free surfing. I did all right in different surf contests here and there. I enjoyed the sport of surfing more than competing. I was always too nice: "You want to go right? I'll go left."'

Yet, by the time he was seventeen, Jesse was rated one of the top 100 junior surfers in the world by US *Surfer* magazine, and sponsors were keen to send him on the world pro tour. To surf and travel and get paid for it was his every childhood dream fulfilled.

Jesse was acutely aware of his good fortune. He'd survived a serious car accident when he was sixteen that threatened to end his surfing career. He'd worked as a deckhand on a fishing charter boat, and as a lifeguard, always keen to pay his own way and not averse to an honest day's work.

Then, in March 1996, during an otherwise idyllic surf session at his local beach, his world stopped. Tube-riding is sometimes seen as a metaphor for rebirth — and Jesse emerged from a solid beachbreak barrel that day into a whole new reality.

'The waves were really good, six- to eight-foot faces, over a shallow sandbar that I surfed all the time,' Jesse remembers. He pulled into a good-sized tube breaking close to the beach. 'I fell when I came out of the barrel, and didn't have time to put my hands out.'

Jesse hit his head on the sandbar and found himself floating face down in the water, unable to move. 'My legs went tingly,' he recalls. He used the force of the next breaking wave to flip himself over and call for help. Friends initially thought he was joking but quickly realised the gravity of the situation and pulled him from the water.

One of those friends, Brett Sanson, later wrote a poem, 'The Birth of Jesse Billauer', which reads in part:

> *I pulled the limp body out of the water*
> *To realise I was holding a new born teenager*
> *He came out of Mother Ocean wet and scared.*

Jesse was airlifted by helicopter to UCLA Medical Center, where it was determined he'd suffered a complete spinal cord injury. Jesse was now a quadriplegic. He had no sensation or movement below mid-chest and limited use of his arms and hands. He would remain in hospital for three months. When he eventually returned home, he required a full-time attendant and a whole new perspective on the world.

The accident happened a month after Jesse's seventeenth birthday. How did he deal with his new reality? 'I had a lot of friends and family that were supporting me. I had a lot of goals and dreams to take care of,' he says firmly. 'The only time I ever got down was when I started thinking, where would I be? Surfing the world.'

But Jesse wasn't about to wallow. He was too busy. Studying, travelling, public speaking, starting his charity, the Life Rolls On Foundation, and surfing. His remarkable return to the waves was poignantly documented in the movie *Step Into Liquid*. Lying on a specially made board fitted with arm straps, and aided by a collection of surfing friends, Jesse discovered all his old surfing instincts were still intact. He'd decide which wave to catch, friends would push him in and, with subtle shifts of his weight, he found he could trim and turn and ride waves with remarkable control.

'To be able to feel that freedom out in the water, to get back to doing what I loved the most, was amazing,' he says. 'I was just a little nervous. The waves were small but they looked big.' As soon as he hit the water, though, Jesse knew this was something he could do. Just being in the ocean, he says, took away the constant pain he'd been living with since the accident. 'Just a lot of burning sensation in my legs and stuff went away totally.'

So confident and comfortable was he in the water, he didn't even wear a life-jacket at first. The scenes in *Step Into Liquid* show him coolly cruising into wave after wave, angling left or right, easing his board through gentle turns, a mix of joy and intense focus etched on his face. Not content with just getting back into small beachbreak surf at home, Jesse has continued to push himself into larger and more challenging surf and pursue his dreams of travelling to the world's great waves. He's surfed perfect Malibu, the famed Californian pointbreak, visited Australia where he's sampled Snapper Rocks, Kirra Point and the Pass at Byron Bay, travelled to Hawaii and Fiji. His performance agenda these days is simple, stripped down to basics. 'It's all about speed and length of ride,' he says. Lying down, close to the water, accentuates the sense of speed: 'It feels like I'm going so fast.' While he has to rely on the help of friends to get in the water, it's important to him that he uses his own instincts to choose which wave he wants, and to pick his line. 'That's a big part of it. All that's really, really important. I'm making those decisions about which waves I want.'

In 2005 Jesse ventured to Hawaii to surf the world-renowned North Shore of Oahu, riding six- to eight-foot faces at Sunset Beach. Later that year he was invited to the Tavarua Surf Camp in Fiji, and tackled the perilous reef waves of Cloudbreak, a spot most able-bodied surfers approach with caution. Towed into solid five-foot waves with the aid of a jet ski, Jesse found he was able to position himself in the tube, skimming over the tropical reef, clearly visible as it raced by just inches below.

'That was amazing . . . a beautiful feeling, amazing, scary, exciting. It's very dangerous, but it was worth it to me at that moment.'

Surfing isn't the only area where Jesse has continued to pursue his dreams. He graduated from San Diego State University with a degree in Communications in May of 2002, majoring in public speaking. He has established the Life Rolls On Foundation to raise money and awareness for spinal cord injury research. He travels around America as a motivational speaker and inspiring others living with disabilities. What's his message? 'To live a full life, enjoy yourself and still do what you want to do,' he says. 'I just want to raise awareness and money for spinal injury research. That's my main thing right now — public speaking. I'm just trying to surf, travel, raise enough money to have a family, have little grommets running round.'

The Life Rolls On Foundation has so far raised more than US$15,000 for spinal cord injury research, donated to the Center for Neural Repair at UCSD. Jesse has spoken to more than 500 groups, including schools, businesses and rehabilitation centres. His messages are simple, yet powerful and universal. Live for today. Embrace change. Cherish family and friends. Happiness is just a positive thought away. Love life because life loves you.

They'd sound trite coming from a lot of people, but not from Jesse.

School groups especially report a phenomenal response to Jesse's talks. 'Believe me, when you can bring 600 students in a gymnasium and hear a pin drop, you've got something special,' writes Malibu High School principal, Michael Matthews. 'Jesse considers himself lucky to be alive and is making the most of everything he has been given. His message to us was to feel the same way. I know Jesse's story. Jesse has been a positive force in my life since his accident. When my son Sean died in 1997, it was Jesse who came to my house many times to offer solace and friendship. Pretty amazing. Yet in spite of knowing Jesse, I was still overwhelmed by the assembly. It gave me a renewed sense of pursuing the important things in life, both in my job and in my personal life. I think that many of our students felt the same way.'

Holly Korbonski, a teacher at Pacific Palisades High School, concurs: 'Through the use of video and lecture, he illustrates how rich and meaningful human relationships have become to him since he was injured, and that his disability struck his body only, while leaving his spirit intact and powerful.'

In a surfing world where crowds fight and squabble over waves, where pro surfers throw tantrums and smash boards over lost heats, where surf-rage confrontations wind up in court, Jesse's messages of gratitude and appreciation are sorely needed.

What has surfing taught him? 'You definitely have to have patience — patience is very important,' says Jesse. 'Go with the flow, and enjoy the time you have because obviously it could be gone at any moment.'

To his fellow surfers, Jesse says simply: 'Ride the waves as long as possible. Surf as much as you can, share as much as possible, explore the world and surf as many waves as you can.'

At the time of going to press Jesse was nursing a broken leg after surfing ten-foot waves in Hawaii, but this wasn't preventing him from completing a national speaking tour of the US.

For more information go to:
www.liferollson.org or www.jessebillauer.com

'Instead of seeing the rug being pulled from under us, we can learn to dance on a shifting carpet.'

THOMAS CRUM, *THE MAGIC OF CONFLICT*

tim winton

{ the novelist }

Surfing and the sea got me through the grimmer parts of adolescence. When life gets overwhelming it's incredible what a few hours in the brine will do for you. It's as though the ocean is this vast, salty poultice that sucks the poison out of your system.

Tim Winton is probably Australia's greatest living writer. His novels, including *Cloudstreet*, *The Riders* and *Dirt Music*, have won numerous literary awards, including the Miles Franklin Award, the National Book Council Banjo Award for Fiction, and been shortlisted for the Booker Prize. His work has been translated into numerous languages, and adapted for stage, film and television. *Cloudstreet* was recently voted the most popular Australian novel in an Australian Society of Authors poll.

He is also a keen surfer, growing up on the WA coast and spending plenty of time exploring its southern and northern extremities, which also provide the setting for many of his books. He even made a rare foray into the public spotlight to campaign, successfully, to save Ningaloo Reef from development.

An intensely private person, Tim preferred to conduct this interview by email. His answers were so articulate, as you'd expect, there seemed no point in tampering with them. Here, then, is a complete verbatim transcript of that correspondence.

What are your first memories of surfing — sensations, emotions, that first child's eye view of riding waves?
I grew up near the beach at Scarborough in the '60s and I guess I always saw people surfing. It was simply what people did where I came from. When I was five my older cousins, both girls, paddled me out on a longboard. I was more scared than anything, but I can vividly remember the greeny colour of the resin and the weave of the volane and the feel of the old paraffin wax and the symmetry of the three stringers. The vehicle itself, I suppose, was

kind of overwhelming. And then the sensation of rushing shoreward. Oh, that was something. That was it. I was gone for all time.

From there I began riding Coolites, the way you did in those days. First without a fin and later with a waxed-in bit of plywood. The rashes we got from those foam boards were epic; it's a wonder I've still got nipples. Nipples aren't that useful in men but I would have been a little disappointed to have had them drop off at age eleven. The best thing you can say about the Coolite is that you could surf it between the flags and keep your mum and the clubbies happy all at once. I surfed for hours, until my face and back were roasted and my chest was a grated, weeping mess. The last hour was spent studiously avoiding eye contact with my poor old mum who'd be madly waving me down from the beach. (Years later I'd be in her position, knowing damn well that my kids knew I was calling and semaphoring like hell. Some days I nearly swam a snatch-strap out into the break so I could hook them up and slap the F100 into low and hoist the buggers out that way.)

My first glass board was a seven-foot egg with a radical, raked fin. The shortboard era had well and truly arrived but this thing rode like a longboard and had an effect on the way I surfed. Later I went to shorter and shorter boards but I never forgot the pure, gliding feel of the longer board and the graceful way older blokes surfed them. They were the guys I watched, the blokes who became uncool. In the '90s I went back to big boards and I think I enjoy surfing now even more than I did when I was a kid. One of my boards, a wooden one, made by Tom Wegener, must weigh thirty kilos. It's a cruise-beast.

How does surfing make you feel? How do you explain the effect it has on us? How has your relationship with surfing changed and evolved over time?
I guess the obvious attraction of surfing, particularly for younger people, is the sheer momentum, the experience of hurtling towards the beach. It's

a huge rush and it never really diminishes, even though you repeat this experience hundreds of thousands of times in thirty or forty years. It's never exactly the same, but it feels like a miracle every time you do it. I think what you can lose, especially as a younger person, is the wonder of the experience, the beauty of it. This isn't unique to surfing; it happens in many parts of our lives where our senses are dulled by our education, by the dominant obsessions of the culture, by the speed at which we live. Surfing has its origins in Polynesian ritual and play. At one level it seems to have been about power and caste, I suppose — you know, a regal display — but it was also about grace and beauty and celebration. This was the stuff that *haoles* from California and then Australia picked up on. Surfing became an expression of life, an alternative to the rigid social mores of the '50s in particular. It was a gentle form of rebellion. Beach culture was tinged with pre-hippy romanticism which is easy to ridicule but had real things to offer a culture locked in conformity over the love of machinery and shiny surfaces and appliances and suburban dinkiness. It was tribal but it celebrated the rebel. And it honoured nature because surfing depended on the vagaries of nature and an intimacy with it that the average stockbroker lacked.

I came to surfing at the peak of this period and it had a lasting effect on me. Admittedly, we thought we were special when really we were only very lucky. But we surfed, many of us, with a sense of awe and a feeling of kinship with each other and the sea that sustained us. This was before surfing became merely another occupied territory, before it was completely commercialised and just another colony of the business world. How eager surfers were to surrender their freedoms. They wanted to be like everyone else. We had years of dreary contests and chest-beating and sponsor chasing and brawling in the surf. Surfing became nasty and macho and nationalistic. How many five-year-old boys were introduced to surfing in the '80s by girls? None, probably, because women were driven out of surfing almost completely. The dominant mode was aggressive, misogynistic, localised, greedy. Surfers became jocks, morons who trashed beaches and beat the crap out of each other. For anyone whose idea of surfing was different there was nowhere to go. I just gave up and walked away out of shame, to be honest. I went diving. At least underwater you don't have to listen to anyone's bullshit. I'd always loved being underwater as much as being on it and it was my main connection with the sea for most of the '80s. But I missed surfing badly. I lived in Europe for a couple of years and when I came home I moved to the country and went back to surfing and found a bit of that old vibe among the more intelligent fishermen who were my neighbours.

Looking back I think there were plenty of people like me. They really came out of the woodwork in the mid '90s when fun returned to surfing. Some surfers were old enough not to care about being self-conscious. Others simply rebelled against the slavish conformity of the 'sport' and paddled out on weird craft and did nice things with them. Women returned, thank God, and little girls took to it in numbers unseen since the '60s. You paddled out and people in the line-up were actually smiling, talking to each other. The slit-eyed surf-punks were still out there, slashing and snarling and scowling, but they were no longer the only game in town.

For me surfing is about beauty and connectedness. Riding a wave to shore is a lovely, meditative thing to be able to do. You're walking on water, tapping the sea's energy without extracting anything from it. You're meeting the sea, not ripping anything out of it. Few other water pursuits have this non-exploitative element. As a boater, fisherman, shell-collector or whatever, I'm always taking something away from the sea, having an impact on it. But as a surfer I'm riding energy that the sea is expending of its own accord, the way a dolphin or seal or sea-lion does. The actual physical sensation of sliding down a wall of water, feeling really awake and alive and in the moment, is hard to describe to the non-surfer. It looks beautiful and it feels beautiful. Knowing that you're not doing any damage just makes the feeling better. For some men in particular, whose lives require a kind of utilitarian mindset that can be pretty unfulfilling, this is one of the few activities they undertake in which they can do something pointlessly beautiful. There's no material result, nothing they can show themselves or the boss. There's just a bit of a rush, an elevated heart rate, a buzz that lasts the rest of the day.

Surfing isn't the only human activity that offers people this natural high. Nor is it the only sustainable recreational activity at our disposal. But I believe that if more surfers tapped into that feeling of connection with the sea, the planet, each other, then their lives and those around them would benefit. There's the roll-on effect of simple happiness, for one thing. And people who love surfing often educate themselves about the sea itself, and those who learn how fragile it is, and how it's affected by our other activities will likely change their behaviours and attitudes to keep it alive. We still use the sea as our sewer. Many people don't realise just how much trouble the world's oceans are in. Water quality, the temperature of our water, the levels of over-fishing, the health of coral reefs, these things have global implications. Surfers should be at the forefront of doing something about this, of saving the sea for our children. We should know, better than anybody, what there is to lose. And if you've been surfing for thirty years or more you've had time to figure out what there is to gain.

Any peak moments in the surf, when the waveriding experience has seemed most profound, moved you most deeply, maybe helped pull you out of a difficult time or helped you see things more clearly?
I guess surfing and the sea got me through the grimmer parts of adolescence. When life gets overwhelming it's incredible what a few hours in the brine will do for you. It's as though the ocean is this vast,

salty poultice that sucks the poison out of your system. I still feel that now. Admittedly it's addictive, but there are more destructive addictions to be had. I just think it's a way of slowing down and processing stuff without consciously addressing it. A lot of the time we're forced to live in the future or the past. Surfing is something that keeps you in the present tense. Some of that is just the immediacy of the problems it sets you, physical adjustments you make every half second to stay on your feet or avoid physical injury (or discomfort, at least). Some of it is just the energy required that dulls much of your other problems. And some of it is the pure dance of it, the sensual pay-off, the feel of the water, the shapes of waves and the colours of the sky and the reef and the water itself; all these things are like money in the bank mentally for me. And even though I'm mostly a solitary surfer these days, there are social pay-offs even for a grumpy loner like me. Sometimes you'll be sliding down this beautiful long wave and you'll hear some person you don't know, some man or woman sitting up in the channel just hooting for you, happy for you. Man, that's nice. I'll take that to the bank, too. There are people whose names I don't know who I see in the water or on the beach nearly every day and we smile at each other and say hello and talk simple, civil stuff and I value that.

I think surfing has, at times, saved me from doing self-destructive things. It's pulled me out of depressions the way only nature can. And for me, the sea really helped me to be a parent. It gave me something precious to share with my kids and my wife. It's a fabulous thing, if you're lucky enough, to be able to paddle out with your family and laugh and fart about. It's not always about the quality of the waves; it's that feeling of being in it together. You have to treasure the things you have in common. My wife took up surfing at forty. Nowadays we're keener than our kids. I think they're pretty amused at this. We're two stoked old farts who spend far too long wondering what the weather will do.

Honestly, I can't imagine what my life would have been like without the water, without surfing.

What lessons do you think surfing and the ocean have imparted to you? Do you agree the ocean can be a powerful teacher and metaphor for life?
If there's something I've learnt from surfing it's about connection. When you sit out in the line-up you're bobbing in seventy per cent of the earth's surface. Seventy per cent of your own body is water. Water connects you, internally, to yourself, and it links you externally to everyone else. I really feel the gravity of that. And I think feeling joined to nature, knowing how much I depend on it, and how it's affected by me and my species, has been very important. As an artist, as someone who writes stories and tries to make words into beautiful forms, it's vitally important to me, especially in a culture that's forgotten the value of beauty. It's a primary source of inspiration, I guess, when so much of what goes on around you is only about money and big swinging dick capitalism. It's important for blokes to be able to do beautiful stuff, impractical stuff, that adds to life. That's an early life lesson from surfing.

Watching a little girl or a middle-aged woman smiling like a maniac as they come cruising by on a one-foot wall of mush. Or a pod of dolphins doing jumps off an empty pointbreak. Or surfing with a couple of whales spouting and tail-slapping just behind the break. All this is good for the soul. To me it's not a sport. The professional sport side of it bores me to death. It's mildly more interesting than golf. To me, surfing has always been soul-business. It's the pointless things that give your life meaning. Friendship, compassion, art, love. All of them pointless. But they're what keeps life from being meaningless. Catching a wave and turning and dancing and looping in towards the beach is one of the nicest forms of pointlessness I can think of.

I've heard you described as an 'indigenous' writer because of the way you evoke the Australian landscape. Do you think surfing can be a way of enhancing your connection to a place? Have you ever marvelled at those surfers who seem to almost magically appear and paddle out at the precise time and place to snare the wave of the day, as if they are picking up some unseen signals the rest of us miss?

I don't make any claims about being indigenous. Never have. But I am interested in the mysterious business of belonging. People who take note of where they find themselves and make a commitment to that place, a compact that demands something real from them, have a chance of feeling properly at home. Yeah, you're right about some surfers, the way they know what the sea is about to do, how they show up at the right place and the right time so often. This is experience becoming instinct; it's intimacy. But it requires more than just time. It requires respect, I think, a bit of humility, the ability to watch and wait and listen and learn. That's wisdom. We should celebrate these people, value them. There is a tribal sense in which this knowledge can be passed on to younger surfers, but we need to go back to fostering a culture that values wisdom and age and experience rather than youth and 'attitude'. Surfing is only one area where this is needed, I think. You see it more readily now in music. I think it's beginning to happen in surfing again, but I'd love to see it grow faster. Surfers need to broaden, I think, to see the bigger picture, and there's more hope for this now that we're not forced to pretend we're all fifteen. Much of what comes from the surfing media is deadly embarrassing, but I think men and women who are passionate about surfing can bring something grown-up to the wider culture. I'm talking human wisdom here, not market share.

'The knowledge you get in schools and colleges is second hand. The wisdom and know-how you get from the sea and waves and water is virgin, new and fleeting. By all means, get some of this kind of education . . . Try to co-ordinate with nature, or God, by studying the waves, riding them, finally making an almost perfect ride.'

TOM BLAKE, SURF PIONEER, IN 1990, AGED EIGHTY-EIGHT

SURF LESSON #18
Jumping through windows

Windows of opportunity. They float invisibly around us all through life. Hesitate, and they'll pass you by. Jump through them and previously unimaginable possibilities open up. I used to doubt such cosmic waffle, but no longer. And I have none other than 1966 world surfing champion Nat Young to thank.

I was in Makaha, on Oahu's westside, covering the Oxbow World Longboard Championships. There, exposed to the traditional, laidback, ocean-oriented Makaha lifestyle, I felt like I'd been granted access to some kind of living surf museum, almost untouched by time. It's just as well Makaha localism has such a fearsome reputation. The place must never be allowed to change. Where else do the contest crew lovingly affix palm fronds to the contest structure to hide the unsightly metal scaffolding?

The biggest bummer was the hour-long drive each way to and from the North Shore to get some waves when the swell was small, or when you didn't feel like battling it out with a hundred odd loggers. The westside's only a short hop from the North Shore as the crow flies, but an enormous military base — Schofield Barracks — occupies the interior mountains, forcing a wide inland sweep around the towering, volcanic peaks.

I bummed a ride to the North Shore with Nat and his son Beau (the long- and shortboard ripper who bears an unearthly resemblance to his dad) one such day, Young Senior regaling us with stories from the old Makaha International days in the '60s: the extravagant receptions at the posh Outrigger Canoe Club; getting put up at the Sheraton Waikiki; the concrete bunkers that still squat amid the undergrowth on the Pupukea Hills — left over from the war — where thrifty surfers used to stay. Buzzy Trent, a Californian surfer who had been living at Makaha since the mid '50s, even succeeded in renting those bunkers out to the more gullible visitors.

Invitees to the Makaha International, Nat recalled, used to get a special pass for the duration of the contest allowing them to drive through the military base — reducing the drive to the North Shore to half an hour, along a scenic, winding mountain road through the Kole Kole Pass. This sharp, vee-shaped break in the mountains is where several of the Japanese bombers flew fifty-odd years earlier before dropping their explosive cargo on Pearl Harbor.

But those days are long gone and we braved the maze of freeways and exits to find our way to the North Shore. Even in October, the mass invasion of the Seven-Mile Miracle was well in evidence. To escape the crowds, we surfed some nondescript close-outs and occasional lefts at one of those anonymous breaks past Jocko's but before Waimea, and headed back a little underwhelmed at the thought of a two-hour round trip for such average surf. As we approached Wahiawa and the unsightly military base, Nat appeared to have some kind of spontaneous, nostalgic rush of blood.

'Let's try the Kole Kole Pass,' he barked. Who was I to argue? He swung the rental van hard right and, as if in slow motion, we passed through the imposing military gates.

Nat gave a cursory wave to the soldier on duty, who saluted mechanically, and we were in. Just like that. I figured Nat must have that regal, senior officer air about him, even from a distance.

Inside, it was like stepping through the magic looking-glass to some Hollywood set for a movie like *An Officer and a Gentleman*. Soldiers jogged in formation under the barking command of sadistic drill sergeants. Jeeps and trucks trundled about. Whole battalions hid beneath enormous nets of camouflage, practising for a jungle invasion of some long-suffering, Third World trouble spot.

I was waiting for an alarm to go off or stormtroopers to descend, heralding our intrusion. Nat, profoundly calm, stopped several times to ask bemused soldiers for directions to the Kole Kole Pass. We cruised through a veritable suburb of military houses and apartment blocks, past young kiddies happily at play, family men washing their cars, housewives hanging out clothes.

We had to wind our way up the mountainside to a second security check at the apex of the Kole Kole Pass itself, tantalisingly within sight of the westside, before we were home free. If we were busted there, we'd have to retrace our steps, turning the potential shortcut into a two-hour marathon. We practised our excuses as we approached the pass.

A guard came out from his box as we mounted the ridge and waved us down. I cowered in the back of the van among the surfboards, picturing our imminent arrest.

'This a hire car?' the guard asked dryly, looking us over impassively. Nat nodded. 'I'll write you a visitor's pass,' he muttered, as if impatient with another carload of lost tourists, before we had time to utter any of our elaborate explanations. It was a miracle. We were through. Nat was euphoric as we drove on, pulling over at a scenic lookout, leaping onto a low stone wall and roaring into the lush green recesses of the majestic valleys like 'the Animal' of old, his guttural cry echoing back at us.

Beau took over the wheel and flew down through the sweeping s-bends like a slalom skier, fatherly urges to slow down emanating from the passenger seat, around the protruding noses of the longboards separating them.

Before I knew it we were out of the rural foothills and back on the highway, zooming past McDonald's and Taco Bells, and jacked up four-wheel drives thumping out menacing rap bass lines. We pulled into the Makaha car park just before sunset, brilliant golden lines of swell combing the famous point, as the locals gathered for the traditional arvo beers and strum of the ukuleles. Caught up in the magic of the moment, I was ready to join them, but Nat had other ideas.

'We're going canoe surfing,' he announced, and marched off to fetch lifeguard Brian Keaulana to instruct us in the ancient art. Soon, I was stroking out through the busy line-up, furiously trying to keep time with my fellow oarsmen — Nat and Beau in front, and Brian behind me, skippering. Paddling into a rolling swell in an outrigger canoe is a surfing sensation unlike any other. I have a new respect for clubbies and their ridiculous craft, though they are patently ill-designed for waveriding. The outrigger canoe on the other hand is an amazing waveriding vehicle. The Hawaiian bobsled, Brian calls it. 'I get as big a rush on an eight-foot wave in the canoe as a 20-foot wave on a surfboard,' he reckoned.

We caught five waves, only flipped once, and found it remarkably easy to get whatever set waves we wanted, despite the crowded line-up. 'They can't really get mad with me. I might have to pull them out one day,' Brian reassured us. Brian would bark us into the biggest sets, even when I was convinced the seemingly sheer drop would surely end in disaster, and expertly steer us through the bowl, out onto the shoulder, and even execute cutbacks. I felt like I was tripping.

Back on land, the ukulele jam session was just warming up. I thanked Nat for making the magical afternoon happen. 'You've just got to do these things,' he bawled, a grommet-like fire sparkling in his eyes. I hovered in the shadows as Nat pulled a chair into the circle of Hawaiians drinking beer and playing music. Buffalo Keaulana (Brian's father), the Makaha patriarch, was holding court, just as he would have been thirty-odd years ago when Nat first came to Makaha. In the dusk half-light, they could have been in their twenties.

I tried the Kole Kole Pass scam again some days later, without Nat, and failed miserably. We got onto the base but got sent back at the pass itself by a brusque security guard who was aghast at our nerve and left us in no doubt that we would be severely dealt with if we tried it again. I can only imagine the ramifications of such a stunt in these post-9/11 times. It was as if the magic mountain had yawned open for that one instant to allow us through, and slammed shut again. A window.

No doubt about Nat — he knows how to jump through 'em.

'It's worth remembering what John Paul Getty said when he was asked in an interview what was the best thing he'd ever done in his life. He said it was when he was a teenager, when he and his friends picked up surfboards, paddled out and rode the waves. This was an old man, who'd been the richest man in the world and done whatever he wanted, and surfing was better than all of it.'

CHRIS HINES

[Founder of Surfers Against Sewage, UK, and Sustainability Director for the Eden Project which has developed an environmentally friendly surfboard made entirely of natural materials.]

bob mctavish

{ the shaper }

I feel very comfortable in the ocean, in big surf and stuff. I've learnt from fifty years of surfing that it's only water. As long as you flow with it, you're pretty safe. Life is just like water too. If you hang on you'll come through. No matter how hard a situation is at the time, you'll come through. Just flow with it and you'll come out the other side.

At sixty-two, Bob McTavish knows he probably shouldn't be swinging around under the lip and taking off late on ten-foot waves.

At an age when some folks are contemplating hip replacements and choosing nursing homes, the legendary Australian surfer/shaper is as fit and gung ho as many surfers half his age.

'I got hurt last time I surfed ten-foot waves . . . Took a ridiculously late take-off,' chuckles Bob.

Having recently passed the milestone of fifty years of waveriding, he seems resigned to the fact that he simply can't help himself. 'I feel like my personality has been moulded a lot by the ocean, in the sense that I take chances. The way I surf, I'll have a go at anything. I see a looming section, a bowl, it's only ten per cent makeable, I'm going. Same with a vertical drop — I'm a bit too close in but I'll give it a go. I might go over the falls but what the heck? I'll try and I'll pull it off sometimes. It's translated into feeling like I'm surfing through life. There's tight sections and bowls in life all the time, and I see in myself I'm probably too much of a risk taker, especially at sixty-two. I'm a bit of a fool that way. I jump in a bit too quickly. I'm so adrenaline pumped in the ocean, it's reflected in my life. It's the adrenaline lifestyle. You ask my wife. It drives her crazy.'

As a younger man, McTavish helped redefine surfboards, surfing styles, the whole surfing lifestyle, language and culture, during the pivotal '60s era of sudden consciousness expansion, freedom seeking and shortboard revolution. He turned on, tuned in and dropped out, as prescribed by counter-culture guru Timothy Leary, then rejected the new drug culture as a con and found meaning in God and a settled family life instead. He's made and lost fortunes in a business career filled with dizzying peaks and troughs. That he has ridden through it all with body, spirit and family intact is some kind of validation of his 'surf your life' philosophy.

'I feel very comfortable in the ocean, in big surf and stuff,' reasons Bob. 'I've learnt from fifty years of surfing that it's only water. As long as you flow with it, you're pretty safe. Life is just like water too. If you hang on you'll come through. No matter how hard a situation is at the time, you'll come through. Just flow with it and you'll come out the other side.'

When I call in at his Byron Bay surfboard factory, I find Bob out the back in the shaping bay, disc sander in hand, mask and ear muffs on, dancing around a blank with the grace and deft touch of a much younger man — the Gene Kelly of the blue room. I watch for a few moments as he neatly cross-steps from one end of the blank to the other, as he's been doing for over four decades now. He notices me, switches off the sander, removes mask and ear muffs and greets me warmly. I wonder aloud how many laps of these small blue-walled rooms he's trodden over the past forty-odd years. 'Well, I've shaped 40,000 boards and there's about a hundred laps per board, so that would make . . . four million,' he laughs.

Bob started surfing at the age of twelve, inheriting a love of the ocean from his father. 'Dad was a keen bodysurfer — he bodysurfed until he was eighty-nine, he's ninety-two now — and he took me bodysurfing from an early age. We lived in Toowoomba so we were only at the beach for holidays. We moved to Brisbane when I was twelve, and every weekend we were bodysurfing. Then he bought a toothpick, a 16-foot toothpick [an old-fashioned hollow plywood paddleboard], and I can remember the first sensation of paddling out the back. After years of bodysurfing I went, this is so much better. You can see what's coming. You never went out the back bodysurfing, but once you went beyond the breakers, you could see. The sensation of being up high . . . I started to get addicted from then on.

By the time I was fourteen I was a mess. I was a surf junkie . . . I wanted to live the life. I wanted to be on the beach. I wanted to be in the water every day for as long as I possibly could.'

Bob left home when he was fourteen, and slept in the first aid room of the Caloundra Surf Club, hovering around the older surfers and spending most of his waking hours in the water. He took advantage of the free accommodation in surf clubs for members, drifting from one club to the next. It was a time of regular new surf discoveries, as surfers struck out to explore the coast to the north and south. Noosa, Burleigh, Kirra, Lennox, Angourie — it seemed there was another empty, perfect, pointbreak to be discovered around every bend. Bob recalls iconic surf identity Pa Bendall picking him up from Caloundra one morning to introduce him to the delights of Noosa. 'Pa Bendall rocked up in the morning. "We're going somewhere different today, chuck your board in",' Bob mimics the gruff old surf pioneer. 'He drove me up to Noosa. I couldn't believe it. There was one guy in the surf club. He went, "Great, someone to surf with." Four of us went out at First Point. I couldn't believe these little zippers. I was paddling back out going, "It's a bit lonely here. It'd be good to have some mates here." That was in 1960. I just felt it would be really lovely to have some friends come here. I always dragged people back to Noosa whenever I could.'

Meanwhile, these early surfers were beginning to attract some unwanted attention from that other emerging youth tribe, the rockers. 'We were their exact opposites so we had a really hard time. The first few surfers had a really hard time, 'cause the coast was run by the rockers, the bikers, so we got beaten up, we had rocks chucked at our cars. But it didn't bother us. We had a great time anyway. Bodgies and rockers didn't hang around Angourie, they didn't hang around Noosa, they didn't hang around Bells or any of those coastal spots. It was only in the towns we had these problems. We just discovered the coast.'

Bob vividly recalls the first time he saw a surfer get tubed, riding inside the hollow curl of the breaking wave, at Tallebudgera River mouth on the Gold Coast in 1960. 'I was staying at Tallebudgera Surf Club, and I woke up one Saturday morning and saw a guy streaking across the shore-break. He goes past the first flag and it curls over him and he's going and going and going. I could see him backlit through the wave, and he popped out past the second flag, and I went, "What was that?" So when I went back to Caloundra the next week, I started going for the tube every wave. I started looking for the tube. It was really early days of tube riding, it's not like today where you can steer and navigate. It wasn't until '68 that we started to master it a bit, with shortboards, and started to manage tube rides really well.'

In 1963, at the age of nineteen, Bob became obsessed with a desire to get to Hawaii and challenge himself in the huge waves of the North Shore. With the fare hopelessly out of reach, he decided to stow away on a cruise ship, and enjoyed four weeks in the islands before eventually being deported.

'The stowaway was typical of my life,' says Bob. 'There was a chance I could get to Hawaii. A chance — there was no other way I was going to get there. We threw away careers. I was going to be an architect, chucked that in. I ended up working at a radio station for a while spinning discs. I was pretty intrigued by all that. They wanted me to be a DJ, that would have been fun, a bit of advertising, I found that interesting . . . but I chucked it all away to go surfing. I started shaping boards to make a living, took me thirty years and I got pretty good at it,' he laughs.

In 1965, Bob's mother was killed in a car accident and in his grief his surf addiction only deepened. 'I sort of turned to the ocean as my mother through the '60s and I'd go there for solace and guidance,' he says. 'I was surfing round Caloundra and the guys were all cool at pulling chicks and I wasn't, so I'd just go surfing, just go to the ocean. I ended up surfing six or eight hours a day, it was solace, and that went right through the '60s.'

The long hours in the water and an inventive, creative approach to waveriding paid off. Bob became Queensland champion in 1964, 1965 and 1966, finished third in the Australian titles in '65, and second in '66, and shaped Nat Young's world title winning board in '66.

'I guess by '65 I actually had a career going as a shaper, which I hadn't really planned on. I didn't plan on having a career, per se. I still don't call it a career, I'm just a shaper and a surfer.'

Bob's leading role in the so-called 'shortboard revolution' has been well documented, collaborating with Nat Young and Californian kneeboarder George Greenough in pushing the boundaries of surfboard design and surfing performance as part of what Bob dubbed 'the involvement school'. Disillusioned with competition, Bob was at the forefront of freeform expressionism in surfing, becoming intimately involved with the wave instead of merely riding it. His articles in surfing magazines at the time, wild streams of consciousness raves, were regarded as the gospel of this new direction in surfing.

In 1967, in *Surf International* magazine, he wrote of this new surfing style: 'Let the mind unshackle, set it free. Let it stroll, run, leap, laugh in gardens of crystal motion and sun and reality. Talk with the caretaker on the Plastic Telephone. Weave and paint with the hand of your imagination, with the fingers of your body, brush of fibreglass. See that Cavity up there? I'd love to be there, upside down, carven' off a cutback. Hey! The horizon's going over, up! Wow!! Sssswishsssss, swoop!! Toes pressed through wax job. Stomach in upper reaches of chest cavity. Feeling the bounce of the re-entry.'

In December '67, Bob and Nat took their deep vee-bottom boards to Hawaii, with mixed results, spinning out at Big Sunset, but surfing perfect six- to eight-foot Honolua Bay with the kind of powerful, arcing, top-to-bottom surfing that would become the template for modern high performance.

Again in *Surf International*, Bob wrote of that Honolua Bay session:

'GET IT ON!! Thrust! Move it out! Up. Under. Curl. Coming over! Right over! (that noise) Inside! (that feel) A GIANT GREEN CATHEDRAL AND I AM THERE. Positive-Negative Pow!! Infinity. Curl just going further ahead of me, but it's right! This situation is flawless. Now only water visible sky gone — can't see out but who needs to because time is gone. Seconds? Minutes? A lifetime. Crystals. Sound smells. Tasteless. Forever. Now. The door is open. The wave laughs, board breathes, sun smiles. Cruise out into . . . peace . . .'

Bob virtually invented much of modern surf language and its most enduring imagery and mythology — the concept of time expanding in the tube, the phrase 'the green cathedral' to describe the tube, the emphasis on 'thrust'. He once described a session at Noosa as like 'having a cup of tea with God'.

I mention to Bob that his writing reminds me of those other cutting-edge cultural forms of the time, beat poetry and improvised jazz, in its rhythms, unstructured form, its uncensored attempt to convey nebulous feelings. Bob is a bit embarrassed by a lot of this stuff these days, but he likes the comparison. 'We were into jazz, that was our music — and the Beatles and the Stones and Van Morrison. But jazz was our night music. We were beatish characters. It was the lifestyle of surfing, we were the foundation of that lifestyle. We no longer went for careers, we kissed the surf club goodbye, and it was beatish for sure, was crazy, pursuing surfing at a million miles an hour because it was the greatest thing on earth, and surfboards . . . The '60s was just tearaway, full-speed, adrenaline, as fast as you could power it. I had a pretty chaotic life.'

And as with the Beats, drugs were embraced as a gateway to higher levels of consciousness. 'When Timothy Leary said, "Take LSD and you'll reach instant nirvana," I was a spiritual sort of a dude, I popped acid — no nirvana. It was a con. So after popping acid for six months I thought, "Nuh, it's not on." The same with smoking pot. [Californian surfer] Bob Cooper got us all loaded in '65, '66. There was no one else smoking dope in Australia anywhere. Before the musos or anything, we were smoking pot thinking there was going to be insight and revelations coming from it, but nothing. So, by '69 I dropped all drugs and everything but I was still searching for spiritual truth. The Jehovah's Witnesses knocked on my door and I grilled them for two or three years before I finally realised they were making sense.'

In the space of a few years, Bob gave up drugs, became a Jehovah's Witness, and met and married his wife Lynne. 'In retrospect, I don't think I was complete until I met Lynne,' says Bob. 'In the '60s the ocean was my completion, it did the job. When I met Lynne and I was in a stable mental state, I'd given away drugs and had a pretty happy positive attitude to life, she was everything I wanted. We've been married thirty-five years and have five kids, so what I'm getting at there, is after that it changed, my relationship with the ocean changed. A couple of years later I became a Jehovah's Witness and developed a really strong belief that there is a creator, Jehovah, so then I started to view the ocean as one of the wonders of his design, one of his gifts to mankind. So I had a different perspective of the ocean, as a playground, a wonderful gift from our creator. The surf was a direct creation of God. He knew we would enjoy all that action on the shore, so I'm very thankful that we have a generous, loving creator.'

But those who look to Bob today to rekindle that mystical, quasi-religious surf fervour of the late '60s era are likely to be disappointed. He's moved on and is very clear about where surfing fits into his priorities these days. 'In the '60s, my life was chaotic, dedicated to surfing 100 per cent. But now I'm not dedicated to surfing, I'm dedicated to serving my creator. Surfing comes in line behind my wife and kids, and my responsibilities to my fellow man. Surfing's had to take a bit of a back seat for the last thirty years, but I feel blessed that I'm a shaper, that my career, for want of a better word, was making surfboards. I love it.'

Can surfing be a religious experience? 'I used to think so in the '60s, but I reckon it's a lot of crap now,' he snorts, before conceding, 'though the ocean has so many mysteries.'

What about the transcendental, time-expanding, consciousness-raising powers of the great green cathedral, the mystical tube ride? 'During the very brief acid period, I wrote that crap, got barrelled at Honolua and wrote in a magazine about time slowing down and it's been exaggerated ever since,' he laughs. 'I tell you what's freaky, being a Jehovah's Witness, I go knocking on doors trying to give people hope for the future. Some young kid, I knocked on his door a few years ago in Byron, and he went, "No, man, I've got the ocean. You get tubed, you see God." And I couldn't even say to him, "But I wrote that crap." All he could see was an old guy with a tie on.'

What about Timothy Leary's famous labelling of surfers as 'futurists' who had awoken to the idea that life is a dance, to be enjoyed in the now, not spent in servitude to the grim work–earn–spend–die grind of modern capitalism? As one of the surfers who helped break down the austere work ethic of the times, does Bob see some truth in Leary's words? He sighs heavily, as if reluctant to give the evil Acid Guru credit. 'Yeah, yeah, I do, but only a little bit,' he concedes eventually. 'When we tossed it all in in 1960 and the first years of the '60s got the surf culture rolling, we realised that the nine-to-five, buttoned-down thing was a hoax. American marketing, go live the suburban dream, it was a hoax. Have kids, get the big mortgage, just die. That's not what we're here for. We're here to enjoy this planet. Surfers picked up on that early. I remember that article by Leary, that was in the early '70s and I was starting to get a bit suspicious of all the marketing of dope and stuff. He wasn't on my favourite list . . . but, yes, we rejected the nine-to-five thing. It had everyone duped.'

Imagine back to Australia, specifically Brisbane, in 1958. It was a pretty radical move for a fourteen-year-old kid to quit school and leave home for an itinerant life bunking down in surf clubs and chasing waves. Where did the conviction come from, that he could carve out a life doing what he loved and not succumb to the grind? 'I think my dad helped me out a lot. In 1956, when I was twelve, he chucked his job in as a bank manager in Toowoomba and said, "We're going to go to Darwin." Bought a Chevy ute and a big caravan, didn't have much money, chucked all the kids in and away we drove. The wheel fell off the caravan before we got to Brisbane, so he ended up working in Brisbane. But his action of tossing his job in and going somewhere for a new life was a big lesson for a twelve-year-old. I realised what he was trying to do. He got caught back in the system for the next twenty years, work, work, work, so I took the lesson on board. So did my brother. He took off to Hong Kong and has been there for the last thirty years. I think Leary was right in that sense — that the early surf culture was rejecting the system. I hate the system. The system is bad. It's destroying the planet, it's so unjust, there are so many suffering people, it's a rotten system. Surfers saw that really early. Enjoy creation. We need to be much more in tune with our environment. We tried the hippy thing too but that didn't work because selfishness and greed come into it, and the system, we are all dependent on it to some extent. You just can't escape that, so you just try and minimise your footprint. You might ask why I make surfboards because of the pollution factor, but I have tried all my life to come up with better ways to make surfboards, more environmentally sound ways, and I'm still trying. I'd like to see one day that boards are recyclable.'

In 1992, Bob poured every cent he owned and large sums from investors into developing a new process for making moulded replicas of top surfers' boards, using polystyrene foam and epoxy resin. More durable and less toxic than conventional, hand-shaped polyurethane foam and polyester resin, Bob's Pro Circuit Boards were released to the market with great fanfare. But the boards suffered from production problems and potential buyers resisted the idea of mass-produced 'pop-outs'. Bob lost everything. Ten years later, an almost identical process was successfully developed and marketed by Surf Tech in the USA, producing a vast range of models by many of the world's top shapers, and gaining widespread market acceptance. Bob may simply have been ahead of his time. 'I feel like in my life I've taken big chances. I've had a couple of failures but in the process I was vindicated because the processes I developed ended up in Surf Tech.'

Bob has mixed feelings about the mainstreaming of surfing, the growing crowds and publicly listed surf companies, even as he has ridden this new wave of popularity with his classic longboards, funboards and retro models.

'In general, the big picture of where surfing is at, it's pretty darn buttoned-down straight,' he laughs. 'There's nothing alternative about it. The only thing that's true about it is when you actually hit the water, preferably with very few people and a good vibe in the water. That is true surfing. If someone is carrying on and whistling at you, I'll go somewhere else. That's not surfing to me. It's just another bitch fight and greed. To me there's still nothing better than a good eight- to ten-foot, good clean swell. The crowd thins right out and you can still pull half a dozen big, good waves on the east coast of Australia. To me that's heaven. Warm water, boardshorts — love it!'

On small days, he'll take his longboard out at the soft, gentle rollers of Watego's among the kids, learners, the moneyed middle-aged beginners and old folks, and enjoy the communal surfing experience. 'It's a pissy little wave but it's great — everyone's kept it fun. No yelling, people run over each other all the time, no one gets upset. Everyone's preserving the pleasant atmosphere of the origins of surfing. That's what Waikiki used to be back in the '60s. Watego's is like that today. Everyone keeps it happy. It's a rare break.'

After fifty years of surfing, for all kinds of reasons — solace, competition, consciousness expansion, design research, simple fun — Bob still marvels at how fresh it remains. 'It's a gift. You can go and de-stress, have a physical workout in this beautiful creation. Every day's fresh, every surf's different, every time I go surfing I have a ball.'

In this era of mounting crowds, when the waveriding dream sometimes seems in danger of being forever sullied by greed and aggression, Bob suggests our lesson as surfers might be to see past our selfishness, to embrace a sense of the common good of a surfing community enjoying a shared experience.

'Most sessions I go out and try and make it fun for everyone. Give them a wave, make it fun, share the experience,' he enthuses. 'There's more happiness in giving than receiving — Bible verse. Eddie Aikua [legendary Hawaiian lifeguard and big wave rider] taught me that — twice. He gave me a wave at Sunset. I'd been sitting there for half an hour, hadn't pulled a wave. This beautiful wave came and he says, "Bob, be my guest." "Really?" "Yep, be my guest." So I took this magnificent wave. Then a couple of years later, he saw me sitting at Trees at Waikiki and it was crowded and I'd been sitting for an hour without getting a wave, and Eddie said, "Bob," and I paddled over to him. When a couple of guys paddled for this set, he said, "Uh-uh, Bob's wave," and they pulled back, these big mokes, and gave me the wave. And I went, "Why did he do that?" And then I started doing it myself and realised what a wonderful thing it is to give people waves at your break. You're the host and they're the guest. You feel great. You're the host and you're sharing your little corner of the world with them.'

richard tognetti

{ the classical violinist }

The whole genesis of surfing was somewhere between a performing art and a sport. Surfing's always had that for me.

It's not a problem most classical violinists face. But for Richard Tognetti, the prospect of salt water dripping from his nose during a performance is a very real concern. Especially when he has a $10 million Giuseppe Guarneri del Gesù violin, built in 1743, resting under his chin.

'It's happened during rehearsal,' admits Tognetti, 'but not during a concert.' The saline nasal drip was a result of his long hours immersed in the ocean chasing waves.

The rare violin, known as the Carrodus, was recently purchased by an anonymous Australian benefactor and made available to Tognetti, creative director of the world-renowned Australian Chamber Orchestra. That is the kind of devotion the ACO inspires in its fans.

It would surprise many in the classical music world to know that Tognetti has had things other than rare antique violins occupying his attention lately.

'I couldn't have done a concert yesterday because I'd surfed for two or three hours,' says Richard. 'It's been a great month of surf in Sydney.'

A phenomenal run of swell has been playing havoc with Richard's schedule. Quick bolts south to Sandon Point, near Wollongong, have interrupted practice sessions.

'I think it's a damn blessing to have both music and surfing in my life,' says Richard. 'It's like the Ancient Greeks: body and mind.'

Richard says these twin pursuits, and the release surfing provides from the focused and disciplined world of classical music, have had great benefits. 'It's the ultimate Zen experience. I used to think I'd solve my problems by going surfing, but it's better than that. You can't even consider them. You just get lost in a dream. It's a brilliant release.'

Not too many surfers get lured away from the waveriding lifestyle by the delights of classical music, but Richard is one such rare creature. He grew up in Wollongong on the beach and naturally followed his older brother into the surf at Puckey's, North Wollongong. 'There was a gang of groms, I wasn't part of it but my brother was. He was always a terrific surfer.'

What does he remember from those early forays into the waves? 'Sitting out the back and trying to catch a wave and finally catching one and being overwhelmed by it,' he recalls. But when he was eleven, Richard moved north to study violin at the Sydney Conservatorium of Music, and surfing took a back seat.

'Then I didn't surf for years and years until I was seventeen. I found it too hard to do intermittently,' says Richard. Eventually the pull of the Bondi beachbreaks proved too much for the city-bound music student. 'I can remember the gradual improvement that comes with being an intermittent surfer. It's the hardest thing I've done,' he says. What kept him persevering? 'Just the common thread of that thrill, being lost in it,' he says. 'Just getting pummelled is so important, I reckon. If you get pummelled once it's no good, but if you get pummelled over and over you get used to it.'

Regular trips to southern Western Australia, and opportunities to combine touring and surfing fed the habit. 'When we tour regional areas — places like Shell Harbour — surfing there and doing a concert in Kiama that night, that's a pretty nice thing to do.'

But while Richard's surfing progress may have been gradual, his musical career surged from one peak to another. He trained under esteemed teachers such as Alice Waten and William Primrose at the Sydney Conservatorium, and Igor Ozim at the Berne Conservatory in Switzerland, where he was awarded the prestigious Tschumi Prize as the top graduate soloist in 1989. That same year he became artistic director of the Australian Chamber Orchestra, when he was just twenty-four. His was a controversial appointment, particularly because of his youth, but his bold and adventurous leadership of the ACO over the last seventeen years has earned it an international reputation for expanding the boundaries of classical music. Now over forty, Richard is widely regarded as one of the great classical violinists in the world today, and was made a National Living Treasure in 1999.

Richard is a very physical violinist, conducting as he plays, crouching and extending with the peaks and troughs of the music, riding the sound waves. He walks on stage with the surfer's easy gait, cracks jokes, hitches up his pants or gazes about casually when not actually playing. In another time or place, the stuffy world of classical music might have found his informality too much. But his talent redeems all.

A review in the London *Telegraph* in May 2006 is typical of the kind of praise the ACO and Tognetti earn: 'This concert was that rare thing, a beautifully shaped whole in which all the parts were absolutely in tune with each other and with the space . . . The orchestra played like angels throughout, with springing rhythmic grace and impeccable style . . . [Richard Tognetti] is one of the most characterful, incisive and impassioned violinists to be heard today.' Or this, from *The Times* in London: 'The Australian Chamber Orchestra is a ticket to musical bliss.'

These days, it is the idea of combining his surfing and his music that has Richard excited. He recently collaborated with Tom Carroll and Ross Clarke-Jones to produce a soundtrack to the big wave surfing video *Horrorscopes*, which documents a dangerous mission to surf a huge offshore reef near the Cape of Good Hope in South Africa.

Working with composer Michael Yezerski, and ex-Midnight Oil guitarist Jim Moginie, Richard's haunting violin provides a suitably eerie soundscape for the images of the cold, lonely, shark-infested waters.

'That was just so fortunate,' says Tom Carroll, who was won over to the power of classical music as a surfing soundtrack. 'It goes hand in hand with tow-in and big waves, the romantic side of it and the reality. The awesome power of the ocean, it's best married with music with real full-on, unadulterated emotion.'

Richard also performed on the recent album *Look*, by well-known surfing musician Pico, who recorded the album in a mobile studio while on a surfing road trip down the east coast of Australia.

Close followers of professional surfing may even recall an appearance by Tognetti at the Rip Curl Pro at Bells Beach in 1993. Close friend and ex-pro surfer Derek Hynd convinced Richard to play electric violin as accompaniment to recordings of past Bells winners discussing the event — a kind of spoken-word classical-music performance art. Most of the surfing crowd didn't quite know what to make of the experimental artform, but Richard remains excited by the synergy between surfing and music. In 2007, he's staging a tour of regional surfing centres to take his music to a younger audience.

'We've only just started,' he says. 'The whole genesis of surfing was somewhere between a performing art and a sport. Surfing's always had that for me.'

He imagines playing live at the beach to accompany a surfing performance — almost like an aquatic ballet. 'I'd love it. I've always dreamt of it. It's one of the most difficult things to do but one of the most appealing and one of the most satisfying.'

At the same time, he stresses, he's not on any mission to convert the surfing world to the virtues of classical music. 'I'm not into the tribal thing of surfing. I'm not much of a missionary. It's always refreshing when people talk about their musical experiences and they happen to be surfers. It was edifying when Tom Carroll started coming to the concerts and was blown away by the experience of sitting in a concert hall. The only difference when you're at classical music concerts, you are expected to just shut up and listen. For some that can be quite frustrating, but it can also be powerful, when you are exposed to yourself like that.'

There have been times when he's played violin spontaneously after a good day of waves and made a profound impression on his surfing friends who aren't normally exposed to classical music. 'I remember playing for a group of friends in WA. I'd been surfing the Farm . . . and instead of losing the energy, by the time I played, I was fuelled by the experience of surfing. And I played in the Maldives once to one of the surf guides there. He'd never heard a violin before. I started playing a few notes and he burst into tears. Those kind of things are pretty powerful.'

Richard reckons his own musical tastes are broad and he'd like to see a wider definition of surf music and a broader understanding of the kind of soundtracks that can best complement the beauty and drama of surfing. He cites the example of Pink Floyd's ambient soundtrack to '70s surf movie *Crystal Voyager* as an early influence in his understanding of how surfing and music can work together. 'I can listen to thrash metal if it's well played but I don't see the marriage. The soundtrack in my head [to surfing] isn't thrash metal,' he says. He once used footage of the late Tahitian surfer Malik Joyeux [who drowned at Pipeline, Hawaii, in 2005] on a huge wave at Teahupo'o, in Tahiti, and set it to a Beethoven symphony, to see how it worked. 'I thought that was overwhelming,' he says.

Tognetti has been seen as something of a maverick in the classical music world, but has won over even his most ardent critics, breaking down barriers between musical genres and taking classical music to new audiences. A recent documentary on a year in the life of the ACO was appropriately titled *Musical Renegades*. 'We feel Richard and the ACO are "renegades" from the stale, closed-off world that is sometimes associated with classical music and musicians,' says the film director, Tim Slade. 'We took the word *renegade* in its more everyday usage not as a "defector", as such, from a cause, but a breakaway who changes the status quo.'

Among his many groundbreaking collaborations and projects, Richard has also worked with former Midnight Oil singer (now Labor MP) Peter Garrett and cartoonist Michael Leunig in the performance and recording of *Leunig's Carnival of the Animals*. He also worked on Peter Weir's 2003 film *Master and Commander* — as composer, soundtrack soloist and violin tutor to Russell Crowe.

Does he think his taste for the adventurous and unusual in his musical career is influenced by his surfing? 'That's a very difficult question to answer. Let's say, yes. A Wollongong surfer doing what I do?' He leaves the question hanging, ponderously.

It has been a remarkable journey for a surfer from Wollongong and Richard's in no doubt surfing has played a large part in fuelling that journey. 'As Terry Fitzgerald once said, it's good to outlast the bastards. Coming from Wollongong, so many people are either mulled out or they've hit the plonk or they've turned to fat,' says Richard, 'but those who have kept surfing have kept living.'

'Life is like a day at the beach, and history moves like the waves of the ocean. Inevitably, a big, dangerous wave comes. Of those people who just sit there passively, some drown and some survive, according to chance. Those people who fight too hard usually drown. But those people who swim with the wave, feel it coming and add their strength to its currents, are moved forward and upwards. They ride with the wave and relish its ripples and currents, gently kissed by the sun. And the wave doesn't care. It is moved by forces beyond human perception according to the rhythms of the universe.'

NUSAPIENS BLOG

SURF LESSON #26
Paddle in the troughs, rest on the peaks, enjoy the ride

I am a kilometre or so out to sea, halfway between Currumbin and Burleigh Heads, paddling an enormous clubbie board, and I am starting to get a bit stressed.

'I reckon you're paddling at the wrong time,' Dave Rastovich observes.

A strong southerly is blowing and Dave has suggested an ocean paddle to take advantage of the wind swell out to sea, as a bit of sport on this otherwise surfless day. Paddleboarding has enjoyed something of a resurgence in recent times, as increasing numbers of surfers explore their roots — paddlers travel long distances on enormous, sleek boards, parallel to the coast, riding wind chop and rolling swells in the open ocean. This — as a form of transport between neighbouring Polynesian islands — is thought to have given rise to the sport of surfing. As you came in to shore, you would have naturally caught and ridden the breaking waves as the quickest route to the beach. This 'wave sliding' as it was traditionally known, proved such fun, provided such 'supreme pleasure' as Captain James Cook once famously observed, that it soon became a sport in itself.

As soon as we take off, Dave streaks ahead, catching little runs in the wind chop that I can't seem to find. It's like we're playing snakes and ladders and he's landing on every ladder. He stops and waits patiently while I flail breathlessly along.

'You're paddling on the top of the peak. You've got to paddle in the trough. When you see a steep bit in front of you, that means there's one behind you too. That's when you paddle. Once you're on them, you rest. You've got to paddle in bursts,' he explains. We set off again and within seconds he's caught two little runs and leapt ahead by fifty metres. At one point, Dave catches a full-on rolling swell and gets to his feet, surfing in open ocean, silhouetted against the skyline of Surfers Paradise in the distance. It is a surreal sight.

Slowly, I begin to get the hang of it and start to understand why Dave, and great watermen like Laird Hamilton, are such fans of the paddleboard thing. And it begins to occur to me, bobbing about out there in the ocean, that Dave may be applying this same shrewd strategy to his apparently blessed and effortless path through life, riding each little cosmic wave as it picks him up and propels him forward, paddling in the troughs, resting on the peaks, and enjoying the ride.

Dave, you see, is a professional 'free surfer', a wonderfully talented waverider who dislikes competition yet is handsomely sponsored simply to travel and surf for film and photo shoots. A blessed path if ever there was one. It made me wonder, how many of us struggle through life like the untrained ocean paddler, flailing away, bobbing like a cork on the ocean, wondering how others sail by so easily? And it struck me, on my paddleboard, somewhere between Currumbin and Burleigh Heads, that this might be an ability we can all learn. When there is a steep bit in front of us, a daunting climb, it means we are in a trough and there is another wave behind us about to pick us up. We don't have to climb that imposing peak in front of us, just catch the next one coming along from behind. It is in those down times that we really have to work to maintain our momentum, ready to harness the power of the next wave when it comes along. When we are on a peak, soaring along, we can rest and enjoy the ride, while understanding we can't hope to maintain this fleeting realm of the peak experience forever.

And there will always be peaks and troughs — may as well learn to ride them.

'There is beauty in everyone's individual style and how you surf a wave is indicative of your personality . . . sort of tells something deeper about you. Surfing is surfers' art. Surfing is a way to express yourself and a lot of people don't think of it that way. Sometimes that sounds deep and silly, but essentially it is true.'

KELLY SLATER

kelly slater

{ the king }

I really thought the ocean sent all of us signals like smoke signals from the Indians and that it was communicating with me in some way. I had to communicate back with it. It sounds very out there and fruity but as a kid it was reality. And my parents weren't even hippies. No one gave me that idea.

Perhaps enough words have already been written about Robert Kelly Slater, eight-time world champion, holder of just about every record in the history of the Association of Surfing Professionals, greatest surfer of this and perhaps any other era.

The humble beginnings in the small waves of Florida, the broken home, the largely absent alcoholic father, the focused, driven young competitor pouring all his youthful angst into the ocean. The unstoppable sweep to glory on the pro tour — both the youngest and oldest world champion in history, with eight titles accumulated over fourteen years of unparalleled dominance.

When I came up with the idea for this book, this notion that surfing and the ocean held powerful life lessons, Kelly was close to the top of my list of interview subjects. I'd seen enough of him over the years to know he approached surfing slightly differently to many of his peers, a difference that has become more apparent as time has gone on. He has taken time off from the pro tour to explore other areas of life — music, yoga, acting, business. He has largely kept his own counsel, preferring his solitary competitive success to popularity on tour. Despite ushering in the so-called 'new school' era of super high performance, he seems to harbour something of an old-school philosophy which regards surfing as a tool to self-knowledge. 'Surfing is kind of a way to find out things about myself. It gives me really good feedback to my life, where I'm doing good and where I'm doing bad, where I can improve in different ways,' he observed in the 2005 documentary video *Letting Go*, on his record seventh world title season.

Five years earlier, during an extended break from the pro tour, he'd seemed acutely aware of the dangers of letting surfing competition become his whole world. 'The life on tour is pretty exciting. There's always a lot of stuff happening. It's really easy to get caught up in thinking that's what life's about, you know, to not be excited just by everyday life,' he told me back in 2001. 'Sometimes I feel like I'm missing out a bit on pushing myself. But then, I'm probably more healthy physically and emotionally and, at this point in my life, that's more important.'

His outlandish eighth world title seemed to come through a conscious effort to let go of his infamous competitive instincts, to be unattached to surf contest results. This non-attachment has only served to increase his dominance over a whole new generation of competitors, frustrated beyond belief as their greatest career goals are denied by a man who seems barely to care.

His unending success, though, has also intensified the goldfish bowl existence he endures as the most famous surfer of all time. Gaining an audience with the Great One these days is no easy task. I dogged him on the Gold Coast during the Quiksilver Pro, but there was always a pressing media throng and scrum of fans mobbing him — hardly the place for an intimate, philosophical chat. He stalked the competitor's area like a caged lion — instead of bars, surf fans held him prisoner as they incessantly waved pens and paper or snapped photos, hundreds of them standing and staring as if he were an exhibit in a zoo. How must that feel, I'd wonder? In the spirit of this project — to try and unearth surfing's higher potential as a consciousness-raising tool — I could hardly bring myself to join the madding crowd.

Ironically, my then four-year-old daughter found it a relatively simple matter to run freely in and out of the cordoned-off competitor's area, playing as she was with the children of some of the surfers, unobstructed by the burly security personnel. At one point, Kelly squatted down to engage her in conversation, but she brusquely rejected his advances, perhaps the only person present not interested in chatting with the Great One, as she chased the other kids around. Kids and dogs, I remember Kelly once observing, are his favourite choice of company, because they don't care who he is.

The contest came and went, Kelly won without raising a sweat on the way to his eighth world title, and that moment of quiet conversation never materialised. I was reduced to firing off pleading emails, explaining the lofty intent of this book to distinguish it from the myriad other media requests he was no doubt besieged with. And then, one day, to my enormous surprise, in my inbox came a brief but thoughtful and illuminating set of answers.

'I get a lot of interviews and things I have to do and I can't really get to all of these if they keep coming my way and don't want to put you off. Hope you understand,' he explained.

What are your earliest memories of surfing?
Just venturing out into a mixed bunch of waves and lines that I had to figure out the patterns to. I really thought the ocean sent all of us signals like smoke signals from the Indians and that it was communicating with me in some way. I had to communicate back with it. It sounds very out there and fruity but as a kid it was reality. And my parents weren't even hippies. No one gave me that idea.

Any peak moments in the surf, when the waveriding experience has seemed most profound, moved you most deeply, maybe helped pull you out of a difficult time or helped you see things more clearly?
There have been numerous times that surfing was able to help me pull out of being depressed or focused on something that was unfulfilling to me. I have always been able to trust what feedback it gives me and the direction that pushes me. I can't think of one to share right now or maybe don't want to. :)

What lessons do you think surfing and the ocean have imparted to you? Do you agree the ocean can be a powerful teacher and metaphor for life?

The ocean teaches patience and experience. I think if applied in any way it can teach you about whatever you want to know. The laws of energy are nowhere more apparent than in the ocean. If the bottom's there the wave's gonna push up against it. If there's any chop it will affect the wave in a certain way, as will the wind and all the different angles of movement that occur when waves get near shore and start to materialise in an orderly or chaotic way.

How has surfing shaped and influenced you and your life's journey? How different might your life have been if you hadn't found surfing?
I'm not sure what I would've done other than surf. I may have eventually found music and stuck with that but initially I probably would have lived locally in Cocoa Beach for years and had a normal job like anyone else. I'm not sure whether I was destined for stardom in any other way than surfing. Maybe I would have been a fisherman. I don't know. My mind keeps thinking of big things though, and usually that makes you do something away from where you started, 'til you get back there.

How does surfing make you feel? How do you explain the effect it has on us? How has your relationship with surfing changed and evolved over time?
Surfing was initially just a fun thing to do. It became a challenge and a dream and a way of life. Eventually it turned into a job and a responsibility. In the worst of times it has been a real pain in the arse but ultimately it is an ongoing adventure and, needless to say, has provided me with incredible experiences and still remains the most fun thing to do in my life.

'You can't stop the waves, but you can learn to surf.'

JON KABAT-ZINN,
SCIENTIST, WRITER, MEDITATION TEACHER

dr dave jenkins

{ the humanitarian aid worker }

Late in the day, only him and me out, rising swell, four- to six-foot perfection, and the red sky stretched 180 degrees — God putting on a show. The take-off was tricky but if you made it you settled into a barrel. Looking out all you could see was red horizon through the tube. A huge sense of healing wonder washed over me. Euphoria but in a spiritually higher place, not the adrenaline type. This was from a calm place and reinvigorated the soul.

Sitting on a luxury surf charter boat, after a day of great waves, enjoying fresh fish and cold beer, is undoubtedly one of surfing's sweetest and most indulgent pleasures.

When Dr Dave Jenkins stepped out of this surf fantasy bubble into the stark reality of life on land for the people of the remote Mentawai Islands in Indonesia his life changed forever.

'We'd just had a really good session at Lance's Right, and we had this beautiful lunch and a few beers on the boat and were going, "Wow, what an experience this is, this is a bit salubrious",' laughs Dave. 'And just the perfection of Lance's Right, it's such a beautiful wave . . . I think we were all pretty sensitised by that experience when we went into the village.'

After lunch, Dave and several of his travelling companions headed into the nearby village of Katiet to meet the locals. 'And the contrast between our experience and what was happening fifty metres away . . .' Dave leaves the sentence unfinished, as if words are inadequate.

When Dave took time out from his high-powered position with a Singapore-based multinational health company in 1999, he headed to the perfect waves of the Mentawai Islands, looking only for rest, recreation and the surfer's dream of empty, idyllic waves in an unspoilt natural setting. 'I was the education director setting up training programs for a very corporate, quite conservative German multinational, so I was pretty thrilled to get away and go surfing,' he says.

Images of the phenomenal surf of the Mentawai Islands had been broadcast through the surf media for several years, making the islands suddenly top of every surf traveller's wish list. What remained largely unseen was the desperate poverty and health conditions of the islands' inhabitants.

Dave and his companions took the small tender to the beach after lunch, negotiating the keyhole in the reef and coming ashore on the coarse, golden sand lined with palm trees. Set back in the trees, small quaint houses built of exquisite rainforest timbers lined a narrow walking track through the village. Children played happily, locals came out of their houses to welcome them warmly.

'I always take a big medical bag because I'd run a few clinics at Frigate's Passage in Fiji a few years back,' says Dave. 'And also just to cover ourselves for injuries and illness.' But it soon dawned on him that not all was well in this picture-perfect island paradise. 'I noticed a few pot-bellied kids and things that weren't quite right, and I was curious about the health of the village, so I started asking a few questions. And immediately they found out who I was they said, "Can you see some patients?"'

Dave agreed to come back in a couple of hours with his medical bag. 'When I came back there were about a hundred people there. Half the village turned up. They had never had a doctor there.'

He discovered rampant malaria, tuberculosis, cholera, malnutrition — and people dying for lack of basic health care.

'A lot of them have got complaints that they have never had diagnosed or treated or don't understand what they can do about them. So we set up a little clinic at the chief's house. We were overwhelmed. It was a really intense situation. Some people I can remember still — a whole family wasting away with tuberculosis, looking like cancer victims or Auschwitz victims, really wasted. And this one woman came in a wheelbarrow, they brought her in semiconscious and she died. I couldn't save her. Even two days earlier we probably could have saved her. And there were kids I noticed who were malnourished. They had malaria. It was the sickest of the sick. That's the thing when you go into the villages.

There's kids running around laughing and carrying on, but behind there are the ones you don't really see. It was the witnessing of that . . . One of my mates turned green and had to leave. My fiancée was fighting back the tears. And we sort of went back at the end of the day, just, "Phwooo, that's heavy," and just sat with it for a while. No one said anything that night, and I guess it dawned on me that I was going to do something about it.'

What Dr Dave Jenkins did was start a medical charity, Surf Aid International, which has attracted the support of the world-wide surfing industry and community, earned the praise of the World Health Organisation, the United Nations, the US Navy and government aid agencies like AusAID and NZAID. In the space of five years Surf Aid's efforts have reduced malaria by up to ninety per cent in their two pilot villages, spread their health programs to another 200 villages throughout the Mentawais and neighbouring islands, and responded to the Boxing Day Tsunami and subsequent earthquakes with an extraordinary, sustained relief effort in some of the most remote and devastated parts of Indonesia.

That first day at Katiet village still drives Dr Dave's sense of mission. 'I remember that woman, I've still got her photo, one of the worst tuberculosis victims, and thinking, this is so treatable, this is mad, absolutely mad. And being almost angry at my own journey in life that was about career advancement, big pay packets. My dream was to actually buy a boat and sail away. And coming up against the way you're living compared to this madness. With a little bit of education, knowledge and compassion you could turn the situation around. I call on that energy sometimes to keep going.'

When Dave returned on the charter boat to the Sumatran mainland port city of Padang, he started asking around the local surf charter industry to see if he could muster some support for his plans. He was pointed in the direction of Dr Manoo, an Iranian doctor, and his wife, Nita, who had been waging a lone campaign to help the long-suffering people of the

Mentawais for years. 'I went to see him and he said, "Oh we've been waiting for you to arrive." He and Nita both said, "We've just been waiting for someone to arrive, we knew it would happen." That was very encouraging meeting him. He's a very inspiring character, he's quite a spiritual leader.'

Dr Manoo had run clinics out in the islands, like Dave had just done, for years — but had eventually realised that the need was too great to tackle in that way. He decided education and training and self-empowerment for the Mentawai people were the only answers to the problems. Dr Manoo and his wife had set up schools in the islands, adopted numerous Mentawai orphans and helped educate a group of Mentawai nurses, so that they could return to the islands and help educate others, while providing some basic health care. All Dr Manoo needed to carry out the plan was funding for wages for the nurses and a series of small clinics throughout the islands. Dr Dave figured he could approach the fast-growing local surf charter industry and the wider global surfing industry, which regularly used the island's amazing surf for film and photo shoots, to raise the necessary funds.

'He and I sat down and wrote a project plan, and then came over here [to Australia] and went round the surf industry . . . That was the hardest part, raising money for those first two years.'

The surfing industry was initially sceptical about this unknown New Zealander and his grand plans. 'Those guys had all been out to the islands. They knew there was no infrastructure. Where were you going to live? What were you going to do? How were you going to do it? It didn't seem feasible.'

In hindsight, he can understand their hesitation. 'It was kind of mad. It was. It was beyond rational thinking,' he admits. 'What are you doing? This is an ancient culture, this is extreme isolation, extreme levels of endemic disease and just a bunch of surfers who go there surfing. How are you going to fix that? I never really saw it. Only now looking back do I see it as mad. I just thought it was tough and it was something that needed to happen.'

Dave quit his job, sold his house, and put all his time, energy and resources into getting Surf Aid off the ground. Friends, strangers, his fiancée at the time, all were swept up in his sense of mission. 'I always knew it was the right thing and that's energised me. I went back to Singapore, and turned to Bron my fiancée and she was all up for it. She has a really big, warm heart. She was a successful corporate marketing director. She was prepared to give that up. She had some real skills. I didn't know business or marketing or whatever, so she really helped. I tossed in my job, she tossed in hers and we went back to New Zealand to find out about registering for a non-profit organisation and how to build a charity from nothing, and to talk to some of my friends. In particular, Dr Steve Hathaway, who's now chairman, is one of my best friends who has many years' experience in running global programs. He's an adviser to the WHO and the United Nations. I talked to him about what I wanted to achieve. He'd been to the Mentawais. And then my lawyer friend who's now lawyer for Surf Aid, he'd also been to the Mentawais. I said, "Listen, if I do this thing will you join me and help me form a board and volunteer your time?" And they said yes, so it seemed like it was feasible. And then Bron started putting together some information and a brochure and a marketing plan . . . While we were doing that, we were communicating with people in the Mentawais and Dr Manoo and forming a plan.'

Dr Manoo's experience and expertise were central to Dave's plans, so when Dr Manoo announced that he was moving to the larger city of Medan in northern Sumatra to expand his education program, Dave was hit with a sense of dread. 'He said, "Dave, sorry, I can no longer implement this program." So at that point I realised the lip was about to hit me in the head and I'd better duck and rearrange things and get ready for the barrel. I was going to have to do it myself.'

Living on savings and funding Surf Aid out of his own pocket, Dave soon started running out of money. He went to London and got a job to bankroll the fledgling organisation, and it was there he met an unlikely saviour. Andrew Griffiths was a twenty-eight-year-old New Zealand surfer and hotshot in the corporate banking world, who was looking to take some time off to go surfing. The prospect of combining a surf adventure with humanitarian work appealed to him.

'Dr Dave and I met in a little pub in London because, through a friend of a friend, I had heard of his idea to develop a non-profit organisation in the Mentawais,' remembers Andrew. 'Dr Dave unloaded a creative force of hurricane proportions. He detailed for me the childhood mortality rates, the disease, the suffering and the fatigue, and then once he had me down, boom! Out came the fundraising ideas. One that sticks in my mind, "We could get people to paddle around Japan to raise money for this and with the money we could go and set up health systems and quite literally save lives." The lifesaving hooked me. The paddling around Japan convinced me Dr Dave needed help.'

Andrew jumped aboard, brought his business acumen to the table, and turned his upcoming surfing holiday into a humanitarian mission. 'He was amazing,' says Dr Dave. 'He took it on passionately, raised money with his friends and donated money himself. I gave him all the links and he and Andy Lucas [another New Zealand surfer and doctor] and a bunch of surfers distributed mosquito nets up and down the Mentawais as part of our first program. We didn't know what we were getting into, we really didn't. We were quite naive on some levels, but with the combined determination and skill, the complementary knowledge and backgrounds, that's when Surf Aid started to become more feasible. I thought, "Wow, maybe we do have a chance." I think

Andy was just thinking it would be an adventure, something to do that would be useful as well as going surfing. Once he'd been in the villages he was hooked. Once he'd walked down a village and had thirty kids holding his hand and he just saw the beauty of the people out there, I think he was pretty hooked.'

I first met Dr Dave and Andy Griffiths during the Gold Coast leg of the Big Day Out concert tour in 2000. They were trying to sell raffle tickets to stoned fifteen-year-olds, as Dave recalls. It seemed an unlikely setting for a pair of aspiring aid workers but Surf Aid was grasping any fundraising opportunities they could find at that stage. Organisers of the Big Day Out, impressed by their passion, offered them a stall to promote their work and raise funds throughout the Australian and New Zealand tour. A couple of pro surfers gave Surf Aid informal endorsements, donating old surfboards for them to raffle. I'd volunteered to help out on the Gold Coast, and so we stumbled about the thronging Big Day Out crowd, carting one of Luke Egan's surfboards, waving raffle tickets and trying to scream above the din to uninterested teenagers about the perils of malaria in remote Indonesia. It was a hard sell.

By the end of one day I was fried. Dave and Andy endured the entire tour, six cities in two weeks, spurred on by the knowledge that every ten dollars raised would buy another mosquito net and give another Mentawai child or family a shot at good health.

'We spent very little money, we spent it all on the program. Because everyone was just giving so much of their own time and money and energy, we developed a philosophy, if we can't make something work at a pilot stage we shouldn't continue. We should get other agencies with more experience to come and do it. But I'd already tried to do that. I'd already rung World Vision, Médecins Sans Frontières (Doctors Without Borders), to describe the situation and asked if they could help, and for a variety of geopolitical reasons they couldn't.'

Surf Aid's pilot malaria programs went ahead in two villages, but the future was looking shaky. 'Andy and I weren't taking any income from it, we were going to run out of money, and it was a matter of either getting some money soon or shutting it down.'

The cruel irony was that Surf Aid's financial position was becoming most desperate just as they were receiving solid proof that their small-scale programs were working. Baseline data had been meticulously recorded before any intervention was undertaken. A year later, Surf Aid's campaign of education and distributing mosquito nets seemed to have reduced malaria by an astounding seventy-five per cent.

Lonely Planet Publications threw Surf Aid a lifeline with their first significant corporate donation and then, slowly, things started to go their way. US surf journalist Steve Barilotti spent time in the Mentawai Islands, documenting the malaria program, and the resultant article pricked some consciences in the US surf industry. Co-founder of surf company Reef, Santiago Aguerre, got behind Surf Aid and sent out an open letter to the US surfing industry, inviting them to get involved. Dr Dave was invited to address the Surf Industry Manufacturers Association (SIMA) at their annual conference in Cabo San Lucas, Mexico. Suddenly, Dave found himself jetsetting around the world, spreading the Surf Aid message. 'Joe Dowling is a stockbroker in New York, he's one of our biggest donors. He flew us out to New York, met us, spent two or three days asking difficult questions, liked what we stood for, and wrote us a cheque. We'd just done our parasite rates and we had a seventy-five per cent reduction, so I stood up at Cabo [at the SIMA meeting] and said, "This is what we've done and we'd like you to be a part of it." I was in another zone during that speech. I could hardly remember it, as if some other force entered me and helped me express how important it was. This came across powerfully and made grown men cry. The next day we were talking to Billabong and Quiksilver.'

Surf Aid was suddenly a going concern. With solid data showing that their programs were working and some real funding, the young organisation was set to consolidate and refine its operations. But the universe, it seems, had other ideas.

1999 was an interesting time to start an aid agency in the Mentawais, largely dependent on surf tourism as its point of contact with the outside world. In a few short years, they had to deal with the SARS scare, the September 11 terrorist attacks, the first Bali bombing, and the spectre of bird flu, all conspiring to keep Western tourists away from places like Indonesia. Somehow, they survived. On Boxing Day 2004, the ground shifted again, literally this time, and Surf Aid found itself dealing with an unprecedented humanitarian disaster. Some 240,000 lives were lost around the Indian Ocean when a huge tsunami inundated coastlines in Indonesia, India, Thailand, Sri Lanka and Africa. The overwhelming majority of lives lost, some 170,000 of them, were in north-west Indonesia, right in Surf Aid's backyard.

'I was on Christmas holiday with my kids staying in a 1950s caravan on Steve Hathaway's front lawn, having barbecues. We were two days into the holiday when I got the call, so I was packing my bags again and jumping back on a plane,' Dave recalls. 'That was extremely testing of our physical and intellectual endurance, and really stressful.'

Although the Mentawai Islands themselves, and Padang, were spared the brunt of the tsunami, the neighbouring islands to the north were directly in its path. With a fleet of charter boats on hand, and an intimate knowledge of the most remote nooks and crannies of the island chain, Surf Aid was positioned to respond to the disaster in a way bigger and more established aid agencies couldn't.

Boat owners and skippers banded together to donate the use of their boats and skills. The surf industry kicked in with massive donations. Suddenly, this ragtag bunch of surfers were at the front line of a global rescue mission to reach and help survivors in some of the most inaccessible island communities. 'We knew that the threat of epidemic diseases was real because we'd seen them in the Mentawais even without a tsunami. We'd seen measles outbreaks, we'd seen cholera outbreaks. I think having had that experience, we were positioned to respond, and we were motivated and knew what to do. And then the synchronicity that happened between us and the boat captains and the surf industry, that was fantastic. It meant our productivity was way beyond what anyone could have expected — including the UN, who made comments, and AusAID and NZAID. "Who's this Surf Aid? Why are they the only people getting into these remote isolated villages that no one else has got to?" We were the only agency with doctors who had spent time in the field, who speak Indonesian, and were capable and skilled enough to run a program for an extended time under incredibly stressful conditions. The other guys took time to get all those people together.'

Dave is justifiably proud of Surf Aid's performance under such extreme pressure. 'This is the story that hasn't been told. There were no epidemics. If you look at other emergencies on such a scale, there are almost always epidemics. In Pakistan there were cholera outbreaks. We didn't have one significant one. We succeeded in what we set out to do.'

But the gods, or whatever commands such colossal forces, weren't done with the Indonesian islands yet. On 28 March 2005, a massive earthquake, measuring 8.4 on the Richter scale, rocked Sumatra and devastated the popular surfing island of Nias, among many others. Another 3000 lives were lost. More than 500,000 people were left homeless. 'After the earthquake, we had all these injuries. We had kids lying around with fractured femurs on day seven after the earthquake, in little villages in the hills of Nias. They would have died. And we suddenly had eighteen charter boats and a helicopter and I remember a moment flying over Seronga. We had all our boats in the harbour there and I was in the helicopter. We'd just evacuated all these people to the mercy ship. That was a really proud moment. The helicopter was a bit dodgy, and another helicopter had recently gone down and killed everyone on board. I thought, "OK, I'm happy to die now. I'm really proud of what we've achieved and if I go down now we've done something worthwhile."'

Surf Aid made quite an impression on the more established aid agencies it worked with. 'From the first day it seems that they were out in the field going around the smaller islands identifying and moving the seriously injured, days before the rest of the organisations in Medan were able to operate,' says Morgan Morris, head of the UN's emergency field office in Medan, capital of Sumatra. 'Surf Aid were also a valuable source of information because of their previous work in the area even before the tsunami, and it was this information that proved invaluable to the search and rescue operations by being able to help identify landing sites for the helicopters and sites where beach craft could be used. I think it is no exaggeration to say that the Surf Aid teams saved many lives that could have been lost without their prompt action. Surf Aid will be remembered and respected by the people of these islands and the many UN and NGO agencies who worked with them, for many years to come.'

More aftershocks followed. Several volcanoes in the area became active. At one point, Surf Aid staff had to move out of their Padang office because cracks had appeared in the walls. Waves of panic spread throughout the local populace, as rumours of another tsunami would spring up after every tremor. 'I live on the hill in Padang. After the second earthquake, we had people coming up the hill evacuating, thinking Padang was going to get hit by a tsunami. The volcanoes were going off and we had people coming down from the mountain,' remembers Dave.

Slowly, as things have returned to a semblance of Sumatra's precarious version of normality, Surf Aid has returned to its core programs. Central to Surf Aid's remarkable success is a simple, insecticide-treated mosquito net. When they recently conducted blood screenings at their two pilot villages, malaria parasite rates were down by ninety per cent. While Dr Dave stresses there could be seasonal fluctuations and other factors, the results are hugely encouraging. 'It's about creating social demand for the mosquito nets, because they're a culture that hasn't really had much exposure to modern life and education, and they didn't know that malaria was transmitted through mosquitoes. So their understanding of disease was really very low: "So why would I want a mosquito net?" To turn that situation around we needed a multifaceted education program — school songs, plays, dances, really get the whole community in. So, once we created a social demand, we had a very high uptake of the mosquito nets, which meant we had broken the cycle. The mosquitoes land on the nets and they die. Then people would say, "Look at all the dead mosquitoes." And they were pretty excited by that. It was almost like magic. And it is almost magic, the way it creates this halo. If you get about eighty per cent of the community using these insecticide nets you get like this protective halo, and then the mosquitoes smell it and turn away and go bite a rat or bird or pig or something. So that again just adds to this breaking of the parasite cycle.'

Surf Aid's goal of a malaria-free Mentawais suddenly doesn't look as far-fetched as it once did. They are also expanding their programs in immunisation, nutrition and education in health and hygiene. Dave gives the example of a Surf Aid worker who began a small vegetable garden because she couldn't get the kind of food she wanted in the village where she was posted. Soon, the idea caught on and villagers started vegetable gardens. Before long, word had spread and neighbouring villages were following suit, to supplement their staple diets of taro and rice and improve nutrition and general health. This, says Dave, is the greatest goal of aid work, to inspire spontaneous and lasting change and empowerment, for the people to help themselves. Surf Aid's ultimate aim, he says, is to make itself redundant in the Mentawais and move on to other surf-rich but socially disadvantaged regions. Eastern Indonesia, Fiji, the Philippines, Africa, the South Pacific — there is no shortage of exotic locations where surfers travel to find waves and local populations live in oppressive poverty.

'Western individualism and the way society's shaped now and the priorities and goals it fosters mean that other people don't have access to the simplest and most basic health care,' says Dave. 'It's like [wealthy US investment king] Warren Buffett recently said, capitalism is great, it worked for the last few hundred years for getting fifty per cent of the world's population out of poverty, but now a new paradigm is required to distribute that wealth and also save the planet's ecosystems. We need to seek new ways of doing things.'

All these ideas had begun to crystallise in Dave's mind, he says, when the opportunity to start Surf Aid materialised. 'At the time it seemed like an opportunity to express that human value.'

Dave and many others have sacrificed a great deal to keep Surf Aid going and they continue to inspire remarkable support from a wide variety of corporate and private donors from within and outside the surfing community. Such is Surf Aid's standing these days, they were invited to take part in *Time* magazine's Global Health Summit in New York in November 2005, convened to tackle the world's health problems. Surf Aid was represented by big wave rider and honorary board member, Laird Hamilton, who joined speakers such as Bono, Bill Clinton and Bill Gates. It is a long way from trying to sell raffle tickets to stoned teenagers at the Big Day Out.

What seems to have rallied surfers around the world is the idea that surfing might prove to be a blessing to a remote area, rather than a curse. Surfing has been a forerunner of major development in many parts of the world — drawing attention and more travellers to some of the most beautiful destinations on Earth. In many places, unchecked development has been to the detriment of the local environment, has displaced local people, corrupted their cultures, and led young people into drug dealing and prostitution to cater to the tastes of their new guests. This sad reality weighs heavily on the hearts of many surf travellers, who have watched the inevitable waves of modernisation wash up on some of their most treasured shores. Dave knows that the Mentawais, and what he has undertaken there, are something of a test case for the idea that surfing could actually be good for a remote area, bringing economic, social and health benefits to the local people. He takes heart from the interest of Conservation International, a large environmental NGO, which has proposed an eco-marine reserve concept for the entire island chain and convened a conference in Padang for all interested parties. Guidelines for environmentally responsible development would be strict, and the interests of local stakeholders upheld. Their vision is for the Mentawais to be the Galapagos Islands of the surfing world — a place where rare and fragile ecosystems are preserved and local cultures respected. Without such a framework, Dave fears that unchecked development would lead to many problems for local communities. At least if they have good health, he reasons, they have a better shot at advocating for their rights to be respected in the gold rush of land camps and surf resorts that is already beginning.

'There was and there still is a fear of the huge size of the project, and of moving into new areas that you're uncomfortable with and the sacrifices you have to make,' says Dave. 'Concern for my family was the largest problem, but there's also the knowledge that I'm doing the right thing. As a father, even though my kids don't see as much of me, I've done the best thing as a parent in setting an example. And both my kids are very much involved in humanitarian issues. I think that's been a real big motivator recently for me, to see that the kids are really stoked that Dad's doing this work and are inspired to do similar things.'

Dave doesn't get as much time to surf as he would like — he reckons the locals get a bit testy if they see him surfing too much. Why isn't he off saving someone, because there is always someone who needs saving here? He clearly savours the occasional surf, usually in idyllic conditions, when he gets the chance. The perfect waves of the Mentawais have no doubt helped attract many of the Surf Aid volunteers. Andrew Griffiths says surfing itself has instilled in Surf Aid's staff and supporters the very qualities that have made it viable. 'The transformation in our organisation is a credit to the entire sport of surfing — its industry leaders, its athletes, its media, its consumers and the sport itself. It teaches us to take risks, to believe and to have fun,' says Andrew. 'Those lessons and the support of many people have put Surf Aid in a position where we have now started work on an expanded project.'

Surfing is also an important source of renewal when working in harsh conditions, facing grim realities, day after day. Dr Dave recalls surfing E-bay, one of the best waves in the islands, with a fellow Surf Aid doctor, after a tough day in the field, and having what he can only describe as a spiritual experience: 'Late in the day, only him and me out, rising swell, four- to six-foot perfection, and the red sky stretched 180 degrees — God putting on a show. The take-off was tricky but if you made it you settled into a barrel. Looking out all you could see was red horizon through the tube. A huge sense of healing wonder washed over me. Euphoria but in a spiritually higher place, not the adrenaline type. This was from a calm place and reinvigorated the soul.'

Dr Dave's journey from that first dream session at Lance's Right to his spiritual moment at E-bay six years later, is one not many of us could comprehend.

How has surfing helped him endure the innumerable tests and hurdles he's faced along the way? 'It's my place for reverence, my stress reliever, one of the things that centres me. My meditation. Over time it's been more about the paddle out. The waves of course are important but they're a bonus. It's being a humble and minute part of the massive expanse of sea and wind and sky that's most important.'

Surf Aid recently received a prestigious Rainer Arnhold Fellowship, which recognises outstanding achievements in tackling Third World problems. The organisation said of Surf Aid: 'Rainer Arnhold Fellows are people with great ideas about how to save the world. The program is about lasting change and Surf Aid gets it. We couldn't be more pleased that Surf Aid has become part of this network of remarkable people and organisations. Surf Aid rose to the challenge of Indonesia's catastrophes; more than that, they've shown that they're in it for the long haul. Best of all, they haven't rested on their well-deserved laurels; they're committed to the continual refinement and growth of their work. This is an organisation to watch.'

For more information go to: www.surfaidinternational.org

'I was blessed with having understanding parents who introduced and encouraged me into surfing. To date I have been fortunate in having a fantastic life, despite my many pitiful stuff-ups. Surfing has helped shape me as a person: surfing has been my Pieria. Challenging ocean conditions have constantly reminded me of my insignificance: they have taught me about my fears, resetting boundaries, and dealing with people. Surfing has pointed me towards a pathway which leads to an understanding of the universal power, called God.'

DR GEOFF, MEDICAL ADVISOR TO *TRACKS* MAGAZINE

SURF LESSON #32
Be kind to surf vagabonds

Just as the large surfwear companies have their armies of sales reps who go out on the road peddling their wares, I believe the spirit of surfing has travelling representatives whose job it is to roam the world and keep the spirit strong.

You have probably met such surfers, though you might not have recognised them and their role, as they can take all shapes and forms. Yet their travels are characterised by several common, magical features.

They will almost always inspire an increased keenness in your own surfing. They are the house guest who gets you up early for the first time in ages, re-acquaints you with the splendour of a sunrise, tunes you in to some new fitness or stretching regime, maybe psyches you up on ordering a new board or trying out a variety of fresh shapes.

They will have some special understanding of any physical ailments that have been impeding your surfing — dodgy knees, crook backs, stiff necks — and will have some special stretch or remedy for your condition. They will get you eating good food, whipping up fresh fruit smoothies or wheatgrass juice or some other powerful tonic to increase your vitality.

They will see the magic in even marginal conditions, urge you into sessions that you might normally have turned your nose up at, and get you stoked with the infectiousness of their enthusiasm. They will give you some meaningful feedback on your own surfing, noticing the private little subtleties of your style that no one has ever noticed before, suggesting alterations to your technique or things for you to work on.

And their travels will almost always coincide with good waves, as if they are in possession of some special itinerary of the world's magic surf sessions and they simply meander the world according to this timetable.

Like the wise, holy men who wander around India, they may be of simple means in the material sense, relying on the kindness of friends and strangers, and living on the most basic of resources. Their duties have nothing to do with fame or recognition or publicity. They work on the blindingly simple notion that as they contribute to the greater good of the world-wide surfing vibration, the forces of the universe will ensure that they continue to be supported in that lifestyle.

Look for them in their travels, offer them a bed, a meal, friendship, and you will be rewarded with a new lease on your surfing life and a freshness of appreciation for this wondrous lifestyle of ours. It is sacred work they do, and they deserve our thanks.

First published in Surfing World, *1997*

chris lundy

{ the artist }

Everything's connected. I'm starting to see that more all the time. Before, I used to look at it like: there's my art and there's my surfing and there's my music. The more you get involved in all of it the more you start to nurture the linking up of all of it.

The six-foot by ten-foot canvas occupies one end of the main living area. For two weeks, it's been the first thing I see every morning and the last thing I see every night. It taunts me on my resting place on the sofa — somehow making the wild Hawaiian surf which awaits me outside appear both more terrifying and more inviting. When the ocean roars in the dark of night, I know the painting is there looming over me, threatening to come to life and inundate the living room, sweep me down the mud-fringed Kam Highway and out into the booming Pacific.

Chris Lundy has spent two or three days roughing out this piece, and at some point in the future, he will spend another couple of months bringing it to life. His surreal, ocean-inspired art portrays a world of gleaming, cathedral-like, cavernous barrels, blown out to cosmological proportions. Each water droplet contains a universe, subtleties of light and colour and texture that sparkle and intrigue. The sense of motion — the violent, heaving, mindless yet majestic might of the ocean — is rendered with meticulous detail, almost photographic accuracy, yet at the same time with cartoon-like whimsy. It's what Rick Griffin might have come up with if he'd been commissioned to paint the ceiling of the Sistine Chapel.

Lundy's been here thirty years, a US east coast wave refugee who scraped his way over in the mid '70s and never left. Ten years of solid Pipe charging and surfboard building and designing led to a spot in the renowned, so-called 'Pipeline Underground' and to the ill-fated '83 Pipe Masters. In that contest, raging north close-outs nearly took the life of his friend Steve (Beaver) Massefeller in the heat before his. Lundy took one he shouldn't have and found himself annihilated on the reef, a wipeout that witnesses still recall with a shudder, and which Chris remembers 'like a high-speed auto wreck'. Rehabilitation of a shattered knee took him to LA, where he devoted himself to years of cycling and study at the prestigious Art Center College of Design.

Since that life-changing moment, Chris has succeeded in making a living from his art, returned to North Shore surfing, and maintained the great creative adventure, interweaving parallel passions for music, shaping, snowboarding and technology.

He's done more posters for A-list surfing contests than anyone. His paintings are finding their way onto the walls of serious collectors. 'Sneaker heads' in New York, London and Tokyo camped out on the sidewalks last year to be in line for Nike's release of an innovative limited edition of shoes laser etched with designs by six artists, of which Lundy's represented Mother Ocean. When MTV needed a seven- by ten-foot painting/sculpture to command the background in the *Real World: Hawaii* house, Lundy was recruited to pull it off at the eleventh hour.

Lundy appears to spend his time quietly — painting, tinkering in design work or website maintenance, music making and recording, dancing his fingers over his vintage '66 Gibson SG. Or ducking out for surfs when he feels the urge, and senses an uncrowded session somewhere removed from the hustle and bustle of mainstream North Shore surfing. Out of this apparent stillness works of mind-boggling dynamism are born.

There is a natural curiosity, a uniqueness of perspective, at work here. At age four, he observed his foot buried in beach sand and told his mother, 'Look, the whole world is my shoe.' He once dug the hunks of cookie dough out of a tub of Häagen-Dazs and baked them, with scientific inquiry, to see if they would actually turn into little cookies. When a friend heckles him for this latest eccentricity, he passionately and vehemently defends his obligation as an artist to check it all out.

This interview was recorded over six years ago, and lay idle until Chris felt he had the body of work worthy of such flagrant self-promotion. Then, in an intense two-week Hawaiian stint, in between surfing and music making, I managed to coerce and cajole a finished edit out of him.

I should own up right here, the brief times I've spent with Lundy over the years are some of the most enjoyable of my life. I'm in Hawaii, for a start, so I'm already stoked. And Lundy has an infectious ability to make every excursion — a simple surf check or a run to Foodland, late night music making, art rave or story telling — into a hilarious adventure. Lundy's company will make you want to further your art, whatever it is, to be more idealistic, purer in your vision, more childlike in your play. At the same time, there's an edge to his observations, a powerful sense of humour that banishes pretensions and posing, a deft social commentary that can render the most oppressive circumstances somehow comical. A recent email concluded: 'The ice caps are melting and George Dubya is president. My cat, however, is sitting on my bed, licking his butt and appears to have not a care in the world. Aloha . . . Chris.'

He was surrounded by artists and actors as a kid, and creativity was always encouraged. 'It just so happened that most of the adults I was around when I was a kid were very passionately creative people, so I was always around it and it seemed very natural. There were always art materials around and in my hands. I was always encouraged to just go for it,' he says. 'Little kids create really vital artwork before they're inadvertently derailed with questions like: "Why is the dog purple?" Or, "The sky can't be green." Or, especially, "What's that supposed to be?" It's not supposed to be anything. It's a kid with paints and materials and he's just going off at the purest level that it's ever going to be . . . And then he's going to spend the rest of his life trying to get back to that vitality and pure sense of automatic expression that he had when he was four years old. You can't negate life process and formal training, but it's interesting that that's the mode of functioning you strive to get back to.'

Chris grew up on the west coast of Florida, where much of the year the lazy Gulf of Mexico barely laps the beach. 'Every now and then things come together from a cold front or a hurricane and some special things'll happen,' he insists, with enduring loyalty. 'Enough of that happened when we were kids to keep us stoked and constantly on the hunt for anything that moved. That and just being stoked groms with wild imaginations devouring surf magazines and whatever we could get a hold of. I remember when *Pacific Vibrations* came to town my buddies and I checked into the movie theatre at one in the afternoon and didn't come out until nine at night. We watched that thing four or five times over.'

He and his friends would drive to the east coast and surf Cocoa Beach and Sebastian Inlet, in awe of the local elite. 'Mike Tabeling, Jeff Crawford, Greg Loehr and then Juan Rodriguez from our side . . . they were the legends. And when Crawford all of a sudden went from Florida hero to North Shore and especially Pipeline heavyweight, it all of a sudden seemed very real, 'cause before that it all seemed just bigger than life.'

Straight out of high school, his crew loaded up two cars and drove across the country to California, where the hollow summer reefbreaks of Santa Cruz cemented the desire for more serious challenges. After eight months, most of his friends started drifting back to Florida but Chris, only seventeen, wasn't done. 'The pivotal moment for me was

seeing that episode of *Hawaii Five-0* that opens with Gavin Rudolph s-
ing down the face at Pipeline as seen through the crosshairs of a sniper's
rifle. That was it. I never looked back. With my last 400 bucks I bought
a plane ticket and went to the North Shore with a backpack and a
surfboard.'

He washed dishes, worked as a janitor, fixed dings and laminated
at Island Surfboards, Surfboards Oahu and the Kahuku glass shop that
did all Brewer's boards. 'All of a sudden you're here and you see all the
legends that you've ever read about, BK and Gerry Lopez and Reno
Abellira and they're like these immortal characters and here they are
out surfing right in front of you. There was a huge respect. You'd never
dream of dropping in on one of those guys . . . It's such a frenzy now,
you know, and there's a sense that just anybody can come over and just
jump into it. It's just way more accessible in the way the media portrays
it now. People don't seem so intimidated by it any more, but maybe
they should be. It's still dangerous. It's still full-on heavy duty and can
still completely undo your whole world in a split second.'

Eventually, Chris got his own little glass shop at the old Pipeline
house, sparking a period of intense surfboard designing and shaping
with a like-minded crew. 'Cort Gion had a shaping room right next to
my glass shop, and that was the beginning of really intense shaping,
designing, hard-core Pipeline surfing. Every hour of the day at Sunset
or Pipeline, making countless boards, just trying to figure it all out.
They were all Cort's boards. He'd shape 'em and I'd glass 'em, for our
whole crew — Greg Bonner, Paul Dunn, Jimmy Richards, Brian
Bulkley, Bruce Hansel. Cort pretty much set everyone on course. He's
a really good surfer and had his own thing going, but was also kind of
a protégé to Mike Diffenderfer. He brought it to the younger crew and
livened things up quite a bit. They were very much on-the-edge
surfboards for the time, low volume, more extreme templates than most

of what was around. That was how that all went for, I don't know, five or six years. Then I started shaping my own boards because of specific details I was after, and I just had a hunger to make what was going to be under my feet.'

Surfer magazine labelled the crew the Pipeline Underground, for their hard charging and apparent disregard for contests and media coverage. 'That was a magazine thing. We never referred to ourselves that way. There were amazing Pipeline surfers from all over the islands, from all over the world. *Surfer* magazine did a string of mini articles on everyday surfers and alternatives to pursuing the pro tour. There was an article on Phyllis the boogie boarder and a few other things, and there was one on the Pipeline Underground. They portrayed us as the resident, hard-core, papaya-smoothie drinking, stoked-up Pipeline crew that was just on a different plan than pursuing contests. We had the Banzai Pipeline in our backyard and that was our whole world, which was pretty much right on the money.'

Pro surfers Bobby Owens and Mark Foo ordered Chris's boards for Sunset and Waimea, and he formed a strong bond with visiting Aussie chargers Jim Banks and Mitch Thorson, sharing their tastes for finely tuned guns and extreme surf.

'Lundy is a really good shaper,' says Banks, one of Australia's top big wave surfer/shapers. 'I just used to stare at his boards. He has such a good curve. He has the artist's eye and he has the hands to reproduce what his eye wants to see. I thought they were much better than what I was doing. And he was a serious charger. He was surfing giant Waimea from behind the bowl, and going right at Pipe on days when very few other people wanted to know about it.'

Mitch Thorson concurs. 'He made me this board, this 7'10", which I ended up riding for eight years in a row, in the Pipe Masters and all the contests, just a mind-blowing board,' says Mitch. 'He was a credible surfer and was pretty inspiring and was also a magnificent waterman and a great shaper to go with it.'

Simon Anderson's win in the '81 Pipe Masters on his newly unveiled thruster flicked a switch for Chris and the mission of taking the three-fin design into increasingly serious surf gathered momentum.

'It was obvious that everything was gonna change from there on out,' he says. 'Those last few years of single fins had gotten tuned into really beautiful, fluid boards, so I don't think people really had some dying thirst to have their world turned upside down. But all of a sudden, Simon's surfing had a new magnitude. There was a whole different look of speed and command that was just undeniable. And then winning the Pipe Masters on his own design was just about as influential a statement as anyone could make.'

Chris immediately started putting thruster guns together and his curvy, loose boards adapted beautifully to the new fin system. The next couple of years was an exciting time, the new boards opening up new possibilities daily. It peaked for Lundy with the 9'1" tiger-striped thruster he built for big Waimea and then had the good fortune to ride through the huge 1983 spring El Niño season. 'Everyone was saying you couldn't ride thrusters at Waimea, and Lundy proved them all wrong,' says Banks.

When the Hawaiian events weren't sanctioned by the newly formed Association of Surfing Professionals in 1983, Lundy was granted one of the ten additional slots added for Pipeline regulars. He still approaches the subject of that fateful Pipe Masters with some trepidation. He gives me the comprehensive version, every agonising detail still vivid — waking up with the flu and hoping the contest was called off, the north swell 'clamshell close-outs' on the lowest tide of the year, his friend Beaver Massefeller nearly killed in the heat before his, then his own instant of reckoning. After Lundy's nightmare wipeout, Beaver's chopper was flagged down and the medics told, 'We've got another one for you.' But he urges me not to dwell on the subject.

'I'll tell ya what,' he eventually concedes, 'that was a very heavy split-second thing that changed my whole existence in a lot of ways. I did something that a lot of surfers do at one time or another: I went for broke. But things didn't exactly pan out. I got horrifyingly pile-driven into the bottom at big Pipeline like there was no water and it practically tore my left leg off. The whole thing was so surreal as it was happening and it's almost like the whole story is about someone else when I think about it now. From the moment of impact right through that very freaky *Apocalypse Now* helicopter ride over inland Oahu to Queens Hospital. Eight hours in surgery, two weeks in the hospital, two months in a full-length cast, toe to hip, the next ten months on crutches, another year and a half in a steel-hinged knee brace, and a second surgery to remove a bunch of hardware. And then years of serious cycling to get my leg back. The flip side is that those were the years I was at Art Center, which was basically my new North Shore for my art . . . and I got my surfing back, full on. Beaver did too. Last time I saw him he was the farthest guy back on a solid 18-footer at the Bay and the four guys in front of him didn't have a clue.'

While Chris recovered from surgery and immersed himself in art school, his surfboards were still attracting attention back in Hawaii — especially the 9'1" 'Tiger', that first thruster he built for Waimea Bay. Mitch Thorson more or less adopted the Tiger and would ride nothing else at big Waimea. 'I never wore a legrope at Waimea, primarily because the Tiger didn't have a legrope plug. You learn a lot about Waimea when you have to swim in,' Mitch recalls. 'Lundy was really good at the three big spots, particularly Sunset and Waimea. He taught me how to ride Waimea and gave me a line-up point and a strategy and it was amazing. This line-up worked from twelve feet to closing out. I was in the Billabong Pro when it was moved to Waimea (in 1985), and it was fucking huge. Using the Lundy strategy and the Tiger, no legrope, I ended up winning the heat. I was so excited. I won a heat at Waimea. I came in and Tom Curren said, "That board looks insane. Can I borrow it?" And he won his heat. I had another heat on it and won, and he won another heat on it.'

Back in California, Lundy had to get his surfing buzz vicariously, through the pros riding his board. 'It was a pretty neat thing. I was hurt, I was pretty devastated, but all of a sudden a bunch of the top pros were riding my own guns, so it was a kick. Later on, I did some Sunset and Waimea boards for Barton Lynch the year he was world champion. But I was really separated from it. I wasn't even there. I was in California getting into school. I couldn't surf. I was on crutches for eleven months. I was just talking to Mitch on the phone, with him giving me reports on the Tiger at the Bay so it was a buzz. You could really surf that board. They were taking off behind the bowl and doing these big, arcing turns, up from behind the bowl and banking under that giant hook. And a few of my crew rode it too — Eric Merlander was a full maniac charger. He rode that thing for years. And Don Johnston too. A lot of guys got the heaviest Waimea waves of their lives on that board. It's officially retired now. It's earned its purple heart. It has a big crease in it and it would be a shame to break it in half at this point.'

Over in LA, Lundy was feeling wary of the stigmatised 'surf artist' tag in the rarified Art Center environment, feeling like 'a bit of a savage' after a decade of North Shore surfing. It has taken years for him to reconcile the two — to recognise surfing gives him access to some of the most inspiring imagery he could hope to paint. From heavily stylised and designed surf-contest posters to increasingly abstract, surreal wavescapes on huge canvases, Lundy now makes no apologies for the surfing subject matter.

'There's always been surf stuff here and there, but much more so now. The thing that got me past being self-conscious of being pegged as someone else's notion of what a surf artist is, was when I saw the power in connecting that whole universe that opened up with formal training to the other single thing in my life that has been all consuming, which was surfing the North Shore. Talk about raw adrenaline inspiration. It's time–space travel. It's a rare opportunity to treat the subject with the attention it deserves and present this wild, superhuman adventure and virtual religion to many in an optimal way. The whole process is completely intertwined over a lifetime. It's kind of funny. It's like I get to go through it all again in this whole other place . . . kind of like the kid at school drawing waves in his notebook, but hopefully stepped up a bit. There's an architecture to the ocean and there's an unlimited supply of luminous palaces to explore through the eyes of a passionate surfer and some adventurous painting.'

Lundy's work often hangs in the Café Haleiwa, and while plenty of well-known surfers have admired his work over their Veggie El Rollos and hot cakes and coffee, Lundy reckons his highest praise came from a couple of unknowing mainland tourists. 'They said, "We have no idea what it's supposed to be but we love it".' Lundy beams. It is this transcendence of the literal reference to waves that you sense is the artist's ultimate goal, to somehow capture the abstract spirit of the ocean's energy without the baggage of comparisons to corny air-brushed waves and palm trees.

I recall watching big, perfect Pipeline one day with another Lundy cohort, Aussie surfer Robbie Page, and Pagey telling me, 'Look at them, they're just like big cathedrals rolling in.' I suggest to Lundy that's the way he sees these waves too. 'Sure. I think cathedral's the operative word,' Chris agrees. 'The monumentality of those experiences, paddling out to Pipeline and looking straight into the guts of some 15-foot, triple-thick, inside-out cavern . . . or you're inside a 10-foot barrel at Backdoor and ten years down the road you remember specific drops of water that were flying by your head in super slow motion, almost like they each had a name. What's that all about? That's all about taking a step into this other perception of time, and that's getting cosmic. That's getting to the heart of the matter. If you can bring that across to painting, look out. And it's not going to happen through painting literally, it's going to happen through letting all the subconscious links come through and happen and having the confidence to let it happen while automatically adhering to all the formal stuff of painting, the common language. That's where you're hopefully going to take the art to a living, breathing and maybe even spiritual realm.

'Everything's connected. I'm starting to see that more all the time. Before, I used to look at it like: there's my art and there's my surfing and there's my music. And the more you get involved in all of it the more you start to nurture the linking up of all of it. When you gain enough facility in music to make your own sounds, it's just like in surfing where you have a style that's hopefully not contrived, it's from the heart, it's just how you move, you know. It's just how *you* move through the water. Ideally, you want to get that same facility in your music and in your art. The marks that you put on paper or on canvas are just mirroring the same kind of attitude that you might have when you're carving a turn and vice versa. Taking it down to a really core level, everybody's got a style when they sign their name. That's a very artful little activity right there, signing your name. And you can relate that to all sorts of things, like Kelly Slater surfing Pipeline. He's just signing his name all over the place, and it's really improvisational, and it's really artful, and it's not contrived. It's really pure, maybe at a purer level than anybody's ever seen. He's like the manifestation of the cartoon surfer. All of a sudden it's real, boom, there it is, in the flesh. There's the guy that's doing what everybody's been dreaming about. But it's almost expected and everybody embraces it and has a real warm acceptance of it because everybody's been evolving towards and dreaming about surfing like that for forty or fifty years. No one's been able to link it up to that level because there's so much involved — the evolution of surfboards, the evolution of surfing itself, and the arrival of a virtual alien freeing himself of the fear involved in doing that stuff at a place like Pipeline. And he's a Florida boy!' he laughs.

It is this linking up of artforms, of subconscious impulses, unconscious memories, unbridled creative instincts, that drives Chris's artmaking. 'Hopefully it's all heading towards the peak in the end, the defining moment where it really all comes together as automatically as breathing and it's all linked to everything you do. It's linked to the first thing you drew when you were a little kid, to the last thing you paint before you drop, and it's linked to the first wave you ever rode, to the heaviest barrel you ever got at Pipeline, but on a subconscious level, you know. I don't know . . . I hope I'm not babbling.'

Chris grows self-conscious as his conversation teeters on the profound, wary of how difficult it is to put this stuff just right. He pauses, crystallises his thoughts.

'It's nice to think if aliens were to land on earth, the arts would be operating on some kind of an elevated level and that they're collectively going to present the human experience in a way that goes beyond language and literal references and politics and logic and finality. If every creative spirit everywhere was allowed and encouraged to just go off and really do their little Johnny Appleseed thing — across the board, too, not just the visual arts, but that creative and idealistic element in everybody's involvement in everything they do — if there was no inhibition to just go off and take it all higher and farther and better and more out there and, I don't know . . . I guess that's the stuff they invented laws for, to keep all that in check. But man, just imagine!'

First published in The Surfer's Journal.

dorian 'doc' paskowitz

{ the barefoot doctor }

Recreation is easy to understand if you break the word up into two parts — RE-CREATION. Recreation re-creates you, makes you feel like a new person, generates health . . . Recreation is re-creating the spirit, not just playing a game on a polished floor, but somehow going out and re-creating the spirit. We do that in surfing, we re-create the spirit.

The year was 1934. Dorian Paskowitz was thirteen years old, weak and ailing with asthma and bronchitis, when he convinced his entire family to sell up and move from Texas to California, on the strength of one surfing photo.

'I was a typical, nice, pampered little Jewish boy, born and raised on a small island in the Gulf of Mexico off the coast of Texas, and I was destined for a really nice, overprotected life,' recalls Dorian 'Doc' Paskowitz, now eighty-five, as we chat in the foyer of the Sheraton Hotel in downtown Waikiki.

'I've been sneaking into these fancy Waikiki hotels for sixty years,' he'd reassured me earlier, as we sought shelter from a cool onshore breeze on the beach where modern surfing began.

That journey, from a chronically ill youth in Texas, to the magnificently robust patriarch of one of the world's great surfing families, is a powerful testament to the health-promoting properties of waveriding. It's a journey that took him to Hawaii in the '30s, surfing alongside many of the great pioneers, medical school at Stanford University where he was so poor he ate the laboratory animals, fatherhood of fourteen children, a nomadic existence living out of a camper van meandering from surf spot to surf spot, introducing surfing to Israel, founding one of the world's first surf schools and, eventually, developing a whole new concept of human health, espoused in his own self-published book, *Surfing and Health*, which took fifteen years to write.

'At nine I learnt to swim, at ten I learnt to bodysurf the waves, at eleven I was able to cockroach the boards off older guys and by twelve I was a surfer,' says Doc, picking up his story. 'And once I was a surfer two things happened. One, what I felt in my body or my soul or wherever the hell it is, was unbelievable, riding the waves. And secondly, my destiny as a nice, normal, little pampered Jewish boy, my destiny was forever changed . . . When I got to be thirteen years of age I'd already begun to surf well enough that I wanted bigger and better waves.'

His chronic illness threatened to thwart those youthful dreams of travel and adventure, but ultimately it was his illness that saw them fulfilled. 'I was very sick, because ever since I'd been an infant I'd had bronchial asthma, and my island was very bad for that, so I suffered quite a bit, and of course my mother, who also had asthma, really suffered, and I don't think anyone suffered more than my dad, who watched me wheeze and choke and not be able to catch my breath, and he couldn't do anything about it . . . I began to go downhill, and then I got bronchitis on top of it and I was on my way to getting pneumonia and that was a dangerous thing. My mother was very worried about me, and I was languishing in my illness.'

Doc vividly recalls being laid up in bed when his mother brought him the Sunday paper. 'This little magazine section fell out. I opened it up and there on both pages was a magnificent picture of three guys stacked on a wave, which must have been about six feet high. They were riding this beautiful white wake. Oh God,' he effuses, eyes sparkling with the recollection. 'I sat up and in an instant — I am not exaggerating, this has happened to me two or three times in my life — in an instant I was free of disease. My lungs went up and down with no squeaks and no squeals; my fever suddenly plummeted; my eyes grew bright. I called out, "Mumma, Mumma, come here, come here." Mother came running in, horrified that I was dying. I said, "Look at that, look at that. If you take me where that wave is I'll get well today." She said, "Dolly boy," that's what she called me, "if you get well today I'll take you there tomorrow." Well, she didn't take me there tomorrow but she did within two weeks change our entire lives. We sold everything we could sell, bought a car, got everybody together, said goodbye to friends, and headed out on the highway from Galveston Island, through Houston, all the way across the country . . . It was an epic journey, weeks, weeks, weeks. We finally got to Mission Beach, California, and she said, "OK, we've got to get to Los Angeles. You folks have your swim and we've got to go right away. You've got one hour." And we stayed twenty years,' Doc smirks with the satisfaction of a child who got his way, even seventy years on.

Unable to coerce their son out of the surf, the Paskowitz family simply decided to settle in Mission Beach. Doc's life path was set. 'I was in the mainstream of surfing then . . . I was a genuine surfer.' True to his word, Doc found his health improved the more he surfed. 'My asthma didn't improve. In fact it got worse over the years, but my health improved. Health can exist in the presence of illness and disability. Even though I would wheeze and cough and splutter, and lie awake at night wheezing, still I was a world-class paddleboard racer, I was a surfer, I went in contests, I was as strong as an ox.'

His own health problems, and the benefits he'd experienced from surfing, led him to study medicine.

'When you've been suffering from some ailment, the first thing that comes to your mind is, maybe I can try and help other people not suffer like I've suffered,' he says. 'I wanted to show how surfing had led me not to a wisdom of disease but a wisdom about superior well-being which I call health.'

Doc's parents were not wealthy — his father was a shoe salesman and his mother worked in a dress shop — so he had to pay his own way through medical school. To fund his studies, and to increase his ocean time, he became a lifeguard. He looked up to the great watermen of the Californian lifeguard scene, enthralled by their ocean skills and their tales of Hawaii. And he eventually met the three surfers who had been on that wave in the photo that had inspired his family's migration west.

'They became surf buddies of mine ... During that time in California, these guys were fairly manly sort of men, good watermen. That was a big thing for all of us. You had to be able to ride a surfboard, paddle a surfboard, make a surfboard, skin dive, get abalone and lobsters, row a surf dory, lifeguard. The people who were good at all that, they were great people, they were heroes of mine: Preston Peterson, Lorrin Harrison, Peanuts Larson, Johnny McMahon, Bud Morrisey ... These guys were really great.'

He soon became disillusioned with academia and student poverty, and grew restless to widen his surfing horizons. 'I had become disenchanted with college education and my work trying to be a doctor. I wasn't very smart. I didn't learn things easily. I had to work day and night, day and night, day and night. There was nothing like parties, or drinking a bottle of beer, and I was pretty poor.'

Doc resolved to get himself to Hawaii whatever it took, and painstakingly saved up the fare from his lifeguard's wage. 'First I have to paint a picture, a portrait, of how we in California in the 1930s felt about Hawaii,' he insists. 'We felt about Hawaii the same way the Greeks felt about Olympus. It was the realm of the gods. So I was part of all Californian surfers' affection for, if not passion for, if not addiction for, anything Hawaiian. We'd give Hawaiian names to one another, sing Hawaiian songs, do Hawaiian dances. Duke Kahanamoku was our god. So when I said I was going to Hawaii it was the same as saying, I'm going to go see what heaven's like.'

'When the unspoilt shoreline of Waikiki came into view from the deck of the passenger liner, I almost dove off the ship right out there. I came so close. I thought, "Fuck it, I'm not going to wait for this thing." The ship has to wait for the pilot boat. I looked down at that purple blue water and I looked out to the shoreline, and I thought, "Why don't you just jump over here and swim to the shore? Go ahead. Don't be chicken." I was so awed by the beauty, the colour, and in those days if the wind blew out from the land to the sea it carried a fragrance. Today it blows diesel smoke, exhaust from automobiles, but in those days when you were out at sea, whether you were on your surfboard or a sailboat or a passenger liner, you could smell flowers.'

He worked odd jobs and surfed alongside the giant figures of the day — Duke Kahanamoku, Rabbit Kekai, Wally Froseith, George Downing. But despite the realisation of his surfing dreams, he hadn't given up on medical school and a friend suggested he join him at Stanford University in Northern California.

'I said, "I don't want to go to some exclusive school. I want to go to the University of California." He said, "You're going to have a hard time getting a job along with all the other poverty-stricken students at the University of California. At my school nobody takes a job. They're all too rich. One of my buddies brings ten polo ponies from Venezuela." He was right. I got a job right away. I had no idea that Stanford University was the Harvard of the west coast.'

He sat an entrance exam and got in, despite being told by one lecturer that he was 'too dumb to be a doctor'.

'I don't know how the fuck I got into Stanford medical school. Once I got in I don't know how I graduated. I was so poor I ate the animals.'

Driven by hunger and poverty, Doc took to bagging the discarded animal carcasses from laboratory experiments, taking them home and cooking them up. 'These big chubby beautiful rabbits — they were thrown in the garbage can. I'd chop them up and fry them, and for days I'd have beautiful fried rabbit,' he recalls with relish. 'Frogs, big giant frogs, with great big legs like chicken legs. I'd collect all the dead frogs, just fry 'em in boiling oil.'

But his adventures in laboratory animal cuisine came to an abrupt end the day a recipe for baked pigeon went horribly wrong. 'One day in biochemistry we had pigeons, and they must have killed dozens, beautiful big-breasted pigeons, so I told my friend, "We'll keep all the birds and have a feast, bake 'em in the oven." So I had all these pigeons, sprinkled them with pepper and salt.' He put the pigeons in the oven and ducked out to get other ingredients. When he came back the fire brigade was outside his apartment. 'I asked a guy, "What's going on over there?" He said, "There was a terrible explosion." It was my apartment. It stank to high heaven. What I didn't realise was they'd killed the pigeons by putting a cone of ether over them, so each pigeon was supersaturated with ether fumes. When I put them in the oven and it got to a certain temperature, the whole fucking oven exploded.'

Eventually, he managed to graduate. 'I don't know how the hell I did that. I always thought I was next to last in the class. But then I realised that even though when it came to remembering stuff I couldn't remember yesterday's text books, when it came to the practicalities of seeing patients they gave me good grades for that.'

Back in the outside world, Doc found his personal ethics unsuited to private medical practice. 'I just didn't feel that I wanted to support myself and make my living off of the misery of sick people,' he says. 'Medicine has not been a source of livelihood for me.'

Instead, he found himself drifting, from surf spot to surf spot, up and down the Californian coast, back to Hawaii, struggling to come to terms with marriage and parenthood. Eventually, when his first marriage fell apart, he went to Israel to connect with his ancestral roots — and inadvertently introduced surfing to the Mediterranean.

'I got in a bad spin in life. One of my previous wives divorced me, took my kids away. I thought, "What the hell am I doing sitting around here? I'm going to go where my people are fighting wars. I'm going to go over and join the army." When I got ready to go I thought to myself, "I might take a surfboard." Well, they weren't a damn bit interested in me as a soldier, but they fell in love with that surfboard. They wouldn't let me go with the board. Finally I had to go without it. I had to leave the board with them. And then I suddenly had a mission in life. A little later my new wife and I were living in a little car together with one child. We lived in that car for three years, just a tiny little car, a '29 Studebaker. Then these Israeli guys said, "Please send us whatever you can to help us start to surf. So I went back. For the next three years Mom and I worked collecting all kinds of stuff so they could start a surfing industry, and I took it back to them. Now there are 25,000 surfers in Israel. After I gave them that second bunch of stuff they just took it and ran with it from there on.'

Doc's wife Juliette seemed to accept the nomadic surfing existence, and despite the lack of money or a family home they brought up nine healthy children. 'I didn't send them to school. We lived in a camper, what you'd call a caravan, from surf spot to surf spot. My four boys became pretty good surfers. As the boys grew older they began to look for greener fields, and I thought, "How can I keep my boys close to me?" I knew they wanted to go surf with their buddies here and go surf with their buddies there. And I said, "Look, how would you boys like to have a new surfboard every year, surf wherever you want to surf, as much as you want to, have fresh sandwiches and drinks and get paid a buck a day?" Holy mackerel! And I said, "OK, I've got a job for you." "Where? Where?" "Working for me." "Oh, I knew there was a catch."'

And so began the Paskowitz Family Surf Camp. The family would take groups of beginners camping up and down the coast, teach them to surf, feed them nutritious food and introduce them to Doc's philosophies on surf safety, etiquette and good health. 'We never made any real money, just enough to keep us going,' says Doc. 'We charged a good price but we spent it on them — the best tents, the best sleeping bags, the best food, the best surfboards. When it was all over there wasn't much left. Once at the end of the summer we had $4000 cash, but mostly we'd come out with $200, but we'd been keeping ourselves afloat all summer.'

The pro surfers of the day would regularly come along as guest instructors — Shaun Tomson, Rabbit Bartholomew, Kelly Slater, Christian Fletcher — such was the Paskowitz family's standing in the surfing community.

'Because my kids surfed from Hawaii to Tel Aviv, they met a lot of kids, and being themselves world-class surfers, they were naturally looked up to, considered equal to other world-class surfers. So Kelly Slater would come and just hang out. Kelly was beginning to be a pro champion, so just his being there meant a lot to the students.'

Thirty years on, thousands of students have been through their surf camps. Doc's son Israel, a former champion longboarder, is still running the family business. Israel and his wife Danielle also run a charity, Surfers Healing, introducing autistic children to the calming effects of the surf, which they started after they realised their own autistic son Isaiah benefited greatly from his time in the ocean. Surfers Healing run free surf clinics up and down the coast, and families with autistic children flock to them. Poignant testimonials tell of children's lives transformed.

Doc has distilled his seventy-five years of surfing and sixty-odd years of medicine into his own theory of human health, as outlined in *Surfing and Health*. Part surf anecdotes, part homespun philosophy, part nutritional guide, part motivational text, it's a radical and entertaining call for a new view of wellness. Central to Doc's philosophy is the idea that health is more than the mere absence of disease'. He says the first time he heard this in medical school it sparked an epiphany.

'We all know we can walk down the beach at times sad, forlorn, hurting, aching, feeling shitty. We go surfing and we come back from that experience bright, cheerful, shining, as if we've been remade. We all know that. But to me ... that commonplace experience is a sign of a sophisticated physiological phenomenon. If one sat down to dissect it one would see that everything from pulse pressure and cardiac injection to hormonal reaction of adrenal glands is affected. But what strikes me most of all is it is governable, it is predictable, it is creatable. That's what gave me one of my most profound insights into the nature of health. It is more than the mere absence of disease. It's the presence of a state of vigour, vitality, pizzazz, that can be purposely come by, by working at it day after day. That realisation gave me an awareness of the real dimensions of health, that this almost superman feeling could be actually created by your deliberate action.

'When you come out of surfing, there is this euphoria, which is part of an actual physical sense of well-being. It's not that suddenly you hear angels, it's that you feel physically remade. If you started out from normal, or if you started out feeling shitty, you feel entirely remade. You're not only remade but remade with refinement, exactness, so that things feel inside you to be gearing and meshing effortlessly. You feel lighter, you feel that you move with more agility. You have more positive feelings, you talk faster. How much more this is than not being sick; how much more this is than just being normal. If you could bottle it, you would have a whole population of enviably vigorous people. So I said to myself, "OK, how do you achieve that? What is happening here that can be reconstructed in other parts of life?" For example, surfing is remarkable for the fact that there are periods of intense exercise followed by periods of intense rest. There are periods of advanced agility, balance, coordination, and periods of mere watchful waiting. There are periods of fear and trepidation that, overcome and triumphed over, give you a sense of victory and strength. So when you analyse what goes into surfing and what comes out of it, you realise that there's a template there, there's a paradigm where one can reconstruct what is happening.'

Doc prescribes five pillars of good health: diet, exercise, rest, recreation and attitude of mind. His book elaborates, with wry humour, exactly how to achieve this state of superior wellness. Doc still surfs three or four times a week, hasn't eaten sugar for forty years, doesn't drink coffee or alcohol, and keeps himself at fifteen per cent body fat, which he believes is optimal for good health. What does he do for kicks? 'Surfing and sex,' he grins.

'My life is built around the attempt to take a mass of almost amorphous physiological material and put it in scientific context to the extent that ordinary human beings can go out and, not with pills and potions, but with their own self-motivation, achieve a state of well-being that is not only capable of preventing disease and even curing some diseases, but is capable of making them into superior human beings in all walks of life, from sex to surfing.'

Doc believes his book may have been more successful if he had called it something other than *Surfing and Health*.

'The book is aimed primarily at fat Americans, and once they see the word surfing they say, "I'm not a surfer. I don't give a damn about surfing." It immediately wipes out a whole audience. But surfing had taught me so much, that to leave it out was almost as if I had failed to put one of the most important research workers on the research paper as a contributor.'

What has he learnt from surfing?

'I tell you, if I sat here and I tried to explain the things surfing taught me, it would be a whole book in itself. Let's just take a few simple things. Every surfer has his markers for every break he goes out in [fixed points on land that allow you to orient yourself in the water]. When you go out into really big waves, your markers are your lifesavers. George Downing wrote a whole philosophic text about what he called alignment. I have used that same concept of alignment to try and get a fix on things in my life generally, realising that one has to have some unmoving points around which life can be fashioned or else you become a kind of a scatterbrain.'

He says his Hawaiian surfing friends have imparted some of his greatest life lessons. One, Alfred Kumalae, a great surfer and waterman, helped develop the modern catamaran, but never received any recognition for it, says Doc. 'He was a man of such greatness of spirit that when people talked about others as if they were the ones who did it, he wouldn't care. He just took life as it was. One day we were working on a new type of catamaran, that was being paid for by Henry J. Kaiser, one of the world's wealthiest men. This titan of commerce came up to talk to Alfred who was barefoot, in a pair of cut-off jeans and no shirt. And I thought, Henry J. Kaiser, you will never be the man that Alfred Kumalae is. When they finished, I said to Alfred "Let's go get a drink." We each had enough money for a soda pop, and as we walked across the sand I looked down and there was a bright shiny fifty cents. I reached down and scooped it up and went, "Alfred, look at this! We're not only going to get soda pop, we're going to get pancakes. Hooray, let's go." But as we kept walking toward Mamma San's his demeanour changed from brightness and sunlight to shadow. I said, "Alfred, everything OK?" He said, "Yeah." I said, "Look, Alfred, something's bothering you. All of a sudden something's bothering you. Won't you tell me?" And he said, "I don't mean to offend you, but have you given any thought to the person who lost that money?" Well, it was as if I'd been slapped with a wet towel. I said, "You know, Alfred, if I lived to be a thousand years old I would never have thought of that, but I promise you this. If I live to be a thousand years old I will never forget it." Alfred was a surfer, he was beyond a surfer, he was a man who learnt to surf in the open sea. That's another example of how surfing taught me.'

Doc sees a kind of greed and selfishness at work in the increasingly crowded, modern surfing world — a clawing need to hoard and accumulate waves, wealth, experiences, mindless of the common good.

'That is not an attitude of mind that leads to health and well-being. It may lead you to be a very rich and powerful man but it will not lead you to be healthy, because the human body cannot violate cosmic law. We have to somehow co-operate with other people, share the wealth, in order for the species as well as the planet to get ahead.'

'I believe that surfing and snowboarding, to a certain extent, can create a space where we can contemplate moments in a pure state of mind, where our spirit is free to soar and head towards its true nature . . . The level of concentration necessary to surf successfully is very Zen-like. The empty mind you seek when you sit zazen is the same empty mind you have when you surf best. Surfing is meditation, pure and simple, but it throws in the fluid element of the sea.'

GERRY LOPEZ, PIPELINE MASTER

SURF LESSON #39
Don't think about other stuff while paddling for a wave

A few years ago I found myself on assignment in Hawaii, with the formidable mission of gaining an interview with the Great One, then six-time world champion Kelly Slater. Only a hundred or so of the world's surf media, camped out on the North Shore of Oahu in prime surf season, had the same goal in their sights. Imagine my delight, then, on my first morning on the North Shore, with a handsome yellow seven-footer under my arm, and a fresh six- to eight-foot north swell capping on the Sunset Point reef, when I paddled out to the line-up and spotted none other than Mr Slater himself stroking into an inviting peak, leaping to his feet and disappearing off down the line. Somehow, magically, the crowd seemed to part as I approached the take-off spot, and the next wave in the set was inexplicably mine. This was too good to be true. I spun around, already anticipating the glorious scenario. I would backdoor the peak, squat casually through the tube to be spat out into the channel, where my quarry would be regarding my ride with stunned appreciation. I would cruise off the shoulder and paddle up to my old pal with a wry grin and request an interview. He would be so impressed by my bold tube threading that he would immediately and enthusiastically accede.

Unfortunately, as I entertained this rosy picture, my particular set wave was continuing its relentless march shorewards and in the few moments I was distracted it had begun to crest and pitch out into a barrel of outrageous proportions, with me neatly embedded in the leading edge of the lip. I had only an instant to register a sense of impending disaster — like the hapless coyote suspended in mid-air — before I was pile-driven into the trough and sent cartwheeling underwater across the Sunset reef, dragged behind my surfboard by the legrope like a rag doll. When I eventually surfaced halfway to shore and clambered, breathless and spluttering, onto my board, it collapsed under me, neatly creased across the middle. A wall of whitewater steamrolled me shorewards as I clung to my newly hinged surfboard, floundering in the crook of its now v-shaped form, the front half flapping up and smacking me square in the face as we bounced to the beach. I was thus deposited, breathless and bleeding, onto the steep Sunset foreshore in front of a packed car park and public gallery. I limped away with damaged board and body, leaving the Great One out at Sunset oblivious to the carnage he'd unwittingly inspired.

dave rastovich

{ the professional free surfer }

In surfing, you need wave knowledge and wave sense. All the best surfers have that ability to see things, but also to sense them with all senses at the same time. All faculties are at call, which is just another way of saying they are totally present.

It is late, at a throbbing surf industry party in New York City — surf label Billabong having just opened their opulent new flagship store in Times Square.

This might once have raised eyebrows — surf city coming to the Big Apple — but the surf industry's tireless march to world domination knows no borders.

An air of eager debauchery prevails, fuelled by free drinks and beautiful young people looking for advantageous pairings, or just career-advancing shmooze opportunities.

It's all water off a duck's back for Dave Rastovich, Billabong's freewheeling gypsy team rider. Dave, who's happily married and barely drinks, has other things on his mind. He's decided he is going to sit on the traffic island in the middle of Times Square and meditate to wile away a couple of hours, with a video camera running to record the event. Condensed into a few seconds in time lapse, this unlikely spectacle will form a scene in his new surf/music movie, *Life Like Liquid*. A young surf magazine writer, torn away from an imminent romantic conquest, is recruited to turn the camera on and watch over it, while Dave drifts off to other levels of consciousness.

All goes smoothly — the traffic circling and whizzing by, the neon signs blinking on and off and people bustling by as Dave sits through it all, cross-legged, hands folded in his lap, like a slim Caucasian Buddha — until a cop stops to ask what's going on. Dave doesn't stir and the young surf writer does his best to explain their lofty intent. Satisfied the pair of young surfers pose no threat to homeland security, the cop moves on.

Dave Rastovich may just have the best job in the world. Simply, he is paid, very handsomely, to surf. Not in contests. Not judged and rated for his performance. Not forced to follow some dizzying contest schedule, and perform in a coloured singlet for a faceless panel of judges, his success or failure dictated by fickle competitive fortunes. Just . . . to surf.

It's hard to imagine one of the world's great athletes in almost any other field — an elite tennis player or golfer or swimmer — turning their backs on organised competition and still being well supported to practise their art. Would anyone sponsor Tiger Woods to play golf on his own as a form of creative self-expression? Would any of us pay attention if Lleyton Hewitt quit competitive tennis to tour some of the world's finest tennis courts and whack a ball around with some of his buddies as performance art? Yet that's basically what Dave has done.

After a stellar junior career in surfing and surf lifesaving, Dave made a decision in his late teens that competition was not for him. He'd won numerous state and national junior lifesaving titles in ironman and paddling events, and a swag of junior boardriding titles. And in his first few outings as a wildcard in the top-level World Championship Tour he'd shown enough form to virtually guarantee a long and lucrative competitive career. He very nearly defeated world champion Kelly Slater in his first appearance as a teenage wildcard, at his homebreak of Burleigh Heads. He managed a credible fifth at the Billabong Pro in Mundaka, Spain, against the world's top-rated pro surfers. He sparred successfully with the highly touted 'Coolangatta Kids', Mick Fanning, Joel Parkinson and Dean Morrison, on the Australian pro junior series. The pro surfing world was his oyster.

Yet Dave almost certainly took a sizeable drop in his potential earnings by opting for the far less certain path of the professional free surfer. To their credit, his sponsors Billabong stuck by him and have happily sent him on a tour, largely of his own choosing, to the world's great surf spots for film and photo shoots, and continue to support him as he forges his unique career path. Meditation, yoga, experimental surfboards, music and spiritual growth, rather than winning contest heats, have been the focus of Dave's energies. Surfing seems a tool to foster self-knowledge, as well as simple fun, rather than grim athleticism and competitive sport.

'Surfing forces me into being present. It's really simple but it's really complex,' says Dave. 'I could be riding a wave and flying along a wave quite successfully and having a lot of fun and as soon as my mind jumps in and starts dictating something that might happen down the line — most of the time, nine times out of ten, I eat shit, fall off.'

This, Dave reckons, is the great lesson surfing has to offer — the need to be fully present in the moment, attuned to constantly shifting circumstances. 'When I'm present for anything there's always something profound and joyful and expansive going on in that moment. Always. It's just the nature of life. It's the feeling of actually being alive . . . That's probably the most significant thing surfing does for me in my life.'

As life philosophies go, it seems to work. There's not much he turns his hand to that he isn't good at. When he quit competitive surfing, he turned his attention to paddleboard racing and won the pairs division of the gruelling Molokai Challenge, the world's longest paddleboard race over fifty-seven kilometres of open ocean, at his first attempt. Paddleboarding appealed, he said, because it had clean and simple criteria — first across the line — rather than the subjective judgements of surf contests.

He's recently devoted his energies to music and film-making. With no musical training he's picked up the hung, a kind of steel drum, and numerous other percussion instruments, and gathered a loose collective of fellow surfing musicians — including tube maestro Jim Banks, drummer and Shark Island charger Terepai Richmond, modern bluesman Ash

Grunwald, funk/soul brothers Shannon and OJ from Affro Dizzi Act, and reggae/dub crooner Tony Hughes from King Tide.

This eclectic bunch, known as Band of Frequencies, spent two weeks in a beachfront house in 2005, filming and recording a surf/music DVD and double CD album. Completely improvised, unrehearsed and spontaneous, they ended up with fifty hours of live music recordings and a tonne of footage. Then, without having ever rehearsed or played a live gig, they opened the world-renowned Woodford Folk Festival, toured California, were invited to tour Japan and Brazil, and embarked on their first Australian east coast tour. Their movie, *Life Like Liquid*, came out in late 2006, along with a double CD soundtrack, to wide acclaim. In a modern surfing world obsessed by surf star celebrity, logo awareness and heated competition, *Life Like Liquid* tunes surfers back into the essence of the waveriding experience, drawing parallels between the transcendental peak moments in surfing and music making. Dave shot much of the footage, including innovative inside-the-tube sequences with a lipstick camera strapped to the side of his head, and taught himself to edit the footage on his Apple Powerbook.

'In surfing, you need wave knowledge and wave sense. All the best surfers have that ability to see things, but also to sense them with all senses at the same time. All faculties are at call, which is just another way of saying they are totally present,' says Dave. 'That's translated into a lot of things in my life. Like, if I have to do some public speaking, I know fuck-all about public speaking but I feel like if I'm in that situation I can pull it off, just by being there for it, not sweat it, just be there. And the same thing with this music experience. I have no intellectual musical understanding whatsoever. I have no idea what's going on, but that hasn't stopped me from being able to jam with people and making some really enjoyable music and I credit that to just being present, just being there and feeling what's going on and letting stuff happen. It's amazing for me to see that there's almost this formula in life. Whatever it is, talking to a friend, talking to a thousand strangers, or shaping a board, playing music, writing, making a movie, all this stuff I've just fallen into doing, I have no actual intellectual understanding of them. It just feels like just because I'm there paying full attention to them they've worked out in a way that is enjoyable.'

How has Dave learnt such lessons at the young age of twenty-six? 'It happened when I was young with my dad teaching me about meditating, being present just by sitting down and chilling, feeling what it's like just to have a body and be here. I don't know, it's as if by doing that when I was young I gained power in some way, where it feels like I can translate that into everything I'm doing. I was in the lifesaving movement and went very well in that, and then split and joined the surfing thing and started doing well in that, and now I'm going into other areas of life and going really well. I've got a wife and I've never had a relationship fight in my whole life. Hannah and I have never raised our voices once and we've been together six years. Not once, not even, "But you didn't do the dishes again!" And it just feels like there's this formula and I don't know how or why I've cottoned on to it. It's just kind of been there since I can remember. Just be here. Just do your shit. So I trip out on that, just go, "Wow, that's pretty cool".'

Surfing, for Dave, is a constant reminder of the importance of staying present, as well as a supreme pleasure. 'The thing with surfing is it's just so much fun. It's no place to be serious for me. It's just a place of having fun, and being there in this amazing experience.'

It's an approach that even extends to the shaping of surfboards. 'I've shaped a couple of boards now and they've been unbelievable. Thanks to Jim [renowned surfer/shaper Jim Banks] and a couple of other friends, I've learnt to be conscious of every movement with the planer. The boards turned out amazing and I've been riding a couple of fishes I shaped all the time now for about three years when the waves are small.'

Tube riding, that much revered peak surfing experience, offers something else which Dave says remains beyond description or definition. Surfers all talk about time expanding in the tube and marvel at its extraordinary powers to inspire feelings of euphoria and transcendence, an almost sexual ecstasy. 'It's trippy. I think it's one of those things where it's always that which can't be named. I don't think you could ever find a surfer who could accurately describe a tube ride. What's going on really? It's something that's not of the mind so there's no way the mind can describe it. That's how it feels to me.'

A recent snowboarding trip to New Zealand gave Dave the opportunity to return to surfing in the state yogis refer to as 'the beginner's mind', when an entire experience becomes brand new again. Because of the differing biomechanics of snowboarding and surfing, many surfers experience difficulty readjusting to surfing after snowboarding. 'I'd only been snowboarding once before and when I did I came back to surfing and I couldn't surf. I could barely bottom turn, just an absolute shocker. I could not surf, so I was really keen this time to see if it was still like that because I really enjoyed that feeling. I went out for a surf, and I couldn't surf again. I was cracking up, feeling like I'm a ten-year-old again. I managed to stuff my head in a tube and get like a three-second tube, and it was just like total bliss in the weirdest way. When it went over me and was wrapping me up all around it was like being in the middle of sex or being inside your mother's belly or something. I felt totally embraced and totally surrounded, like held, and it tripped me out. Until that point I was going, "What am I doing? Why do I surf? Is this all there is to surfing, just doing tricks and riding waves and stuff?" And then that happened and I just went, "Aaahh!" It had been a good two or three weeks since I'd been tubed — that's a long time for me — and I was just tripping out, going, "This is something very different from everything else that we experience in life. This is something totally different." I'd been in the mountains going through valleys of snow, really beautiful, no one around, and that was great, but it was nowhere near the level of intensity of a three-foot, tiny little tube sitting around me like that. There's something going on when the mind isn't present in that wave, and the mind isn't interfering, that you get that incomprehensible feeling, and that is the magic . . . and that was never more present to me than the other day. Three seconds — one, two, three, bang — and you're totally changed. It's so potent.'

Dave continues to marvel at surfing's restorative powers — that wave-riding can be a strenuous physical activity that actually generates rather than depletes energy.

'Hannah's always tripped out on me when we travel. We've done a few trips together, one in particular to South America, and we did this thirty-six-hour journey on a plane, a twelve-hour drive, six of which were being lost at night, so we drove from sunset to sunrise, just totally lost. We got there at sunrise, absolutely physically wrecked. The waves were pumping and I went straight out for a surf. And she just went, "You are fucked up. You are a tripper. You're a weirdo. I'm going to bed. See you in a day." And she went straight to bed. But there was no second thought in my mind. I'm going surfing. I got a couple of little tubes, had some waves, had some fun — totally revived, totally sparked, full of energy. It's unique in that way. If you were a footy player and you'd done that travel you wouldn't run onto a field and throw a ball around. I'm not taking anything away from football. There's just something else going on there where you can do all that physical activity and expend all that energy but you get something else from the ether. It's a totally different kind of energy. It's not that muscular physical energy, it's like an electrical kind of energy. Like, the end of a day of big surf, your body is fucked, you're so tired, your body can't handle any more activity, but there's like this electricity in you. You're just sparking, sharing your experiences, like, ahhhh, a totally different kind of energy.'

Dave enjoys musing on the great cosmic forces at work in the formation of ocean waves — it's a wild line of thought that could easily do your head in if you let it, but Dave seems to thrive on this kind of stuff. 'I was sitting out the back one day and there were these small little waves coming in. The immensity of the moment really struck me, even though it was only a one-foot day of waves. It was like, wow, this is phenomenal! All the forces that have gone into me being fortunate enough to ride a wave are so huge. It starts off as solar wind or some kind of activity in the sun, and then from out of that comes all this radiation and magnetic rays and whatever kinds of movements of energy, and they might bounce off something else and they go past the moon and the moon pulls them a little bit this way, and then they hit the outer atmosphere of our planet and create some kind of torsion with what's emanating from our planet and move through the layers of our atmosphere and then that torsion turns into wind and that wind is spiralling around the same way the spirals in the centre of the sun are moving, the magma or whatever . . . And then it hits the water and the water starts spinning and moving, and there we are sitting at the end of that journey. For me, that was like, wow, what I'm seeing now is the last visible action of this vast journey before it turns into some energy wave, whatever it does, like a wave of oxygen that comes out of a breaking wave. I really don't know the science of it, but it seems that motion is the last physical thing we can see, and here we are sitting there riding it, sitting in amongst it. That spiral motion, that little vortex thing that goes on and is gone in a couple of seconds, and that stoke, that energy, comes into my body in some way . . . And then walking up the beach, I feel like the wave is still with me, and then I sit down in the house and tell Hannah or tell my buddies about the surf, the way we all do. We all like to tell our stories of, oh, I caught this epic wave, I did this or whatever, but essentially it's like the magic of the wave and its energy is transferring and passing on and maybe that's the next stage of the movement of waves, going on forever and ever, and then it moves into us — that's how it feels to me a lot of the time.'

Cynics might sneer that Dave is simply an indulged and highly paid pro surfer with plenty of time on his hands to entertain such esoteric lines of thought, spared as he is from the grind of daily work. It's nothing he hasn't heard before. Indeed, the pleasantness of his existence is a running gag with family and friends. 'I definitely hear those kind of statements,' says Dave. 'I always go, "Hey, well, we're all given the same dirt, water, light and oxygen. I didn't come here with a surfboard in my hand. We all have the same stuff to work with." Everyone owns their own ability to do stuff. I don't really listen to people when they call me on stuff — "Oh, you've got it so easy." Everyone's got their abilities. I just laugh at my situation. I think it's hilarious. It's classic, that it's turned out this way and I can do the things I can do at this point, and I'm just loving it. I definitely marvel at the situation.'

phyllis o'donnell

{ the women's pioneer }

I always kept up with the bodysurfing and I have a little boogie board, and I used to go out on that, but I'm really glad that at sixty-nine I'm making a comeback.

As governments agonise over our ageing population, gnashing their teeth about how to keep our senior citizens fit and healthy, active and engaged in the community, maybe someone should talk to Phyllis O'Donnell.

At sixty-nine, Phyllis swims eight to ten kilometres and works out in the gym every day. After a recent holiday in Hawaii she has taken up board-riding again. 'I'm making a comeback at sixty-nine,' she beams. She's in the ocean every day anyway — bodysurfing or bodyboarding, if not stand-up boardriding. She's an honoured guest at pro surfing events and hands out the trophies at the Roxy Pro on the Gold Coast each March — a treasured pioneer and inspiration to a new generation of surfing girls.

Over an extraordinary surfing life, she's collected state, national and world titles, travelled to mainland USA, Hawaii, Puerto Rico and Tahiti, hitchhiked around California, romanced some of the most legendary surfers of her day, but never married, preferring the freewheeling surfing lifestyle. This must have been radical for the times. 'Yes, it definitely was,' she admits. 'I would never have travelled had it not been for surfing.'

We've all heard of Midget Farrelly and Nat Young, Australia's ground-breaking '60s surf champions. But it might surprise some to know that our first world champion was a woman. Phyllis took out the women's division of the 1964 world titles at Manly, only four years after she took up surfing, shortly before Midget Farrelly took out the men's division. With 60,000 people on the beach and sponsorship from the Ampol petrol company, Australia's first homegrown surf champions were big news, splashed all over the front of newspapers.

Perhaps even more surprisingly, given women's surfing's long and arduous fight for financial support, Phyllis regarded surfing as a career, providing a modest but exciting livelihood. 'Considering that era, I did pretty well out of it,' says Phyllis today, as we chat in the lounge room of her neat apartment overlooking Kingscliff Beach in northern New South Wales. 'I started writing for the *Sunday Mail*, so that paid me quite well. And I won many boards so I'd sell them and get the money, and there were numerous Craven A cigarettes. Every contest, ciggies. In those days I did smoke. I haven't smoked now for thirty years, but the Craven As came in handy.'

Phyllis grew up in Drummoyne, in Sydney's inner west, and only took up surfing at the age of twenty-three, when she borrowed her sister's boyfriend's board.

'The first time was down there at Harbord,' says Phyllis, the very beach where Duke Kahanamoku introduced surfing to Australia in 1914. 'All I wanted to do was have a paddle. I didn't care about standing up. Actually my sister got up before I did. But the first experience at Harbord was a jolly shark. Yeah, a shark came in close. I could hardly paddle the thing let alone get away from a shark,' she laughs.

'I did pick it up quickly. I had a lot of hassles, as you can imagine. I was older, and the guys, they just used to aim for me. I didn't even know you could turn the jolly thing, and with no legropes in those days, they'd aim, I'd lose the board, have to swim in, go out, and they'd aim again. But I persisted. Oh, it took a couple of years but I eventually learnt how to surf. There were quite a few girls down in Sydney at the time and, oh, these little fifteen-year-olds, they used to swear like troopers. After two years I learnt how to do that too.'

When Phyllis moved north to Kingscliff, just south of the Gold Coast, her surfing development accelerated, as she surfed all day every day in the warm sub-tropical waters. 'When I first moved up here I'd be down at six o'clock at Snapper. There'd only be two of us out there. None of the locals went early. They'd arrive later. So basically living up here changed my surfing life.' Surfing the Gold Coast's famed pointbreaks in solitude, where 300 or more surfers regularly clog the line-ups these days, must have been amazing.

'Surfing the points was wonderful,' she agrees, wistfully. 'Once I came up here that's when I improved. I could go surfing every day because I got a job at the tenpin bowling alley and I worked mainly nights. I won my first Queensland title and was eligible for the world titles in '64.'

The first official world surfing championships were organised by Sydney surfer Bob Evans, founder of *Surfing World* magazine, who managed to persuade Ampol to sponsor the event. America's Linda Benson was runaway favourite to take out the women's division but Phyllis felt supremely at ease in her old hometown and surprised the field.

'It was only small, but they were playing this real bouncy music, and that made me feel totally relaxed,' Phyllis recalls. 'I used to do a lot of spinners and that was probably what won me the title.' Phyllis stands and demonstrates in the middle of her lounge room, shuffling about on the spot through 360 degrees. 'I used to spin like a top,' she laughs.

Surfing World reported at the time: 'Phyllis was completely at ease on the swell. Her placement in the waves was ideal and her trimming and arching through the hollow sections pretty to watch.'

'No one thought I'd beat Linda Benson,' says Phyllis. 'She and I became very good friends then, and we had a little celebration drink down at the Manly Pacific.'

Phyllis went on to finish sixth at the world titles in San Diego, California, in 1966, and third in 1968 in Puerto Rico, and she won three Australian and eight Queensland titles.

'In Puerto Rico you're against a lot of talented girls . . . I got as much of a thrill beating those high-ranked Americans as I did when I won the world title.'

Phyllis lived in California for two years, as a team rider for Dewey Weber, one of the largest surfboard manufacturers of the day.

'I was glad to get home. Over there it would be a bright sunny day and then all of a sudden the fog would roll in. I was sitting at Huntington Beach, never been there before, and the fog rolled in. And you know there's a pier, and I could not see a foot in front of me. But luckily I made it into the shore,' she recalls. 'We used to do a lot of hitching. Once, in San Diego, I said to my friend, "Don't worry about me. I'll thumb back to LA." But luckily she didn't go, because how do you thumb in the fog?'

Phyllis must have been quite a livewire for the times — admitting to a fondness for drink and cigarettes, hitchhiking, travelling widely. She admits candidly to a romance with a legendary Hawaiian surfer of the day, who should probably remain nameless: 'I had a bit of a fling with XXXXXX, even though he was married and had about six kids,' she chuckles. 'He was a big guy. I could write a little book about my time over there. I was living on Sunset Point for about three months. Bit of an experience that one . . . wild all right, especially when those big Hawaiians came after you. I was used to the aggro Aussies. The Americans were such gentlemen in comparison. They'd open the door for you when you got in the car.

'I get on very well with Hawaiians. I met the Duke over there in 1964. He's an icon. One of my friends was actually [Australian surf pioneer] Snowy McAllister. He was actually my mentor, and he'd told me a lot about the Duke.'

Phyllis is full of surprises, tales that are hard to equate with the frail-looking, white-haired grandmotherly figure she presents today. Like a surfing trip to Tahiti ten years ago. 'That was my vodka trip. Everywhere I went the vodka went,' she laughs. 'I don't know how I got there and back, I really don't. I was plied from the time I left to the time I got back.

My sister was absolutely disgusted with me when she picked me up at Brizzy. And then from the airport I went straight over to the bowls club and had a few more. I used to love vodka. I don't know how I got through customs that trip. Eight years ago I totally reformed. Haven't had a drop of anything.'

In 1996, Phyllis was inducted into the Australian Surfing Hall of Fame, only the second woman to receive the honour, after Isobel Latham, who surfed tandem with Duke Kahanamoku on his historic first surf in Australia. Thus, in a little-acknowledged quirk of history, Australia's first surfer and first world champion were both women.

'Getting into the Hall of Fame really meant something then, because for all the guys that got in there's only Isobel Latham and then me, then Gail Couper, Pam Burridge and Layne [Beachley]. So there's only five of us.'

Did she ever have any other career than surfing? 'Basically, no. I went into the bar trade, served down there at Twin Towns when it was only one level, going around with a double-decker tray remembering all the orders in your head. Don't know how I did it — couldn't do it now. I can't remember one day from the other. That was a very good lifestyle — when there were titles on I could have time off.'

In recent years, Phyllis's surfing has been a stop–start affair but she keeps on returning to the pull of the ocean. 'I stopped surfing when I was about forty-four because I got very thin and when I'd lie on a board my ribs used to stick in. And then I took it up again for a little while and then I stopped again. I went over to Hawaii in July. One of my friends has got a surfing business here, [former US surf champion and surf coach] Nancy Emerson. I had a go on a softboard, and had a fantastic time. Nancy had a soft deck about 7'10". I didn't think I'd be able to stand up but I did quite good, yeah, so I've started up again. We had a reunion, about thirty girls. I hadn't seen them for about thirty years. It was great to catch up with them all, and I hope to go back next year because I've got friends on Maui and I've got friends on the Big Island, and Kauai, so when Nance goes back next year I'll go over again.'

Suddenly, Phyllis is sounding like a stoked grommet, frothing on her next surf trip and the quest for the perfect board. 'I've got a little six-footer but it's a bit too small, so today I'm getting a 6'10". I'm going to sell the six-footer and I've also got a 7'10", so I'll be out there again, only when it's small, of course.'

Phyllis works out more strenuously and keeps herself in better shape than some pro surfers I know. 'I always kept up the bodysurfing. I have a little boogie board, and I used to go out on that, but I'm really glad that at sixty-nine I'm making a comeback.' She smiles. 'I do a lot of swimming. I do about eight to ten ks a day. Not freestyle. I do a lot of work on a kickboard. And I can paddle my kickboard, it's so big, so when I get on a board they're so easy to paddle. Even some of the girls I was surfing with in Hawaii, I could get on a board and paddle quicker than they could, because I'm so used to paddling a little kickboard. I do a lot of work at one of the local gyms, swimming and gym work basically. I used to be only thirty-five kilograms and since I've been going to the gym I'm up to forty. When I first started I could only push at the most twenty-five kilograms with my legs. Now I'm up to seventy-two, so I've improved the strength in my legs, hence it's going to be easier when I stand up on the board. I get up early in the morning, twenty past four, because we open at twenty past five at the pool. I go to three pools, I've got my passes to all three. Sometimes my sister says I overdo it. Perhaps I do, but while I'm fit and healthy I'll keep going.'

She remains as up to date on the pro surfing scene, the latest ratings and contest results, as any starry-eyed kid. 'I always follow the pro surfing and I go to the awards presentation when they have it up there at the [Gold] Coast. That's a very good night. And I go to the Hall of Fame presentations every year at Casuarina. We had a great roll-up last year, and it was great to see Layne get into the Hall of Fame . . . But the one who's going to take over is Stephanie. She's going great.'

Remarkably, the latest women's surfing sensation is another slight, blonde natural footer from the sleepy town of Kingscliff, fifty years Phyllis's junior. Stephanie Gilmore, eighteen, looks set to sweep all before her — already a world junior champion and the first surfer in history to win two World Championship Tour events as an unrated wildcard. 'Ah, we can produce them down here at Kingy,' laughs Phyllis. 'I met her when she was fifteen. She's a girl with her head screwed on. She won the Roxy Pro a couple of years ago. She got quite a bit of money and what did she do? She went and bought a house at D-bah. Another kid would have spent it on a snazzy car . . . She said one day she's going to be a world champion. Well, the way she's going she could get it next year. She's done very well money-wise.'

But you won't hear any sour grapes from Phyllis about missing surfing's era of big-buck professionalism. And she's not one to obsess over past glories. 'I had some fantastic trophies. I got sick and tired of cleaning silver . . . They all got chucked in the wheelie bin. The only ones I kept are the majors.'

She has a few surf trophies on display, along with a couple of contest posters signed by the current crop of female surfers declaring the inspiration Phyllis has given them, and a few old surfing photos. If you imagine women's surfing in the '60s was all about grace and dainty posturing, think again. One shot shows Phyllis in a strong, crouched, backhand bottom turn, arms splayed out at her sides, longboard up on a rail with only the fin and the tail grabbing the water on a head-high left. 'Where do you think that is?' she asks when I stop to admire the grainy sepia-tone shot. 'Kirra! There used to be a left out there,' she declares keenly. 'I used to love Kirra. It used to be fantastic in the old days.'

One gets the impression surfing the Gold Coast points before crowds has been reward enough: day after day of empty, spinning, warm-water barrels — the elusive idyll that drives every surfer's fantasies. 'I just enjoy it, it's very vitalising, and I love watching them surf,' she says simply. 'I couldn't imagine me going inland. Definitely once you start it grabs you.'

GRAMBEAU

LEFT: With a devilish glint in the eye, and rugged up against the southern elements, Ross Clarke-Jones embarks on another big wave mission.

BELOW: Free-falling through the tube at Tasmania's Shipstern Bluff, Ross takes big-wave bravado to surreal extremes.

GRAMBEAU

MARK METCALF

Quadraplegic surfer Jesse Billauer expertly navigates the cavernous recesses of the Cloudbreak reef in Fiji.

MARK METCALF

MARK METCALF

Jesse (ABOVE) takes the boat from Tavarua Island out to the offshore Cloudbreak reef and (RIGHT) is all smiles after another successful ride.

ALICE WINTON

Novelist Tim Winton with his Tom Wegener-shaped timber board, the 'cruise beast'.

COLONEL/WWW.OZSURFSHOTS.COM

Bob McTavish, surely Australia's most barrelled senior citizen, enjoying a booming swell on the north coast of New South Wales in winter 2007.

GRAMBEAU

A pre-teen Kelly Slater quietly reading the ocean's signals, before fame and riches descended on his young shoulders.

JOHN FRANK

Eight-time world champ Kelly Slater drops into a glassy barrel at an offshore Tahitian reef.

JOHN FRANK

The world's greatest competitive surfer and the look that can make his opponents wilt.

JOHN FRANK

Kelly Slater tow surfing a huge Tahitian reef break.

SEAN DAVEY

Richard Tognetti and friends in an impromptu performance at the King Island town hall for an audience of farmers and fishermen.

SEAN DAVEY

Richard Tognetti putting one of his unorthodox finless surfboards through its paces on a surf trip to King Island.

BOB BARKER/ROVING EYE

Surf Aid founder Dr Dave Jenkins confers with locals on child health in a Mentawai village in Indonesia.

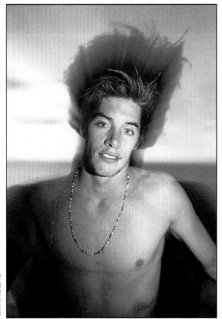

GRAMBEAU

A young pro surfer with an open and expansive mind, Dave Rastovich is a rare bird in the modern surfing world.

COURTESY *SURFING WORLD* MAGAZINE

Midget Farrelly and Phyllis O'Donnell won the 1964 World Title and were featured on the cover of *Surfing World*.

BAKER

Dorian 'Doc' Paskowitz, proud patriach of a surfing dynasty.

COURTESY FINS

Steve Snow, your host at Fins restaurant — a man who has genuinely surfed his menu.

JULIAN SMITH

Surfing artist Chris Lundy in his living room/studio works at 'On The Road to Equilibrium' on Oahu's North Shore.

'Going to get a Kombi and go from beach to beach. Be the kind of people the authorities can't reach.'

THE GO-BETWEENS, 'SURFING MAGAZINES'

SURF LESSON #47
Straying from the herd

OK, two weeks, all expenses paid in the Canary Islands doesn't sound like a bad gig, right? But hang on, what's this? A catch? Also on the quaint Spanish territory of Fuerteventura Island will be 100 or so of the world's top longboarders.

Now, if I want to go surfing with dozens of crazed loggers I can just duck down the road to Currumbin Alley. To fly to a windswept bunch of barren atolls in the Atlantic on the other side of the world, when most migratory surfers are heading to Hawaii in the middle of the swell-drenched North Pacific — this sounded like something approaching lunacy. But, hell, I'm a sucker for a free air ticket. And just think of those frequent flyer points.

The occasion was the world longboard titles, and the contest sponsors, French clothing label Oxbow, were kind enough to offer me paid employment writing a few press releases.

So, there I was, undertaking the unfamiliar marathon by air (thirty-six hours and six airports) from the Gold Coast to Fuerteventura, which, appropriately enough, roughly translates as 'strong adventure'. Instead of flying into the modern highrise of Honolulu, I found myself stopping over amid the beautiful, historic architecture of Madrid. Instead of the familiar drive through canefields and pineapple plantations to the North Shore, Fuerteventura provided an eerie landscape of low, dusty shrubs and endless, grey/brown rolling hills on the bumpy drive out to its own North Shore. The mighty volcanic peaks were reminiscent of Hawaii, but stripped of their lush tropical vegetation, like some post-apocalytpic wasteland.

My quarters were in a strangely sterile holiday resort occupied predominantly by enormous, pasty-white Europeans escaping the northern winter, who lolled about by the pool all day and waited anxiously for the dining hall to open at six o'clock each evening. 'They fly 'em in, turn 'em from white to pink, and fly 'em out again,' one local told me, of the packaged holiday crowds that are the Canary Islands' staple industry.

The contest was cool enough — I found myself surprisingly entertained by the surfing, and the varied and contrasting styles of the modern loggers, like old footage from the world contests of the '60s. And the contest site featured a stylish pair of enormous Moroccan tents, where the delighted competitors reclined on elaborately woven rugs and cushions, like Arab Sheiks. As far as my own recreational surfing was concerned, however, it was slim pickings. I began sniffing around for less well known options. My mission on this trip became to try and score a quality, uncrowded session somewhere amid the chaos. Rent-a-cars piled high with longboards were crisscrossing the island and the chances of any secret spots surviving the onslaught seemed remote.

Then Aussie longboarder and former world champ Marty McMillan, told me about the island, just a short ferry ride from the mainland, that supposedly hosts the longest right-hander in Europe. You could see it, wrapping around a towering volcanic peak off in the distance. Ferries ran twice a day, at 10 am and 4 pm. It needed a huge swell and winds that were straight onshore at most of the breaks on our island. I filed away the information and bided my time as the contest rolled on in reasonable, sideshore, six-foot surf.

When the swell hit, accompanied by howling onshore winds, I was amped. I drove down to the wharf where the ferry departed and, to my horror, saw fifty or so longboarders neatly lined up waiting to board the ferry, then filing on like penguins. I couldn't bring myself to join the queue. The stories that drifted back of the mayhem in the line-up that day were frightening and I resigned myself to defeat. They could have the island. I stayed in my hotel room and sulked, wishing I was in the actual Hawaii, in the North Pacific. Crowded Rocky Point had never seemed so appealing.

The next day was a similar scenario — again I drove to the wharf, and again I couldn't bring myself to join the ranks of longboarders growing by the day as they were knocked out of the event. Now, there should have been another way out to the island, I know, but the locals weren't exactly stoked on the contest and I was short of cash, so the chances of arranging private transport seemed slim. I was watching a Legends Tennis Tournament on cable TV (John McEnroe versus Yannick Noah — a thoroughly entertaining affair that should give inspiration to surf promoters everywhere), when my friend Marshall came knocking. Marshall is a fine American fellow who was travelling the world making a surf movie with a stirring spiritual theme to it, starring longboarder Stephen Slater (younger brother of Kelly) and his pretty Roxy model/surfer girlfriend, Veronica. His concept was to pluck them out of their American, white-bread, shopping-mall comfort zone, drag them through a world tour of exotic and Third World surf spots, feed them a super-healthy diet, train them in yoga and Eastern philosophies, and document the personal transformations, consciousness expansion and heightened surfing experiences they go through on the way. They were all a bit over each other by this point, and Marshall was keen to strike out on an adventure of his own.

His logic was blindingly simple but brilliant. Catch the 4 pm ferry over as everyone else was coming home, score the late session, take provisions and camp on the beach, score an early session, then catch the 10 am ferry back when everyone else was just arriving. I had a 1 pm flight home the next day, and the airport was an hour's drive, so it was cutting it fine, but I was desperate by this stage. We grabbed boards, packed essentials, fanged to the supermarket, grabbed a few things in a blind rush, and just made it to the wharf on time.

We boarded the ferry with two other English surfers who had cottoned on to the same scheme, and bucked and swayed across the channel in the booming swell. As we approached the island, there queued up awaiting the ferry was virtually the entire cast of the world longboard championships. I have rarely felt so exultant. We marched off the ferry, boardbags under our arms, backpacks slung over our shoulders, issuing cheery greetings to our longboard friends who could only stare incredulously at our cunning. The surf was six foot and going off when they'd dragged themselves out of the water en masse to make the ferry. We had two hours of light left, with only a handful of local surfers in the water, who had their own dinghies or Zodiacs. There was nothing on the island; even camping was prohibited unless you had a permit, but we trudged across its rocky, arid surface triumphantly, confident no ranger would bust us on our noble quest.

The wave was like a cross between Burleigh Heads and Lennox, or a softer version of J-Bay, wedging and peaking off the end of a craggy headland, and wrapping in long, fast walls down the island's rocky flank, accelerating, steepening, growing hollower as it ran and shrank for hundreds of yards. I'd brought only a 7'4", figuring I'd rather be overgunned than undergunned, and swooped and climbed my way along the brilliant, grey-green waves in the fading light, feeling like a seabird in flight, barely turning, but spreading my arms wide and opening my heart through dreamy speed runs and bottom turns. The waves were good, but with a slight warp from the stormy conditions out to sea. The morning session tomorrow . . . that would be the one, I reasoned.

We enjoyed a simple feast of yoghurt, bread and cheese spread, fruit and water in near darkness, then wriggled into blankets and boardbags in a little dip in the terrain, out of the howling winds that whipped across the bare island. We talked and laughed and looked at the stars, huddled against the cold, and drifted off to sleep. I must have lain awake for hours the next morning, imagining it was beginning to get light, before a glimmering smudge finally began to paint itself across the eastern sky. It was grey, freezing. My wetty was still damp, and my body tight and sore from the cold, but I couldn't get out there quickly enough, and picked my way gingerly up the point over the jagged rocks in the dawn half-light.

The morning session was a bit of an anti-climax, to be honest. The swell had dropped a touch, the wind was a little sideshore, and half an hour after dawn a boatload of a dozen or so locals descended on the line-up and pretty much took over. I was ready to hustle a little for some waves. Hell, I was getting on a plane back to Australia in a few hours and I wanted to fly out with water dripping out of my nose and a few sweet rides replaying in my head. I got a couple before I caved in to the weight of numbers and went in. Marshall, meanwhile, was having a shocker. He broke a fin just getting out through the rocks and figured maybe he wasn't supposed to surf that morning. He decided to video, and when he turned away for a moment his camera and tripod blew over in the wind and smashed. He was magnificent under pressure, quietly puzzling over the lessons contained therein.

And I, like Bobby Brady at the end of one of those 'Brady Bunch' morality tales, had learnt a couple of things myself. First, the evening session was the one, as it turned out, and I might have appreciated it more fully if I hadn't wasted time anticipating the next day's early session. Second, never despair in your quest to score good, uncrowded waves, no matter how seemingly oppressive the odds. There is always a way, and magic sessions have a habit of popping up at the most unlikely, unexpected times.

And, finally, at the risk of stating the obvious, even though it can be a lonely road at times, and you might feel lost and adrift and unsure of your next move, there's a lot to be said for falling out of step with the herd. For that is where magic dwells.

steve snow

{ the chef }

It's like I should thank surfing and every country I've been to. Without being into the ocean and surfing and going to all those countries and seeing all those different far-flung cultures I wouldn't have a menu like I have today.

Want to know award-winning chef Steve Snow's favourite surf destinations? Just look at his menu. Snow, the owner and chef of Fins seafood restaurant in Byron Bay, wears his culinary influences on his sleeve, over a career that has been defined by his surfing travels.

His Mauritian seafood sambal has its origins in a humble streetcart vendor selling chilli octopus rolls, which Steve would devour between surf sessions at the legendary Tamarin Bay, in Mauritius. His arroz de marisco (seafood risotto), bacalhau (salted cod), Lisbon paste and cataplana of seafood were all learnt during extended surfing holidays in Portugal. His famous Fins Fish, with its lemongrass and prawn paste, takes its inspiration from an elderly Balinese woman cooking on the beach at Nusa Dua. His use of coconut comes from his surf trips to Fiji. African influences were gathered while surfing the mighty right pointbreak of Jeffreys Bay, South Africa. Traces of French cuisine were picked up while surfing and cooking in Lacanau. Steve Snow has literally surfed his menu.

Without any formal training, Steve has steered Fins' unique and multicultural treatment of gloriously fresh seafood to national and international renown, earning a swag of awards (including two chef's hats from the *Sydney Morning Herald Good Food Guide* since 1998, and Best Seafood Restaurant in Australia, 2004) and guest-chef gigs at exclusive holiday resorts from Europe to Fiji to Tasmania.

'Without surfing I wouldn't have a restaurant and a lifestyle like I have now, so I would have to say it's been the major influence in my life,' says Steve. What has surfing taught him? 'A love of seafood, an absolute love of seafood. Love of travelling and, as a result of travelling, learning so many tricks from people near the ocean and seeing the way they play with fish and other seafood. It's like I should thank surfing and every country I've been to. Without being into the ocean and surfing and going to all those countries and seeing all those different far-flung cultures I wouldn't have a menu like I have today.'

Steve was born in Southport on Queensland's Gold Coast, spent his early years in Bangalow in northern New South Wales, before the family moved to Cronulla, south of Sydney, where he discovered surfing at the age of thirteen.

'I remember having a Coolite. I painted stripes on it and I remember how stoked I was the first time I stood up on that . . . and taking off on a wave and being on the top and being really really scared, and going down and thinking, "I'm going to nose dive," and making it. That feeling in the stomach and being scared and all of that, it kind of hooks you. I remember the first time I progressed from a foamie to a green wave. I caught the foam and it re-formed and I remember getting out and sitting on the beach going, "Wow, this is one of the greatest moments of my life".'

As a grommet, Steve cut his teeth on the Greenhills beachbreaks, stuffing his bed with pillows so it looked like he was still asleep, climbing out his bedroom window and catching a train from Miranda to Cronulla, swiping a bottle of milk somewhere along the way for breakfast. 'We'd take a sausage and stick a stick through it and put it on the fire and sleep down there and wake up and go surfing. That was good.'

As he got older, and he and his mates got cars and licences, the surfing lifestyle took hold and the wave-rich New South Wales south coast beckoned. 'I realise now it was dumb — we'd go to the pub all night then jump in our cars and go down to Ulladulla, which was three or four hours. Either sleep in the car or, if we were capable, put a tent up, and then spend all weekend doing the same stuff and going surfing. I surfed a lot down that way.'

Despite a growing surf addiction, Steve managed to finish high school and a business degree — a career in restaurants still the furthest thing from his mind. 'I was working at Nestlé as a product manager, and I was so not into getting a train to work and turning up,' he recalls. 'What happened was, my version of the boss's pedigree and his version of his own pedigree didn't correlate, so one of us had to go. As he was the boss, I was out the door. A guy from the Maggi line that I knew there, the chef that you'd ring up and ask about recipes — he rang me and said, '"I used to like your creativity in coming up with the ads. I'm opening a restaurant. Can you market it for me and do the business side?"' I'd had nothing to do with restaurants, but I'd always loved cooking.' Steve jumped aboard and eventually found himself helping out in the kitchen of the modest Chez Gourmet, serving up good, honest, unspectacular fare like schnitzel and pasta. 'Then the *Cheap Eats* people came by. Valerie Lawson wrote an article in *Cheap Eats* and said it was the best food, so I ended up staying in restaurants.'

Steve's lack of formal training was supplemented by a relentless surf travel lust, which informed his evolving cooking style. He found himself hauling fishing nets in Lacanau, France, by day and cooking in a local restaurant at night 'The chef there used kelp. He put the fish on top of it, and then added onion and wine and whatever else, covered it in foil and put it in the oven. It would cook in its own juices and the kelp would add another flavour. You'd put it on the table, and because you eat with your eyes first, it was like, wow! It was a great thing. Without surfing I wouldn't have learnt that one.'

In Portugal he met his future wife and encountered his greatest culinary influences — inspiring several of his signature dishes to this day, including his famous cataplana of seafood: 'Originally it was all the food that the fishermen or the fisherladies couldn't sell, and that became their dinner. So they'd throw it all into a big cauldron and put in potatoes. The

Portuguese put wine in everything so they put wine in, and then all the odds and ends. We've adapted that and mongrelised it and bastardised it. And we've added the best king prawns and all that . . . bugs and prawns and bits of fish and mussels. I learnt the Lisbon paste — that's what we call it — from an old Portuguese lady over there. I watched how she was cooking and I thought, "Wow, that's a fantastic thing." I've showed it to a lot of guys, like [Japanese-born chef] Tetsuya [Wakuda], who can really cook in Australia and they've gone, "Wow, that's such a different thing." It lends a level of authenticity, so it actually tastes like, wow! Because the flavours are different, people come to our restaurant. Same with Indonesia. Another old lady was cooking on a beach in Nusa Dua. She had this paste she made up, it was all with rehydrated prawns, lemongrass and all of that, so now I use a blachan, that's what we call the paste, and get heaps of different flavours.'

Steve's in no doubt that it's the nature of surf travel, the intimacy with which he's been exposed to foreign cultures and come to know local people, that has given him such rich insights into different cuisines. 'Surfing has been a major influence on where I live, who I got married to, who I might go out with these days, my kids, my menu. I run a seafood restaurant. I wonder why? I love the stuff. I never get sick of it. I went to Morocco and did a week of *la cuisine Australie* in Casablanca. You can go to Casablanca now and have a spanner crab chowder. I teach those guys things when I'm there but I also learn a lot from them so now I've got a Moroccan tagine on my menu that I learnt when I was over there. In Mauritius, I remember surfing Tamarin Bay; it's such a serious wave that one. You take off and you can't go to the bottom, you've got to do a turn at the top because it's just too fast. You've got to get tubed to make it. It's extremely fast, quite dangerous, real heart-in-your-mouth stuff. I'd go surfing and I'd get out and there was this lady with one of those little carts like in Asia. She had this octopus that was so hot, ridiculously chilli hot.

And I'd have three rolls every day. I've added other things to it like good quality fish, and I turn it out with a green pawpaw salad and rice steamed in a lotus leaf — and that's a Mauritian seafood sambal. I make my own fresh paste to go with it, but there's more than a passing nod to that lady because I just loved those rolls that she had. There's lots of things like that.'

Back in Australia, Steve moved around the Sydney restaurant scene, earned some good reviews, but found himself drawn back to his north coast roots. He cooked at the Byron Arts Factory, the Railway Hotel and the Brunswick Pub, before taking a chance on a failed restaurant on the banks of the Brunswick River.

'It was a bankrupt place, had been shut for six months. Even the landlord had got food poisoning there. It was real bad when we bought it. Everyone was going, "No way." I paid eight thousand bucks for it, which wasn't a lot of money, and I thought, "Wow, look at the location, right on the river." That was a funny restaurant. I remember thinking, "I've got to give this place up. I'll never pay the bills." And then — you know, journos have been good to me — [food critic] Terry Durack came in and wrote the place up as the best food he'd had outside any capital city anywhere. Suddenly it went from struggling to get twenty people on a Saturday night to people wanting to book six weeks in advance. Just ludicrous.'

Terry Durack, one of Australia's most renowned food critics, still recalls his meal at the original Fins vividly more than ten years later. 'I was in Byron Bay writing on the local eating scene for the *Sydney Morning Herald*,' he says. 'From what I remember, it was all fine, a bit hippy-zippy, without any blow-you-away highlights. Then we drove to Brunswick Heads, and here was this wacky, wonderful riverside place where you sat under mango trees at tables set with Rid as well as salt and pepper, and pelicans strolled proprietorially between the tables. Halfway through the meal, the chef came out with a long broom, knocked a mango off the tree and went back to the kitchen with it. But what really got me was the food.

The fish and seafood were flapping fresh. There were glorious local oysters with Kaffir lime, ginger and tamari, hours-old char-grilled Moses perch — such bright, fresh flavours. I was intrigued by the distinct Portuguese influence on the menu, including a stunning caldeirada, a with-the-works fish stew of bug tails, spanner crab, mussels, scallops and fish. A celebration of freshness, sunshine and sea. Then I met Steven Snow himself, and realised how the natural style of cooking evolved from the honesty and enthusiasm of this local-boy-made-good with his Byron Bay combination of energy and laidback "peace, man" ways. He is an original, driven by his love of . . . well, just about everything. For me, Snow created one of the great Australian restaurant experiences, all about great produce and a sense of place. Naturally, it was influenced by other cuisines and other flavours but quintessentially this was such an Australian way to eat. His food keeps digging you in the ribs, insisting you remember where you are and who you are and why you are such a lucky bugger to be there. I absolutely adored the lack of pretence about the place and remember never wanting to leave.'

Steve, too, recalls those days with obvious fondness. 'It was a pretty wild restaurant. I remember times when the sannyasins would come in and they'd have some fish under their belts and some wine and God knows what else, and they'd all get their gear off. My restaurant full of people with no clothes on. Then they started running across bridges. It ended up being a fairly wild restaurant. There were weird things, like snakes would go through while you were trying to dine, and water rats would do a victory lap through the restaurant. There were complimentary bottles of Rid on every table because you'd get eaten by the sandflies. People loved it, and it went good. And after that we won an award, best seafood New South Wales or something. They flew me down to Sydney and that was all good, people pumping my hand. And when I came back they announced they were putting a highway through my restaurant; they were closing it down.'

The potential blow proved a blessing. The government paid Steve out for the compulsory acquisition of his restaurant and he moved into decidedly more upmarket premises at the Beach Hotel, back in Byron.

You'd be hard pressed to find any nude sannyasins, snakes, water rats or sandflies at Fins these days. Its latest incarnation represents one of Byron's true fine dining experiences. And Steve's love of seafood and international influences are at the fore. He uses only line-caught fish, fresh prawns that haven't been dipped in chemicals, and freshly shucked oysters — an approach he says comes from his love of the ocean and respect for its produce. His passion for the subject is obvious.

'Whereas a lot of restaurants get their prawns and romantically defrost them in the sink, I know all the trawlermen, and my prawns are real and live. They've got no chemicals on them. They've got the sweet of a prawn and the salt of a prawn and they're beautiful. We always get fish fresh. I've never sold a frozen fish in this place. A lot of restaurants pre-shuck their oysters, but I want the taste of the sea and I shuck each oyster to order. I remember I'd buy octopus for fifty cents a kilo and they'd be going, "What do you do with this? Are you joking, mate? As if you're going to use that? That's garbage." And now octupus can cost seventeen bucks a kilo, so gone are those days. And that was a legacy of going to Portugal and cooking in France — over there they were right into octupus and I saw how good it can be.'

Steve jokes that his love of seafood almost borders on indecent. 'I remember going diving up the Whitsundays and looking at all those beautiful fish and feeling I should be put in jail or something because I was looking at them go by and thinking, "How nice would that bit on the back of its neck be to steam?"' He laughs.

On a more serious note, he says he's concerned about the sustainable harvesting and humane treatment of all the seafood he handles. 'I think as long as it gets treated with respect . . . You don't leave a fish to flap on the deck. How would you expect that fish to taste good? If every fish taken from the ocean had to be caught by someone with a line I'd be real sure that that's a sustainable way of fishing. And I want to know that it's killed humanely, such as the Japanese method of *iki jimi* [where the fish is speared through the head with a metal skewer as soon as it's caught]. I've always got something raw on the menu because if the fish is good enough, it's a good idea to serve it raw. So I do nothing to it, put a dakon pickle with it and not much else and serve it raw.'

Even the flavours he prefers are influenced by surfing and the ocean, and a mindfulness of staying healthy so he can keep riding waves. 'I like clean flavours . . . and food that I want to not fight in your stomach. I want it to convert to a good energy. If you throw enough butter and cream at it you can make anything taste good. But that's not what it's about for me.'

These days, Steve travels regularly as a guest chef to luxury resorts around the world, dragging his bag of cooking implements and a surfboard with him. 'I go to Fiji sometimes and consult — great waves I've had there, seriously good waves . . . Wherever they pay me to go as a guest chef now, I go. It's great. You learn so much. But I love places with water, I love to be near water. There was a major stage of my life, well over a decade and a half, where I'd have to go and check the surf before I could do anything. I was that pathetic I couldn't even function as a person. And as for going on a holiday to anywhere there wasn't an ocean, it was like, "Sure? That's ludicrous, what a dumb idea." Now I go to places like Shanghai and cook. But I've found even now if I'm in a place with really nice air and mountains, after three or four days, even if it's a really great place, I'm so hanging to get somewhere near the ocean. It's a funny thing. I go in the water every day, even in the middle of winter when I'm the only person on the whole beach and it's blowing. I go in those days and have a swim. I don't know how many girlfriends have complained, "Oh this stupid surfboard," and then my wife going, "Darling, have we got to take this board everywhere?" The short answer was, yes.'

Eventually, Steve's lifestyle — the demands of running a restaurant, travel and surfing — took a toll on his relationship and he and his wife divorced after fifteen years of marriage, and with two sons.

Steve reckons he went off the rails for a while there after the divorce, but it was surfing and a new commitment to healthy living that pulled him out of a nose dive. 'I did all the things I used to laugh at about Byron Bay — learnt to meditate, do yoga. Now they're all parts of my life that I love. There's not a day goes by I don't meditate. You reckon surfing's good for your head? Well, combine it with meditation and see how you go. It's like you shut your brain down for half an hour. It's like having four or five hours' sleep.'

Steve says surfing has even taught him lessons in business. 'To open a small business you're so sticking your neck out, and if that business happens to be a restaurant apparently the stats are that after five years, only four or five per cent of them are still going,' he says. 'With risk taking, it's like surfing — so many times you take off somewhere like Tamarin Bay and Jeffreys or new places where you don't know how many sharks are there, how shallow the reef is, things like that, you don't just sit there and do nothing. You go for it and take off and go, "Wow!" Risk taking's all a part of it. And it keeps you healthy so at least you're feeling good when you take the risk. If you're a little bit down or not feeling so good, well, the risk can fall apart a lot more. On a wave it's the same. You work it out when you're there: you get really excited when you're at the top and coming down, and with any luck you don't fall over. You've got to adapt all the time. The sort of waves I love especially are when it's a steep take-off and a bit heart-in-your-mouth and you're on your backhand and you're going real fast. It's not pre-ordained, you may bounce off the reef, or will I eat it here? You've got to go with the flow, for sure. I think it affects your every waking moment, if you think about it enough.'

Does he cook better after a good day of waves? 'To engage in understatement, absolutely, totally, yeah, three bags full, without doubt,' he laughs. 'To cook well — if you're angry, you can taste it. Another thing is if you're hungry because maybe you surfed all day, and you're cooking food, you cook so well you almost begrudge the person the fish because you'd love to have it yourself. But when it goes out people go, "Wow!" People make outrageous statements. People on a number of occasions have said, "That's the best fish I've ever had in my life," and usually when you're cooking really because you're happy and you're into it and probably you're hungry.'

And, of course, surfing has brought other more immediate rewards. 'Surfing's about beauty. When you're tired after surfing and you watch the sun set on some island and then you're waiting for your fish to cook, that's paradise,' he says. One recent assignment as a guest chef in Fiji brought with it the rare treat of surfing a remote reefbreak that had only been ridden by one other person. 'The guy who was the builder on the island said, "Oh, I heard you like going surfing, mate." I'd asked before I went, "Are there any waves there?" and the guy who owned the island said, "Nah, there's no waves here." So I was quite surprised when this other guy came to me. I said, "How about when I finish cooking, let's go surfing. Let's get a boat and go and have a look." I jumped in the boat with him and we had waves that were one of those rare moments that stand out in your lifetime. He said he was the first bloke to ever surf it and he said, "You're the second." We were out for three and a half, four hours and surfing shallow reef and clear water. It comes out of deep water and then onto a reef. It was a serious wave. We had extremely good surf and a couple of nicks from hitting the reef.'

It's an approach to life — leaping into the unknown, charging head-on, taking a few risks, reaping rich rewards and copping a few nicks along the way — that seems to have served Steve well. The high pressure world of restaurants, particularly when you've got some sort of reputation to uphold, lofty expectations to fulfil night after night, has claimed plenty of casualties.

'Even with surfing, sometimes it's really hard in the kitchen and that's why so many chefs are like axe murderers,' Steve reckons. 'So many chefs are alcoholics, drug addicts. Take coke too much and you can't taste and you can't smell, so it's all wrong. If there's an alternative like negative ions or being in salt water, well my suggestion would be, do that one. Because the coke one, I've seen a lot of people go and collapse and fall in a heap and yell and scream and make it even more difficult to get by.

'When I go away as a guest chef, I'm a fairly junior event, but there's a lot of expectation, people have paid a lot for their tickets and the people who own the restaurant want this or that. You finish cooking at midnight, and it gets to three o'clock real quick with a bottle of wine and talking to people. And then you've got to be up the next day prepping, and you do the same the next night. By the third day . . . that's why people take cocaine and stuff, because they're actually so tired. It's like, "Give me something to help!" That's why it happens, because you can't tell those hundred people, "Look, I'm so tired, I just can't do it tonight. Not feeling up to it. Just knock it on the head." They'd want to neck you. Better to breathe, meditate, stand on your head — or better than any of that, go for a paddle.'

At the time of going to press Fins was relocating to the Salt Village development near Kingscliff, on the NSW Tweed Coast.

mark cunningham

{ the bodysurfer }

We must never forget how lucky we are, to play, basically play, in the ocean. It's not rocket science. You're not helping anyone. You're not curing any disease. All you can do is get stoked and create good vibes and share the good vibes with the rest of the world when you go in on land, I reckon.

He has been a lifeguard at Hawaii's Banzai Pipeline, the world's most deadly wave, for thirty years, and saved hundreds of lives. He won bodysurfing's unofficial world title at that same mighty wave fourteen times between 1974 and 2000. He's played mentor and guardian to many of the world's most successful pro surfers, schooling them in the volatile nature of the heaving beast, the nuances of its jagged lava reef, watching over them from the lifeguard tower as they found their feet in surfing's most intense arena, lending them swim fins and encouraging them to bodysurf to increase their intimacy with the wave's many moods.

And while surf stars, clothing companies, photographers and promoters have generated untold wealth and glory from this gladiatorial pit, Mark Cunningham has caretaken the whole insane carnage for nothing more than a lifeguard's wage . . . and the boundless respect of the world's elite surfers. He lives in a cheap rental house on the North Shore, drives a rusted old Volvo stationwagon run on biodiesel. With his close-shaven head, slim frame, quietly contented manner and clear deep eyes, he exudes the air of a devoted surfing monk, undistracted by the displays of ostentatious wealth or chest-beating bravado from the colourful surfing characters all around him. He is his own point of quiet stillness in a swirling vortex of attention seeking.

'I feel like the luckiest guy in the world, that here I am at fifty-one still at Ehukai Beach Park bodysurfing, after thirty years, still stoked,' he gently marvels. 'I read these biographies of people who've done well. A lot of the time their advice is to follow your passion, and I guess I did and I guess I am. Consequently, I'm poor as a church mouse but, filled with gratitude for what surfing or what the ocean gave me, what lifeguarding gave me, what bodysurfing gave me. I owe my whole adult life to it.'

Mark Cunningham didn't start out feeling so lucky. Home was a tough environment and the ocean was his sanctuary. 'My parents were alcoholics, both of them, and there wasn't a whole lot of love — there wasn't the embracing or the hugs or pats on the back. They never came to a bodysurfing contest of mine. With my beach friends, my bodysurfing friends, I really belonged. It felt so cool and soothing and comforting and fun. Here's a circle of friends and acquaintances. I really gained a sense of family there.'

Growing up in Hawaii close to the beach, surfing was almost inevitable, but why bodysurfing? 'Because I was a crap surfer,' he laughs. 'I can't surf to save my life. It's true. Back when I was a teen — this was pre-leash, late '60s, early '70s — I spent more time swimming and bodysurfing after my board. I was a gangly uncoordinated teenager, and I was lucky this older guy, who was one of the elders in the neighbourhood and a great bodysurfer, gave me a pair of fins and dragged me to Sandy Beach and said, "Here, why don't you try it with fins on a real bodysurfing wave?"'

Almost immediately, Mark discovered an uncanny natural ability in the waves, freed from the clumsiness of dealing with a surfboard — that gangly teenage body suddenly finding its perfect function as a sleekly hydrodynamic waveriding foil. 'I was real lucky there was some pretty decent contests around the island. I went in these bodysurfing contests against much older guys, and competition was fun and all and I'm stoked for the recognition that it gave me, but there was just an opportunity to surf with five other guys in the water, that was a big part of it. It felt so real and so legit.'

This was, of course, the Summer of Love, and Mark did have occasion to call upon some psychedelic enhancement of his ocean adventures. 'At seventeen or eighteen, we were doing more than experimenting with LSD.

We did a fair amount of it. The summer before my senior year in high school, I spent all summer at Makapu'u and Sandy Beach. Goddamn it if I didn't think I was part fish, one with the ocean and as fluid as can be. It felt so real, so legitimate and I felt so in tune and at one with the ocean. There were moments of absolute clarity that being in the ocean was right for me. I was in the right place at the right time doing the right thing. I went to this prestigious prep school and most of my contemporaries are attorneys and bankers and politicians and doctors, you know, and like I said there were many moments, not just under the influence, where I just felt like I'm so lucky to be doing this because it feels so good, and it's so beautiful.'

His growing skill in the ocean, and a desire to spend as much time in it as possible, naturally led to lifeguarding. 'I studied to become a lifeguard when I was eighteen and "Hello? You're going to pay me to go to the beach? Where do I sign up?" I was lucky the bodysurfing went hand in hand with the lifeguarding, especially here at Pipeline. Pre-jet skis, a lot of the time you'd have a hard time getting the rescue boards through the Pipe shorebreak so you had to be a really good swimmer. Luckily I was.'

All day he'd sit atop the lifeguard tower, watching many of the world's best surfers, and an ever-growing cast of aspirants, vying for waves — swimming into the tempest and dragging the fallen from the fray. In quiet moments, at dawn and twilight, he could be seen indulging a blossoming romance with Pipe and its cavernous contours — with none of the grim posturing of many of the stand-up crew, but with a pure sense of simple play.

'If you aren't smiling and laughing and enjoying yourself bodysurfing you're doing something wrong. Go back to the beach and try again. We must never forget how lucky we are, to play, basically play, in the ocean. It's not rocket science. You're not helping anyone. You're not curing any disease. All you can do is get stoked and create good vibes and share the good vibes with the rest of the world when you go in on land, I reckon.'

We are, of course, all made up of seventy per cent water, but I wonder whether that fact was amplified for Mark, in his apparently seamless dance with this ferocious wave — whether he had to move like water, become water? 'Getting back to those psychedelic times, that was very apparent to me, oh yeah. I was the ocean, I am the ocean and I just have to get my gills wet,' he laughs. 'I felt so embraced. The ocean just surrounded me and hugged me, and loved me. Like I said, maybe I wasn't getting enough of that at home, but when I got in the water I was just surrounded by it. Genetically we crawled out of the shorebreak, maybe we bodysurfed in to the beach, I don't know, and we're still trying to go back there. I call it the greatest impact zone in the universe: it's where the earth, the sea and the sky come together. Those are three pretty damn powerful forces of nature. We go to the beach and we step off the land and we get in the water. Good God, we're floating. How weird is floating? Most of us are dragged down by gravity on land 99.9 per cent of our lives, and surfers and waveriders and swimmers realise you can get in the water and take a break from being anchored to land.'

While any surfer of note who's ridden Pipeline in the last thirty years is acutely aware of who Mark Cunningham is and the critical role he plays in overseeing their safety, the majority of the general surfing public have never heard of him. Such is the underground status of bodysurfing. Surf video watchers may have been surprised then to see this rangy fifty-year-old bodysurfer turn up in a recent surf movie, on a star-studded boat trip to the Mentawai Islands in Indonesia, alongside modern surfing greats Kelly Slater, Rob Machado and Tom Curren. *A Broke Down Melody*, the latest offering from surf-movie maker Chris Malloy, juxtaposed Mark's graceful, endless trim lines in the spinning Indonesian tubes alongside the high-performance ripping of the greatest boardriders of the modern age. It seemed to be a powerful statement, both of the respect Mark's held in, and perhaps of a hunger to reconnect with the clean uncluttered lines and simple play of surfing's original and purest form.

'I was touched and honoured to be asked to participate in that. I'm a huge fan of surfing. I love the sport and the cast of characters — they're like family, most of these guys. It was just a surf trip. I had no idea it was going to become a movie, much less what the theme or the vibe of the movie was. When it came out and I saw the riff behind it, I was stoked because the vibe was just, "Go out and ride it and have fun, and don't make too big a deal out of it." I was stoked and honoured that my philosophy about waveriding fitted in with the program, especially thirty years past my prime. Here I am, fifty-one. Will I ever grow up? I'm the most stoked grom, and I'd be pinching myself. What am I doing on a surf trip with Curren and Slater and Rob Machado, for God's sake? How'd this happen? But they're all normal people and they're modest and they're humble, so we all got along really well. There was no fighting over breakfast cereal or what movies to watch or stuff like that.'

More than a few high-profile surf stars have sought solace in Mark's wise counsel over the years, or just a loan of a pair of swim fins and a gentle shove in the direction of the Pipe shorebreak. 'Some of my pro surfing friends have told me, "It felt really nice to go out there and not have the spotlight on me." There's something about standing up on a surfboard, it's like, "Here I am, centre stage, look at me, now watch me perform." There's not a whole lot of that with bodysurfing. There's not a lot of pressure to perform. You're just out there for a good time and a good glide and seeing all your friends out there.'

Mark retired from full-time lifeguard duties two years ago but is still hired for water patrol at the big pro contests at Pipe, because of his unequalled mastery in its treacherous line-up, and he still competes occasionally, schooling competitors half his age.

'I'm stoked to be still playing the game. I have friends who aren't here in this world any more, and others who've had health ailments where they couldn't surf if they wanted to. And I've got friends tied up with work and family responsibilities who have lost touch with the ocean. I feel very fortunate: if a bodysurfing contest comes along I can still sign up and have some fun . . . And I do it selfishly for empty water time. At fifty, in this day and age, to surf Pipeline with five guys in the water, are you kidding me? That only happens one day out of the year so I try pretty hard because I want to go to a quarter-final and a semi-final and the final for another twenty minutes worth.'

It was once suggested that every surfer who has owned a three-finned thruster surfboard should send a dollar for each board to Simon Anderson, the great Australian surfer/shaper who invented the thruster and unselfishly shared it with the world — a kind of voluntary tax. Perhaps in the same spirit, every surfer who has ridden Pipe in the last thirty years should send Mark a dollar for his guardianship over the break. But it's not a concept you'll find Mark endorsing. He seems to feel he's already been well rewarded for his tenure.

'I felt very fortunate that I could be a lifeguard. There was a lot of pressure to be a bit more successful. I don't have a brand new SUV, I don't own the home that I live in, and I sort of knowingly made that sacrifice many years ago. This fits me to a tee. I could have been a bit more savvy with business and investments but I definitely made the decision that I'm not going to work the second or third job so I can have a big-screen TV, the white picket fence around the house kind of deal. I don't know if that's a surfer's mentality or just mine, but I'm happy with the path that I chose. I knew what I wanted to do and I did it. I'm so stoked that I did it while I was young. We need to give ourselves a pat on the back for pursuing what felt legitimate to us. Most people in the world struggle and life's hard. Rarely is it as beautiful as the surfing lifestyle.'

Out of the kaleidoscope of outrageous surf sessions, spinning tubes, contest winners and wipeouts, rescues and tragedies, are there any peak moments of his thirty-year relationship with Pipeline that stand out?

Mark pauses, and you wonder what incredible visions must be flashing through his mind. 'My session this morning, because it's most fresh in my mind,' he eventually answers. 'There it is, the accumulation of everything I've learnt, one- to two-foot Ehukai Beach sandbar, and I went out with my buddy Mike Stewart who has a beachfront house right there. This little shifting sandbar was right in his backyard, and we just went for an hour swim. In this day and age, North Shore 2007, we had this little peak to ourselves for an hour or so. It was so fun, and then he disappeared for a while and comes back out with his five-and-a-half-year old son on his back. He didn't have his boogie board — he was bodysurfing, with his kid hanging on with the biggest shit-eating grin on his face. It was wonderful to see a great ocean athlete like that passing it on to his children.'

Does he recognise any common traits in his long-time surfing friends, characteristics etched by a lifetime in and around the ocean?

'I hope it's gratitude. I'm coming to that point in my life, in the last five years or so, that things in my personal life have made me realise how fortunate I am. And I think there's sort of a humility too. A lot of times we could meet our maker out there and a few of our contemporaries have. There's a sense of appreciation that we get to do what we do. We're healthy and we're fit. That's one thing surfing sure gives us, a real all-round level of fitness head to toe.'

But it's the gratitude that seems to have etched itself most deeply into Mark's weathered features. 'That's what I'd like to emphasise, how filled with gratitude I am for every person who's stopped and talked story at the lifeguard tower or shared a smile or a laugh, or that I screamed at the top of my lungs at as they came flying out of a barrel.'

'The timing that is necessary to turn up at the right place on the right day at the right time to experience that really great ride, that timing goes with them, helps them ride the waves wherever they are, the energy waves, to be in synchronicity with them.'

JOHN PECK, PIPELINE PIONEER,
FROM THE FILM *RIDING WAVES*

SURF LESSON #67
Actions have consequences

I have a screwdriver at my throat and a large, angry Hawaiian man performing his own North Pacific version of the Haka inches from my face, issuing graphic descriptions of my imminent, bloody demise.

Welcome to the exciting world of surf journalism.

Up until that moment, the surf magazine game had been a merry lark, a spectacular magic-carpet ride through the rarified world of my boyhood heroes and dream-like surf spots. Sure, we'd occasionally offended people with an irreverent and ribald editorial tone, but the worst threat I'd faced was a surf label pulling their ads or a piqued pro surfer refusing to grant an interview. This was all part of the game. But it still felt like just that — a game. As a kid from Melbourne's eastern suburbs it was hard to fathom that anything I could do or say or write might have any real, tangible repercussions out there in the heady world of pro surfing. I felt like a spectator to it all, a kid watching TV or playing a video game. My Hawaiian high noon shook me abruptly out of that illusion.

Only the day before, I'd been cheering Johnny Boy Gomes on in the final of the Pipeline Masters, the world's most prestigious surfing contest. I sensed some kind of spontaneous, public healing for the enraged Hawaiian surfing warrior as he blazed to glorious victory in the Banzai Pipeline's death-defying tubes and the crowd roared its support. 'We love you, Johnny,' one American woman bawled, as he was chaired triumphantly up the beach.

It seemed a unanimous sentiment. Everyone knew Johnny's gritty story of growing up tough on the rugged westside of Oahu, losing his mother to cancer when he was just thirteen, never really knowing his dad, drifting from neighbour to distant relative, scrounging for stray surfboards in the Makaha shorebreak because he couldn't afford his own. Little wonder then, in later life, that he'd snap and snarl at the oppressive crowds that clogged his home waters every Hawaiian winter. That he'd become one of the great surfing talents of his time was a heart-warming achievement. I felt truly happy for him, awed once more by surfing's redeeming powers, certain this glory and validation would soothe his infamous rage and bury our trifling old rift.

In recent years, Johnny had earned a fearsome reputation as a ruthless power surfer and a blood-curdling hothead with a hair-trigger temper. He once hit a female pro surfer, Western Australia's Jodie Cooper, for daring to object to his hassling in the surf. He could cast a hush upon a surf break simply by paddling out. Non-Hawaiians crossed his line of sight at their peril.

I'd made the mistake several years earlier of documenting Johnny's chequered career in a too-candid profile for *Surfing Life* magazine, titled 'Hero or Villain?'. The provocative cover line, an act of lunacy in hindsight, blared, 'Should we try to like Johnny Boy Gomes?'.

Johnny had been on a promotional tour of Australia for his sponsor, dedicated to turning around his image as a violent vigilante. 'Do me some justice,' he had urged in our interview, with just enough menace to make me wonder what kind of rough justice might befall me if I failed to deliver.

Sure enough, Johnny Boy was unhappy with the result — not so much the stories of his heavy-handed approach to crowd control in the surf, as the fact that I'd quoted his typical Hawaiian accent phonetically. 'I t'ink dis,' or 'I t'ink dat'. His buddies told him I was taking the piss, making him look stupid. I couldn't be allowed to get away with it. He rang up and left an angry message on the *Surfing Life* answering machine. In a moment of madness, I rubbed salt in the wound by giving him Quote of the Month in our next issue. 'I couldn't give a fuck if you guys like me or not. Fuck you and fuck your magazine.' By the time the Hawaiian surf season rolled around again — when people would ask incredulously if I really intended to return to the islands — I was beginning to sense I'd made a serious error of judgement, that this was no longer a game.

That season in Hawaii, I approached Johnny at the first opportunity, heart in my throat, to attempt to make peace. My assistant editor Derek Rielly and I had sat watching in the bleachers as Johnny surfed to a commanding victory in the early rounds of the Sunset World Cup. He appeared happy and relaxed as he towelled off at the back of his big black pick-up truck. Rielly, as usual, egged me on: 'Go on, go talk to him.' Rielly later recounted that he watched a shadow pass over Johnny's features as I introduced myself, and he thought with dread, 'I've sent Baker to his doom.'

I'm not so sure. It may well have been, 'Wow, I'm going to become editor a lot sooner than I thought.'

Johnny is not a tall guy, but he stands as wide as he is high, with dark eyes that can narrow and pierce like lasers when his ominous brow gathers in a frown — such as I was greeted with.

'Look, I understand that you were upset about the magazine piece, and I was hoping we could talk about it,' I started out, nervously. Is this how Captain Cook felt, moments before he met his demise at the hands of the Hawaiians, angered that he was not their great returned god, Lono?

Johnny gave me that look, seeming to grow and tower over me. 'So, start talking,' he snapped. And talk I did, at a pace and urgency I doubt I've ever mustered before or since. He'd told me his job was to put food on the table for his family, and our magazine had helped him do just that. We were the only surfing magazine to give him major coverage, we'd even put him on the cover (albeit in the form of a menacing headshot with clenched-fist salute and a cheeky 'GRRRRRRRRRR' coming from his lips). His sponsors would have loved the ten pages of surfing action photos that accompanied the story, I pointed out, for which he'd no doubt received a generous photo incentive. (Many pro surfers are paid bonuses based on the amount of media coverage they generate.)

Today was not my day to die. We were in full public view after all, and he had just won his heat. I was spared. 'Just focus on the positive, not the negative,' Johnny advised me seriously. And with that, he jumped in his pick-up, revved its throaty engine, reversed out of his parking spot into the busy Kam Highway, and was gone with a screech of tyres. I was so relieved I felt giddy. We'd gotten away with our puerile cheek yet again. My guardian angels had prevailed. We were untouchable.

Later that same Hawaiian season I had cause to ring Johnny Boy for another article I was working on, but got his answering machine. I left a message with the number I was staying at. By the time he rang back, on a lazy surfless afternoon, I had succumbed to the quaint local custom of smoking one's own body weight in potent, pungent, island herb. I would have had trouble recognising my own mother's voice. I barely managed to locate and answer the phone. 'This is JB,' he barked down the phone, in his thick accent. I had a good friend in Hawaii at the time with the initials JB, a mainland American, and I could just compute that this was not he.

'That's not JB,' I scoffed.

There was a stunned silence. 'I said, this is JB,' he repeated, with mounting annoyance.

'You're not JB,' I insisted, dissolving into fits of idiotic laughter.

This clearly displeased the caller. 'What's wrong wit' you. This is Johnny Boy.'

I immediately snapped to my senses, the thick fog in my brain instantly, miraculously clearing. 'Oh, JB,' I crooned like an old friend. He was on to me in a flash.

'You been smoking that pokalolo [the local term for pot], getting all stupid,' he chided. He made it clear that I'd been very fortunate indeed to catch him in a good mood at our last meeting and it was not a reception I could count on in the future. I did my best to salvage the situation, but my powers of communication were faltering and Johnny only grew more irritated with my slurred mumblings. My hopes of a peaceful ceasefire seemed dashed.

I didn't run into Johnny for a few years after that, heard word of him now again, whispers that he was still pissed off. My brother, a cameraman, was hired to shoot a specialty surfing event in northern Western Australia that Johnny was invited to and the blood tie was enough to make his position uncomfortable. 'So, this Peter Baker, he's Tim Baker's brother. Maybe I should punch him, maybe that's the closest I'm going to get,' he theorised to a mutual acquaintance. Johnny was never quite as threatening outside of Hawaii, but to my brother's credit he fronted Johnny and defended my reputation, all without bloodshed.

Still, trips to Hawaii were always that little bit more tense for me after that. Sooner or later, I knew, our paths would cross — under what circumstances and in what kind of mood I'd find him I couldn't know.

It was December 1997, over four years since the original article appeared. Johnny Boy was the newly crowned Pipeline Master, and had celebrated long and loud with numerous cases of Budweiser beer in the beach car park with his westside posse. I was so moved by the day's sensational tube riding and sporting fairytale I'd contemplated wandering down to join in the festivities and make my final peace with the big, lovable bear of a man. With Johnny full of beer, and surrounded by his crew, it was probably just as well I didn't.

The next day I was in the backyard of a house at Rocky Point rented by Australian surfer Mark Occhilupo, just down the beach from the scene of Johnny's victory. The swell had dropped overnight and I was towelling off after a playful surf in modest waves. Occy's place, with its sweeping views of the surf, was the favoured hang for a number of well-known pro surfers and I'd been invited to stash my gear there when I wanted to surf out the front. It was a typical, low-key Hawaiian afternoon, with fun waves and good vibes. As I was changing, the back gate swung open and in walked the new Pipe champ and a young buddy, like a pair of gunslingers at a Western saloon. Johnny Boy was greeted warmly and keenly with many congratulations and the local variant of the handshake, gripping thumbs rather than fingers. I have to confess my heart skipped a beat, but I offered my hand in goodwill, so swept up was I in the mood of good cheer. Johnny fixed me with that gaze. 'Don't I know you?' he puzzled. I nodded, tried not to gulp, confirmed my identity. Johnny nodded knowingly.

'Oh yeah, you da' guy. You da' guy.'

In my peripheral vision, I noticed the backyard suddenly emptying as everyone found a sudden, urgent reason to be elsewhere. I'd endeared myself to few pro surfers over the years and this was rightly seen as my comeuppance. I kept my gaze on Johnny, trying to gauge his mood. He took a step closer. I instinctively raised my hands in front of me defensively. He took this as provocation, as if I was shaping up. 'You wanna have a go?' he snarled, swinging his arms loosely by his sides, Ali-style, as if we were boxers in a ring. I was honestly terrified. Then . . . he seemed to snap. From nowhere, he grabbed a screwdriver that someone had been using to fasten their surfboard fins, and held it to my throat. His eyes and veins bulged as he let loose a graphic description of the dismemberment that was about to befall me, his features resembling a fearsome Polynesian tiki.

Somehow, I held his gaze and my ground, trying my best to issue gentle, soothing phrases, like a hostage negotiator, but it felt like my tongue flapped uselessly in my mouth. I now know what it feels like to face the All Blacks on the football field. Johnny seemed to go into some kind of primal warring state that generations of Polynesians have used, most effectively I imagine, to intimidate their foes. I managed a few stuttered, plaintive pleas in my defence — it was a long time ago, I was sorry that I'd offended him, surely we'd all moved on — but they sounded pathetic even to me. Yet Johnny seemed to relax briefly, as if his anger was spent. I involuntarily breathed a sigh of relief, which only seemed to set him off anew. We stood nose to nose, as he switched back and forth from warring Johnny to appeased Johnny, as I flinched and tensed for the onslaught, gulping as the point of metal prodded my throat.

Maybe I failed some test of manhood there and then. Maybe I should have just copped my thrashing and been done with it, or defended myself physically rather than verbally. It's the way things are done in Hawaii. The temperament of the locals can be as volcanic as the Islands' origins, and once unleashed, usually quickly dissipates. Combatants often end up the best of friends. But I was genuinely afraid for my life.

Eventually — I still don't know if it was three minutes or thirty — Johnny seemed to tire of the stand-off and wandered inside. Occy approached me cautiously, as if my wretched condition might be contagious. 'I can't believe he didn't punch you,' he marvelled, with something like disappointment.

I'd learnt a valuable lesson. Every day countless journalists write the most utter bile, lies and slander about celebrities and sports people. Rarely are they held to account. I am grateful to Johnny Boy: what I write has repercussions in the real world and I'd better be prepared to stand up and face them. The game was over.

There is Hawaii's history of invasion and exploitation by one wave of migrants after another to consider too — from the early European explorers to the Christian missionaries, the sugar barons to the US military. Locals have been dispossessed of their land and culture, made to feel like second-class citizens in their own home. All this fed into the depth of feeling Johnny Boy gave vent to that day.

I felt like a muscled arm had reached out of the TV screen or video game and grabbed me by the scruff of the neck. I was no longer a spectator at some amusing sideshow theatre. This was real. One day I was marvelling at his skill in the world's most dangerous waves. The next I thought I might die at his hand. My words became more considered from that moment on.

mark richards

{ the turning point }

It's a strange thing to say but I actually feel more at home in the water than I do on land. I wander around on land sometimes feeling awkward and dorky, and then when I get in the water it all comes together. Even just the feeling of the water on you, diving and paddling, duck diving your first wave, seeing a set come, turning around and stroking into it, that initial rush as you drop down the face, the jolts of acceleration as you go through the manoeuvres. There's nothing like it. The only thing that actually comes close to riding waves is sex.

Waimea Bay was closing out, and a seventeen-year-old Mark Richards had to make a decision.

'I knew it was a life-changing decision. I could either continue my surfing career or end it on that day,' MR says, in his quiet, no-nonsense way.

The occasion was the 1974 Smirnoff Pro and MR had begged and pleaded contest director Fred Hemmings for a place in the event as an alternate. He'd got in, just, but now confronted with the biggest waves he'd ever seen in his life, the cocky teenager wasn't so sure he wanted to be there.

Even the Hawaiian giants of big wave surfing — Barry Kanaiapuni, the Aikau brothers Clyde and Eddie, Reno Abellira — were questioning whether it was surfable. Hemmings, known for good reason as 'Dead Ahead Fred', called them a bunch of pussies and threatened to paddle out himself to show them how it was done. He had done some begging and pleading himself to get TV crews and mainstream media to even turn up, and wasn't about to let this death-or-glory moment go. And neither, ultimately, was MR, with his youthful visions of somehow making a living from this surfing lark.

'I thought I was probably going to drown out there because I'd never seen anything like it. But I wanted it so badly, I figured it was better to go out there and drown and be remembered for that than be remembered as the guy who walked away.'

We're sitting on the back verandah above the Richards Surfboards shop, in Hunter Street, Newcastle. This is a surfboard shop, full of actual surfboards made by Mark's hands, not some surf fashion emporium staffed by pierced and preened young posers who could barely find their way to the beach. Mark's family lived above the shop when he was a kid, and he runs it today with his mum, Val. A semi-derelict block of flats out the back houses his shaping bay. Old mate Mick Adams patrols the shop floor and does a few ding repairs out back. The gleaming MR twin fins are back in high demand, thanks to the whole retro surfboard fashion. MR's just relieved he can shape boards of realistic dimensions again that will actually float their riders, instead of the pro tour model slithers the punters all used to want. 'I went through the whole spectrum of board design — surf-o-planes and longboards, Brewer guns, eggy single fins, twin fins and the modern thruster. I've seen it all from day one, this kaleidoscope of board design.'

It's hard to comprehend that this unremarkable shop in West Newcastle, a five-minute bus ride from the beach, has been the centre of MR's world for the best part of five decades — despite his glorious feats on the world stage. The place breathes surfing history, but it is no temple to his past glories. MR's far too humble for that. Yet, with a bit of prodding, he can conjure a day in Hawaii from over thirty years ago as if it were yesterday.

Back then, Hawaii was all there was if you wanted to make a name for yourself in surfing. Aspiring surfers, rather quaintly, wrote earnest letters to contest organisers pleading their case for an invite. 'Fred Hemmings [1968 world champion, now Senator Hemmings] was the contest organiser and Fred had total power over who was invited to the Hawaiian events,' says MR. 'There were no numbers or ratings system. He had ultimate power. So I wrote Fred a letter basically telling him that I was shit hot: "You owe it to yourself and the people sitting on the beach to have me in your event."'

Two other young surfers, Shaun Tomson from South Africa, and Queensland's Wayne 'Rabbit' Bartholomew had written Fred similarly self-promoting letters. And so the three of them found themselves waiting around at Sunset Beach when the Smirnoff Pro got underway in solid ten-foot surf to see if they could jag a start.

'There was a guy called Tiger Makin from California who hadn't turned up. Shaun, Bugs and I knew Tiger wasn't there but Fred wouldn't tell us who the alternate was. About ten minutes before the heat started, Fred announced, "Mark Richards, you're the first alternate."' Only problem was, MR didn't have the fifty-buck entry fee on him. 'I went, "Fred, I haven't got any money. Can I pay later?" And he said, "No, if you can't pay we go to the next alternate." And Rabbit just went, "I'll pay." It was a pretty amazing thing for Bugs to do. He could have got in.'

MR won both his heats that day in a spectacular debut at Sunset. 'I'd never surfed Sunset but I was just amped, busting to do well. And the next day was the big day at Waimea.'

Thus, MR found himself standing in the Waimea Bay Beach park at dawn, contemplating his own mortality. 'I was seventeen years old. If I chose not to go out that day at Waimea, I would have let myself down. It would have been a decision I would have regretted for the rest of my life. And Shaun and Rab would have been seriously pissed at me for not having a dig, and blowing the opportunity.'

That didn't stop the raw teenager feeling terrified as he prepared for his heat. But as he approached the water's edge, a curious thing happened: 'The fear disappeared the moment I got the coloured singlet on and actually paddled into the line-up. The intense competitor inside me overtook all the fear. It was weird. I was shitting myself walking down to the water's edge. The moment I hit the water it was like, how the fuck do I beat these guys? I've got to beat 'em. I call it coloured-singlet mentality. And once I got out of the water, I was scared shitless again.'

So much so, that for the only time in his career, MR found himself actually hoping he hadn't got through the heat. 'They used to do this countdown in those days. It was six-man heats and fifty per cent progression [the top three placegetters in each heat would advance to the next round]. And they used to go backwards: in sixth place, in fifth place, in fourth place unfortunately not making the cut . . . It's the only time in my competitive career where I've gone, "Sixth place, please." And they've read out sixth place and it wasn't me. "Fuck!" And then I've gone, "Fifth, please." And then they've read out fifth and it hasn't been me. "Fuck, one more chance." And then fourth, and it was like, "Yes!" I jumped like I'd won when I got fourth. Like, "Phew, don't have to go back out there." I didn't come last, I caught waves, I didn't let the other guys down, didn't let myself down. That was a life-changing moment. It just spurred me on, thinking I was semi-invincible. I didn't have to be scared of big surf any more. I'd been out in as radical conditions as I was ever likely to experience on the North Shore and survived.'

Within two winters, MR, Rabbit and Shaun would be regarded as the new performance benchmark in Hawaii, the focus of seminal surf movie *Free Ride*. Once pro surfing kicked off with a unified world tour, Shaun would collect the '77 world title, Rabbit the '78 title, and MR would march on to a staggering four consecutive world titles from '79 to '82.

How did MR do it? It's amazing how many top surfers are from broken homes or troubled family backgrounds, pouring all their adolescent grief and angst into the ocean, driven to prove something to nay-saying elders, carting an axe to grind with life. MR was the complete opposite.

'I was hooked because my parents were hooked. I got taken to the beach whether I liked it or not,' says MR. 'From the moment I got a surf-o-plane [an inflatable surf mat] when I was three or four years old I was possessed with being in the water and riding waves.'

In the Australia of the '60s, this set the Richards family apart. There were few surfers, even fewer second-generation surfers. 'When I was growing up the only two things that kids could do that were sporting orientated were pretty much football or cricket, so if you didn't have a passion for footy or cricket, surfing was an incredible outlet.'

Rarer still were parents who actively encouraged their offspring's surfing ambitions, rather than wringing their hands with grief at the almost certain path to delinquency and drug addiction. 'When I was twelve or thirteen I convinced my mum to pick me up from school in the afternoon and dump me at the beach, and either she or my dad would come and get me when I'd still be in the water at dark. A lot of times they used to pull up and flash their lights to get me out of the water. Whenever I'd speak about dreams or aspirations in surfing, they'd be saying, "Right on," instead of, "Get a trade or get a real job." I wasn't really subjected to any of those pressures.'

And the support didn't end with his parents. 'The one person who really helped was Robbie Wood, who was Nicky Wood's dad ['80s surf star and MR's godson], who was the best surfer in Newcastle in the '50s and '60s. I think when I was twelve or thirteen Robbie grabbed me and went, "Come on, we've got to take you out in some serious surf." He was one of those full-on gung-ho guys. If you could compare him to someone now he was like a Laird Hamilton tow-in guy who was scared of nothing. So Robbie started me surfing at Merewether and Leggy. He'd drag me out in conditions that I thought were too big for my ability or confidence level. But he was just kind of there, always positive: "You'll be right, nothing will go wrong, I'll be there to save you." Not that he probably would have been. He'd be off on a wave somewhere. But he helped drag me into bigger surf.'

Family holidays were invariably spent on Queensland's Gold Coast 500 miles to the north, surfing the warm-water, sand-bottom point waves to the verge of delirium. 'When we went to Queensland for family holidays, I was in the water from dawn to dusk. For me in those days, the Goldy was like going to the Mentawais [the remote Indonesian island chain] today. Coming from surfing Newcastle beachbreaks, which are predominantly close-outs . . . for me it was paradise. And there was no one around. You'd be surfing with MP [Michael Peterson] and PT [Peter Townsend] and Bugs and Peter Bryant and Deaney [Wayne Deane] and all the local guys up there and it was so relaxed and beautiful. The place was still a little more pristine. None of the highrise was there, it was more the fibro holiday flats. I've got photos of surfing Snapper and Rainbow when there were six or seven people in the water. The memory of it is of incredible times surfing really fun waves and this really relaxed atmosphere in the water. People would actually take it in turns on waves and get stoked when they saw someone else get a good ride, in stark contrast to what goes on on the Gold Coast these days.'

With his entire life so defined by waveriding, can he even imagine what his life might have been like without it? 'I can't even imagine it. I feel incredibly lucky that I've led the life I've led. I've been able, through surfing, to travel the world, and actually see it more than someone who sees it on a package tour. I feel like I've seen the country. I haven't been one of the people on the tour buses driving past wondering what it's like on the streets of those countries.'

What has he learnt from surfing and the ocean? 'I think there's a lot of lessons that have been learnt through surfing and through the ocean but trying to verbalise them is really hard,' he says, thoughtfully. 'I guess the one thing that surfing's taught me is how fortunate I am, because it's given me the opportunity to travel to different parts of the world, and meet people of different nationalities, experience different cultures, to see how people live in other parts of the world; it's made me feel very lucky to be who I am and live where I live. It frustrates me a lot of the time when I see the things that are done in this country by our so-called leaders. It's probably taught me a lot about relating to other people. One of the important things in life is to treat other people the way you would like to be treated yourself, to try and be as fair as you can in your business dealings and all the things you do in life. It's probably taught me stuff about strength. Some of the situations I've been in in big surf when I was younger taught me strength and endurance and believing in yourself, believing in your abilities, to have the confidence to follow through.' MR pauses, thinking, as if he's sure there must be more to his answer. 'There's probably a thousand lessons. I wouldn't be who I was without all those experiences, but trying to actually put them into words without sounding like some cosmic hippy is very hard,' he eventually offers, then adds quickly, 'not that there's anything wrong with being a cosmic hippy.' He laughs. 'But I don't really look like a cosmic hippy.'

Despite this disclaimer, MR remains as passionately effusive about the magic of waveriding as any grommet or long-haired beach hugger. 'It's a strange thing to say but I actually feel more at home in the water than I do on land,' he offers, finally. 'I wander around on land sometimes feeling awkward and dorky, and then when I get in the water it all comes together. Even just the feeling of the water on you, diving and paddling, duck diving your first wave, seeing a set come, turning around and stroking into it, that initial rush as you drop down the face, the jolts of acceleration as you go through the manoeuvres. There's nothing like it. The only thing that actually comes close to riding waves is sex.'

It's a little disturbing to learn that even a surfer of MR's stature feels the pressure and stress of increasing crowds in the water — that the masses, if not the waves themselves, don't simply part in his honour. 'The changes I've seen on the Goldy in my forty years of surfing, I've seen it go from ten people in the water, respecting each other, taking it in turns for waves, to more like 200 or 300 people snarling at each other. There's a really bad vibe in the water in those situations. People have got the war paint on and they're snarling. And guys want to fight. If someone takes off in front of you or gets in your way, people want to fight. It's not what the spirit or the feel of surfing is all about. I think deep down we'd all like to think that surfing still has a little bit of that cosmic feel to it. You can leave behind all your troubles, go in the water and feel it actually cleansing all the crap off, go out there and bliss out for an hour or so. But it's getting harder and harder to do that.'

Unlike a lot of experienced surfers, MR doesn't blame the problem on the legions of flailing beginners, over-eager surf-school graduates, invading the waves, but more accomplished surfers simply being too greedy. 'Every beach seems to have its group of resident loonies who'll be out there all day every day, and they're usually guys who can surf well, and can get as many waves as they want through superior positioning ability and knowledge of the break, and a lot of the time they're the worst people to deal with in the water because they get their waves and they also want your waves as well. They don't want to share. It gets back to that localism argument where guys who surf a beach for a certain amount of time claim ownership, and no one else can surf there. But at some point, it doesn't matter if you're the localest local at a break, at some point you will travel somewhere else. It can be very frustrating going surfing sometimes, and my defence mechanism these days is to look for shit surf rather than good surf. A lot of the time I just go the easy option and ride close-outs and have fun and be relaxed. When you paddle out when it's good and crowded invariably someone will paddle inside you and then if you drop in, it becomes an argument. I haven't had the discussion with one person on this planet yet who has grasped the concept that I've been waiting fifteen minutes for a wave and they paddled inside me and took off — it wasn't really their turn. They can't see it.'

At such times, MR still calls on an old gem of surfing wisdom passed on to him in Hawaii back in the '70s. 'It was during the Free Ride era.

There was this guy, I was surfing Off The Wall and I was whingeing to some local guy about how crowded it was. There must have been fifteen people in the water instead of ten. And he told me something that I've never forgotten. He said, "You shouldn't be complaining. Enjoy this winter, because even though it's more crowded than last winter, it's less crowded than it's going to be next winter. So, you're actually lucky. Enjoy it.'"

'You are something the whole universe is doing, in the same way that a wave is something the whole ocean is doing.'

ALAN WATTS, PHILOSOPHER

BAKER

Captain Paul Watson, co-founder of Greenpeace and founder of Seashepherd.

BAKER

One contented waterman, Mark Cunningham reflects on a lifetime of Hawaiian bodysurfing.

GRAMBEAU

The distinctive swooping style of four-time world champ Mark Richards, as he drops into Hawaii's Pipeline.

GRAMBEAU

Pauline Menzcer shortly after securing the world title at Sunset Beach Hawaii.

John DeMartini back in his hippy
surfer days.

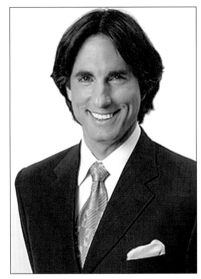

And today, Dr DeMartini the cleancut
public speaker.

DISABLED SURFERS ASSOCIATION

Eight-year-old Sarah Walsh at a Disabled Surfers Association hands-on day, not about to let the little matter of a prosthetic leg stand in the way of her surf stoke.

GRAMBEAU

Scouring the desert coast of southern Peru, surf nomad Rob Page finds a clean line through foreign waters.

The cover of Green's politician Ian Cohen's book, *Greenfire*, depicts him bow surfing a US warship in Sydney Harbour.

JOHN FULLER

Ian Cohen on the beach at Middle Head, New South Wales, site of his first action, already showing a fine sense for the dramatic moment.

Ian Cohen charges a cascading Uluwatu wall in Bali with the same commitment he's used to stage forest blockades.

KIM MAHARAJ

LEFT: Surfing scientist Vezen Wu contemplates the unspectacular waves of New York's Rockaway Beach.

BELOW: Pushing 60, Rusty Miller pulls into the slot on a big day at Lennox Head on the New South Wales north coast back in 1999.

SIMON WOOD

RIGHT: Mick Fanning in a
reflective mood.

BELOW: Blink and you miss it.
The world's fastest top turn, as
executed by world title contender
Mick Fanning on the New South
Wales south coast.

JON FRANK

JON FRANK

ABOVE: Brian Keaulana's hands with scoring manoeuvres listed for his father Buffalo's Big Board Surfing Classic

LEFT: Buffalo Keaulana and his wife Momi ham it up for the camera at the same event.

BELOW: Buffalo prepares for a late go out at his beloved Makaha Beach, as he has done for the best part of sixty years.

'The freedom experienced through surfing eventually teaches us the rules of mother nature, the social impact of co-existing, and hopefully it helps to bring about balance in our attitudes on how we treat each other.'

GEORGE DOWNING, HAWAIIAN SURF PIONEER

dr john demartini

{ the public speaker }

. . . I got to live with Owl Chapman. We'd watch him as he'd meditate on the beach and get in sync with the patterns of the waves. He'd close his eyes and listen to the rhythms of the waves and measure them with his heartbeat. He'd sit there for fifteen or thirty minutes, getting the sequence and the patterns and we learnt from that . . . becoming one with the waves.

Thirty-five years ago, John Demartini was just another penniless, homeless surfer scrounging a spartan existence on the North Shore of Oahu, chasing dreams of riding the huge Hawaiian surf.

Today, he is one of the world's most successful public speakers, on what he calls 'maximising human potential'. He speaks 300 days a year across fifty countries for fees of up to $20,000 a day, has written forty books, has reached over 600 million people in the last decade, and is aiming to reach three billion people in his lifetime.

Not bad for a guy who was told by his school teacher at age six that he had a learning difficulty and would never be able to read, write or communicate effectively.

Demartini grew up in Texas and was nine when he surfed for the first time. 'We'd ride these big clunkers at Freeport, Texas. I got up for the first time, and I got in a little curl and it just went and went . . . I was hooked. Done.'

He dropped out of school when he was fourteen and hitchhiked to California in search of more surf. Inevitably, he was drawn to Hawaii and its greater challenges. The lessons he learnt there, pushing himself beyond his fears in life-threatening waves, have informed his teachings ever since.

'There's a science to it, and there are full-on scientists among surfers. Look at Laird Hamilton and the amount of work that goes into riding those big waves,' he says.

'My first idea of going to Hawaii came from reading *Surfer* magazine. I'm sitting there, just about dropping out of school, and I see *Surfer* magazine. I'm stoned in my friend's red Volkswagen. We looked at the school and we looked at the magazine and we decided in that moment we had to get to Hawaii somehow.'

They eventually scrounged together the $86.90 for a 4 a.m. flight to Honolulu and hitchhiked out to the North Shore. 'We got stoned and got on the plane and didn't know anything . . . We got a ride with this cat who just dropped us off in the middle of the jungle. I guess he didn't want *haoles* [white people] going out surfing there.'

They eventually found their way to the North Shore and spent their first night sleeping under the Sunset Beach bridge. 'We got up the next morning and we looked out, and there was giant Sunset, 15- to 16-foot backs, 30-foot faces, two or three guys out taking off on these giant waves. My first day in Hawaii, and I went, "I'm not ready for this".'

They headed down to Ehukai Beach park, next to Pipeline, to watch the huge barrels roll in, buried their few belongings in the sand, and slept in the public toilets.

Realising they needed seriously bigger boards, they managed to get hold of a couple of Dick Brewer guns, and eventually bought an old North Shore surf van for $125. 'It used a quart of oil a day, and had a rusted roof and broken windows. We slept in that. Every day we surfed, whatever it was, and we had to work our way up.'

John applied himself to mastering the art of riding bigger and bigger waves, and one day something clicked. 'I surfed Laniakea one day. It just lined up, 20-foot faces, and I made it. I went, "Wow, I'm getting into this." After six months I'd started to surf 20-foot face waves. The second year we were tackling bigger waves, 12- to 15-foot Waimea, where I got caught in the bowl a couple of times. Haleiwa, Laniakea, Sunset, big days at Pipe. At first I was chicken of Pipe because I wasn't a goofyfoot. I'd surf it up to six to eight feet, but over ten feet I was wary. It took me the whole time I was there (two years) to surf 10- to 12-foot Pipe.'

There was no shortage of inspirational surfing mentors in Hawaii in the early '70s. 'I studied under Gerry Lopez. He had such a beautiful style, he was unbelievable,' says John. 'I saw Gerry on Big Monday caught inside, standing on the coral, six to eight inches deep because the wave was draining all the water off the reef. He was about to face this huge Pipeline wave, standing on the coral. I was sitting there going, man, this is life and death. And he dived into the oncoming wave. He did get crushed into the coral but he survived.'

Some of his greatest surfing lessons came from legendary '70s surfer Owl Chapman, who can still be found living and surfing at Sunset Beach today.

'I didn't realise it at the time, but it's all about balance and being present. You have to be in the wave and be one with the wave,' says John. 'I learnt a lot. I got to live with Owl Chapman and we watched him surf the most outrageous waves at Sunset . . . We'd watch him as he'd meditate on the beach and get in sync with the patterns of the waves. He'd close his eyes and listen to the rhythms of the waves and measure them with his heartbeat. He'd sit there for fifteen or thirty minutes, getting the sequence and the patterns and we learnt from that . . . becoming one with the waves and the sequences and the patterns of the waves.'

Gradually, John's living conditions improved. 'We moved from the car to a tent to a grass house we built in the jungle to an abandoned house at Puna Point. We stole some hose and some electrical wiring and put water and power into the house.'

He dived on flat days to study the reefs and learnt why waves broke a certain way, paddled to keep fit outside surf season, and practised holding his breath underwater to increase his lung capacity. 'I learnt, if you're going to do something in life, you had better study it and master it and go the extra mile,' he says. He also learnt, in traditional Hawaiian style, to pay his dues.

'I was afraid to get in the tube. You have to get launched to get in there. And there were no cords [legropes]. I had to be in good shape. I was surfing eleven hours a day, there's nothing greater. You've got to get beaten up and get your boards broken by the locals. Once they saw you could surf a decent-sized wave, you had earned the right to be there.'

He even made a brief appearance in the classic '70s surf movie *Five Summer Stories* and can be seen flicking his mane of long wavy dark hair — a far cry from the clean-cut public figure he presents today.

But Hawaii in the early '70s was also a drug connoisseur's smorgasbord and John's turning point came when he eventually overdid it in the consciousness expansion stakes.

'I was eating the woodrose plant [a powerful, LSD-style hallucinogen]. I had my woodrose, mushroom and marijuana garden. I got stoned and surfed. I didn't take good enough care of myself. I almost died of strychnine poisoning. I spent three-and-a-half days unconscious in my tent. My guys abandoned me in my tent. A lady found me and took me to the Vim and Vigor health food store, in Haleiwa. I was sitting there having a carrot juice, and this blond Afro guy said, "You're screwed up. You need to take a yoga class." I walked outside and saw a flyer for Paul Bragg speaking at the yoga centre.'

John decided the yoga centre was calling him. The talk by Paul Bragg, a pioneer of the health-food and well-being movement in the USA, changed his life. 'This ninety-year-old wise man, he's the guy that changed my life. He was lecturing on the body, mind and spirit. He helped me to identify my mission in life.'

John says he was visited that night by a series of visions from his past and awoke with a clear sense of purpose. 'I knew what I wanted to do — to travel the world and teach. That was thirty-three-and-a-half years ago, '72, and that's what I've done ever since, diligently focused on what I wanted to do.'

He studied to become a chiropractor, ran a successful practice, grew it into a chain of five practices, and eventually began lecturing to other chiropractors — about health and well-being but also on how to make their practices more financially successful. Soon his lectures were attracting more than just chiropractors. In 1984, he embarked on a full-time speaking and writing career, and has been addressing steadily larger crowds ever since.

What has surfing taught him?

'What surfing taught me is you have to be present, absolutely present. It taught me about perfect balance, staying focused and not letting anyone interfere with you. Embrace whatever happens. If you're riding Waimea Bay and two people drop in on you, you're in trouble. But if you go into that, magical things happen. I came really close to drowning on many occasions, but I learnt to hold my breath for two to three minutes.'

They are lessons that have served him well in his current career.

'I speak 300 days a year. I'm surfing cosmic waves. I did thirty radio shows in the last week. I teach universal laws, I write books, I travel the world, working with people from all walks of life. I'm shooting for three billion people, to touch their lives. I've reached 610 million in the last decade.'

He owns numerous properties all over the world, and bases himself on an ocean liner called the *World*, the only cruise ship continually circumnavigating the globe. I met Dr Demartini through a mutual friend on one of his visits to the Gold Coast. He was keen to go for a surf and my friend invited me along. There wasn't much swell, and the wind was onshore, but we found a little beachbreak to ourselves on the northern end of the coast. I resorted to a longboard to try and generate some glide out of the tiny wind chop. Despite being around fifteen years my senior, John rode a shortboard with speed and grace, finding tiny runners all the way to the sand in the marginal conditions, dancing over the ragged peaks.

It was obvious he still had his line. Did he get the chance to surf much these days, I asked? 'Not nearly as much as I used to. I still love it,' he beamed. 'The universe is my playground. I hope I can continue that as long as I have a physical body. I would love to surf when I'm 100.'

Dr Demartini says he has studied all the world's great philosophies and religions, and synthesised the essential, common elements from all of them. 'I believe it's a magnificent universe and there's an intelligence,' he says. He teaches that we are all masters of our destiny, and that your thoughts ultimately create your life. When we learn to control our thoughts, he says, we are truly masters of our lives. Surfing has helped in this too. 'Nature is a great meditation. In order to master surfing you have to be at one with nature. When you respect nature, you learn humility to nature.'

He sometimes runs into old surfing buddies at his seminars and has one very simple message for them. 'A surfer can make anything he wants out of life,' he says. 'To ride Haleiwa on a big day, you have to hold your vision and not give up. You have to deal with the rip and paddle for hours sometimes and not give up. Surfing taught me a willingness to hold your vision, and not let anything on the planet stop you.'

Even though he doesn't spend as much time in the water these days, he says it's still all about waves. 'I'm still studying waves, but now through quantum physics. I'm riding the cosmic waves, and I'm lecturing about quantum waves.'

'I went to this ashram and there was a sign that said, "Leave your mind and your shoes outside." And I thought, what they do when they go into these rooms and listen to these teachers is the same thing that you get when you go surfing. You're kind of privileged when you ride waves because you don't have to acquire all that knowledge. It gives it to you, when you ride a wave. It just gives it to you. I think that's the magnetic attraction of surfing.'

ALBE FALZON,
FILM-MAKER, FROM THE FILM *LIFE LIKE LIQUID*

SURF LESSON #158
Why tube riding is good for you

At the risk of sounding like a grand, over-intellectualising nob, I would like to present a philosophical explanation of why tube riding is such a euphoric experience.

Imagine for a moment planet Earth without humans. The winds, the tides, the swells, the shifting sands, the movement of the planets, the seasons and the cycles of nature would all play out their rhythmic patterns even if we weren't here to notice them. These natural elements are what we might consider the pulse of the planet — a gentle symphony of forces maintaining the delicate equilibrium of the earth. Even when primitive humans were first around, they would have had no choice but to follow these natural cycles to ensure their survival — to find food, water and shelter, they would have had to study and follow the signs of nature.

Since industrialisation, another whole artificial timetable has governed human activity on the planet: working hours, days of the week, traffic lights, our Western calendar. All these things pay scant regard to the natural rhythms of the planet and so we have fallen profoundly out of sync with the Earth. If you need convincing, consider the fact that we add one day to the length of the year every four years, and we add a second to the world clock in Greenwich every ten years or so, to keep our time-keeping in line with the rotation of the planet. Basically, our means of measuring time is fundamentally flawed and has to be tampered with to stop it from falling out of step with nature's clock.

And so humans go about their day-to-day business, almost mindless of the underlying rhythm of the planet. We have all experienced the blissful release of getting back to nature and feeling like we have fallen back into rhythm with the planet, on camping holidays or during times of quiet meditation in natural settings. As surfers, we are uniquely blessed because we have a reason to pay attention to these natural rhythms. The tides rise and fall, weather systems circle the planet, swells come and go, sandbanks shift and every now and again, in a magical convergence of these natural elements, a perfect tube is formed. The chances of placing yourself at the exact place and time to ride this tube are remote, to say the least, and the tube is going to peel and spit regardless of whether there is someone there to ride it or not.

So, when a surfer successfully tunes in to all these natural cycles and places himself or herself in the right place at the right time to pull into a tube, ride through that watery tunnel, and come out the end, they have succeeded in falling back into sync with the planet. Suddenly, they are tuned in to the timeless cycles of nature, and the more often they do this, the more deeply they feel the earth's underlying rhythm. That's why great tube riders are generally such cool, mellow people.

Furthermore, many psychologists believe our first and greatest emotional trauma in life is separation from the mother. The newborn baby spat out into the world has to come to terms with the fact that it is no longer in the warm embrace of the womb, fed and protected by the mother, and must learn to fend for itself with increasing independence in the big, wide world. Most of us spend our lives searching for something close to that feeling of safety and security. The mother ocean accepts us surfers unconditionally over and over again — for many of us it is one of our most reliable and accepting sources of spiritual sustenance. And the tube ride, as many have noted before, is a powerful metaphor for a return to the womb and a sense of rebirth.

From a personal development perspective, tube riding also obeys the principle of the greatest reward stemming from placing ourselves in the position of greatest vulnerability. When we pull into the tube we are making ourselves most vulnerable to the power of the wave — it is much safer to stay out on the shoulder, but where is the thrill in that? Yet when we crouch under the peeling curtain of the wave and say, 'Ocean, take us or spare us as you choose,' it is then that we are open to the greatest rewards waveriding has to offer. In tube-riding, as in life, we access the deepest sense of peace and well-being and growth when we trust in the natural flow of events and place ourselves in the position to pass through windows of opportunity, not attempting to dominate or control events, but reading them and working with them.

All this potential magic, however, is abruptly shattered when we are reduced to fighting and squabbling for a hit of the tube-riding elixir. We cannot seek to hoard, guard or gobble this fountain of life force, but must humbly accept what the universe is kind enough to offer us. If this all sounds like a sermonising wank, rest assured I write this as much to remind myself as anyone else: remind myself to stay mellow in the water, expect nothing when I paddle out, let waves come to me rather than chasing them, remain unfazed by the hassling of the crowds, and take my signals from the ocean's rhythms rather than the human chaos unfolding around me. Finding your own peace and stillness in the midst of mayhem is a great lesson for life, and a crowded surf break provides the perfect classroom.

We surfers all speak of Huey, the surf God, who blesses us with his waves. Now, imagine us as worshippers arriving at Huey's temple to receive his blessing. Is he likely to be impressed by us pushing and hassling and fighting to get to the front of the queue? Or would he prefer to see us waiting patiently, happily, gratefully for his blessing while we appreciate the natural splendour of his temple, the surf break? I know when I feed seagulls chips at the beach, I never want to give a chip to the loud, squawking, bullying seagull who puffs up its chest and tries to imtimidate and scare away all the others. I always try to throw chips to the cool, mellow seagulls hanging quietly off to the side somewhere. And I like to imagine that Huey sees things the same way.

So, next time you paddle out into crowded, perfect barrels, try a little attitude adjustment. Instead of aspiring to snatch as many waves as possible, make an elevated state of mind your goal, the foundation upon which you create a positive vibe to help you through life back on land. Stay serene, focused, calm, and wait for that one wave that is just delivered to you, by whatever higher force you care to believe in. One good tube ride, most of us know, is enough to put a smile on your face for the rest of the day. Ten tube rides stolen from others, wrestled and snatched and snaked from the pack, are hardly going to make you feel better about yourself or the world.

Be a cool, humble worshipper at Huey's temple and gratefully receive your blessing.

'The ocean has always been a salve to my soul . . . the best thing for a cut or abrasion was to go swimming in salt water. Later down the road of life, I made the discovery that salt water was also good for the mental abrasions one inevitably acquires on land.'

JIMMY BUFFETT, MUSICIAN

pauline menczer

{ the battler }

*They say I shouldn't surf, and I tell them,
if I can't surf I may as well not eat. If I'm
having trouble at least I'll go out there and
just go straight, just to feel the water on your
skin and the smell of the ocean.*

Pauline Menczer recalls being barely able to walk to the water's edge, crippled with arthritis and racked with pain, and yet surfing a heat as if her life depended on it. And it very nearly did.

With no sponsors, Pauline battled away at the women's pro surfing tour funded almost solely by prize money, throughout an illustrious career that culminated in a world title in 1993, and included eleven straight years in the top eight in the world. Hers is an achievement of Occy-like magnitude — having jousted with all the giants of women's surfing, from Pam Burridge and Jodie Cooper, to Lisa Andersen and Layne Beachley, over nearly two decades. At thirty-six, Pauline still mixes it with the best in her occasional competitive forays.

Growing up as a freckly tomboy at Bondi Beach, pro surfing was a far-fetched dream. 'I remember looking and going, "I want to be just like Pam and Jodie and be famous and rich",' she laughs. The reality of the women's pro surfing tour was rather different. 'It's always been a struggle for me,' she says. Because she didn't fit the marketable image of the blonde, tanned beach girl, no amount of contest success could earn Pauline decent sponsorship. And her arthritis meant that sometimes just getting in the water was a battle.

'I suffered silently for a long time. I'd get up really early, do whatever I could to be able to surf,' she says. Massage, a strict diet and medication helped her manage the condition. But there was no escaping the financial hardships. 'We'd jam six girls in a hire car, this little Renault. We used to travel around on trains. We really did do it tough.'

A steely determination to triumph against the odds fuelled her competitive efforts. 'Adrenaline was the only thing keeping me going. I could barely walk down the beach and would still surf my heat as if nothing was wrong,' she says. 'Winning the world title for me was a relief. Some people win it for others, but it was so personal for me. I was very humbled after. I think that's why I never won another world title. I get content quite easy from little pleasures.'

Her world title was sewn up at Sunset Beach in Hawaii, in 1993. She remembers someone placing a floral lei around her neck, and the smell of frangipani flowers can still evoke the memory of that day. 'That smell, every time I walk past frangipanis, makes me think of the world title. It was like yesterday. There are happy and sad moments, because I know what I went through to win it. I have a bit of a sook sometimes, but it's a happy cry.'

One of the most enduring images of Pauline came during the 1995 Margaret River Masters, when she hurled herself over the ledge of a huge, 15-foot wave, and was sucked brutally over the falls. The footage made TV news bulletins across the country, as we winced and grimaced in our lounge rooms. It was difficult to believe the diminutive Menczer could survive such a wipeout, let alone paddle back out for more. 'I fell head-first and I remember getting held under for so long . . . That was pretty insane. I remember wanting to show off and I didn't care about the size.'

Another personal highlight was getting the opportunity to travel to Fiji for a women-only, stand-alone event. 'That was always my dream, to go somewhere like an island, and have the best women surfers on the island together,' she recalls. 'I lost in the contest, and just went surfing. I surfed four different spots, all perfect, the best surfing day of my life.'

France was always another favourite stop on the tour. 'They really make you feel that whole hype of being a pro surfer more than anywhere because they respect women as much as men.'

But within pro surfing ranks, Pauline has had to battle rampant sexism, and a media and industry that still prefer to judge women on their appearance more than their deeds.

'I can understand that the surfing world has their images, and you can't sponsor everybody,' she reasons. Even as a world champion, the most she was ever offered by a sponsor in a year was $30,000, [barely enough to cover travel costs] and even then she never received the full amount. She estimates she's still owed around $30,000 from former sponsors but doesn't have the appetite for a legal battle. 'I'm not a fighter . . . I think it's bad energy,' she says.

As women's surfing has grown, as participation numbers have sky-rocketed, as female surf-school students have begun to outnumber the blokes, and the women's surfwear labels started by the big surf brands have begun to overtake the men's labels in sales, one might have expected a serious cash injection into women's surfing. Yet, for many female pro surfers, just getting to events is a financial stretch. At the time of writing, the number-one rated female surfer in the world, Melanie Redman-Carr, and seven-time world champion Layne Beachley, were still without major surf industry sponsors. 'They always said they'd support the women's when it grew. Now the women's has grown they've given the money to the men,' Pauline says. 'It's gotten huge. I look at what the tour's doing for women's surfing — it's pretty pathetic.'

Still, she's happy for the handful of young female surfers now earning a decent living. 'I love seeing the new generations coming through. I'm proud that now they're getting money. I have no jealousy at all. It's about time someone's getting looked after,' she says. 'I tell them, take care of your money. I'm like a mother hen. Be careful because it can go quickly.'

With increased prize money and better contest venues, Pauline still wrestles with the idea of a competitive comeback. 'I've been invited to go in a couple of events. I want to do it but there's a whole side of the tour I don't like any more. I was thinking about applying for a wildcard as a previous world champ, but I'd rather work as a checkout chick than go crawling.'

As well, her arthritis remains an issue. 'Yesterday I could hardly walk. Today I'm fine. It's not bad all the time,' she says. As if that wasn't enough, she recently developed carpal tunnel syndrome, a painful progressive condition caused by compression of a key nerve in the wrist. 'You've got to manage to hold your head up high. There's nothing worse than if you lose your sense of humour. I always tell myself there are people worse off.'

These days, Pauline lives at Ocean Shores, on the New South Wales north coast, surfs as much as possible and competes occasionally. She plans on getting into coaching, helping the next generation of elite female surfers achieve their dreams. She's got a rich well of experience to draw on.

'I've definitely learnt there's always a positive out of a negative. Everyone goes, "It must be hard not being supported," but I go, "Maybe that's why I was one of the winningest surfers." Surfing's made me look at it that way. It's always made me appreciate what I do and what I have. There's nothing better.'

Doctors tell Pauline that she shouldn't continue surfing, but giving up is simply not an option. 'I need to have a hip replaced, my C1 and C2 are nearly touching, I could be crippled quite easily. They say I shouldn't surf, and I tell them if I can't surf I may as well not eat. If I'm having trouble at least I'll go out there and just go straight, just to feel the water on your skin and the smell of the ocean. If I surf really good I just suffer so I try and cruise.'

Not that Pauline's complaining. 'I'm just so grateful to be living that lifestyle. The thing I love the most is just as a person, what I've become, and how I've grown, through other people I've met along the way. It's been an unbelievable experience.'

'I keep surfing because surfing keeps me.'

DORIAN 'DOC' PASKOWITZ

rusty miller

{ the coach }

After you go for a surf and you come into town, you tend to be a nicer person. You don't kick your dog and you are nice to your wife and kids and stuff like that. I say that kiddingly, but when the surf is good in Byron Bay and a lot of people get a lot of surf, the vibe in the town is actually elevated by the spirit of what you bring in from the water. For most people it seems a little philosophical and spiritual but actually that is what it is about.

It's the late '60s in California and philosopher Alan Watts, leading light of the emerging counter-culture movement, keenly studying Zen Buddhism and experimenting with psychedelic drugs, decides he wants to know more about surfing.

So US surfing champions Rusty Miller, Joey Cabell and Mike Doyle are summoned by Watts to speak and present a slideshow of their recent visit to Hawaii, surfing the big waves of the North Shore.

The young surfers arrive at one of Watts' regular gatherings of his colleagues — the likes of beat writer Allen Ginsberg and acid guru Timothy Leary — unsure why the counter-culture set are suddenly so interested in surfing.

'We came and gave a talk on surfing. We'd just got back from Hawaii,' says Rusty. 'All these academic guru guys, after the presentation they just went off. The question time was like . . . they just went off. This Chinese guy said, "That's how energy moves through the body, like a wave like you guys are riding".'

The encounter left a deep impression on Miller. 'Alan Watts, he was like the guru of the gurus. He was going off on it. That was like the greatest accolade for our lifestyle. I always remember that.'

What had got the counter-culture gurus so excited about surfing was its physical manifestation of the 'be here now' philosophy they were attempting to embrace. These unassuming surfers, they decided, through their simple play in the ocean, were actually living it, pitting their lives on the need for complete presence in every moment in the potentially deadly waves of Hawaii.

Rusty Miller, now sixty-four, seems to have always hovered about this interface of surfing and spiritualism. As a child, Rusty played in the gardens of the great Indian yogi Paramahansa Yogananda, who had set up his Self-Realisation Fellowship centre on the southern Californian coast. The centre overlooked a popular surf break the Californian surfers dubbed Swamis, in honour of the mysterious, long-haired, robed figure who could be spotted wandering the clifftops or meditating with his followers.

'In a very subtle, beautiful way I was introduced to the self-realisation thing and meditation and yoga by observing it,' recalls Rusty. 'There was no preaching. No one came out and said, "Come to our church." I had a friend who was Japanese whose father was the gardener for Yogananda, for the Self-Realisation Fellowship, and I used to stay with them. So I used to play at Swamis. I'd go and stay the night, go down the cliffs and play in the tide pools. We used to sneak into the gardens where you weren't supposed to go and we'd see people meditating like yogis. I don't know if it was actually him [Yogananda]. They'd look up and we'd scamper off, but they never chased us. They were never heavy. I remember that kindness, that understanding, that "Oh, it's just kids". Years later when I got more serious about surfing Swamis we actually used their place, we walked through there. That's where he wrote a lot of his books, so I'm sure they were watching us surf. There wasn't any direct contact, but when I think back on it, that guy was there. I'm sure he was watching us surfing.'

Rusty grew up in Encinitas, entranced by the Californian lifeguard culture, which was itself influenced by traditional Polynesian culture, mimicking its music, dress, ocean skills and lifestyle.

'The lifeguards got me into surfboard riding. The people I admired were into the water,' says Rusty. 'After everyone left, the lifeguards would go for their surf or they'd go skin diving and then they'd come in and have a fire on the beach, a lot of cooking on the beach when it was legal to have fires, and then they'd often make their own music. I remember they used to play Polynesian music over the PA system. They'd all been to Hawaii, a lot of them had been to Tahiti. What I admired about those guys, they did everything themselves. They wove hats, they'd skin dive, they made their own music. And then when everybody went home at the end of summer the lifeguards were still there.'

It's a trait Rusty's maintained to this day. 'That must explain why you always want to be the last one on the beach every day,' Rusty's wife Trish notes.

'There's something about being on the beach when everyone leaves — the beach changes,' Rusty observes.

The lifeguards took the keen youngster under their wing and introduced him to the Californian coastline. 'Lifeguarding was a well-paid job, and after work or on holidays they'd travel up and down the coast. I did a lot of travelling with older guys when I was thirteen . . . up to Trestles or down to Windansea.'

He has magic memories of those surfing road trips — the young kid included in the adventures of his elders. 'What I seem able to remember — and once in a while I get a sense of déjà vu — is the actual atmosphere, the actual feeling. Sometimes I touch on it and I get it, and I think it's like animation, like an actual feeling in your life where everything's floating, without being stoned, you know what I mean? I remember the magic feeling of being with older guys and going surfing. There was an older guy named Tom Kent who would come to my house and knock on my door before the sun came up, like five o'clock in the morning . . . and I'd get up and get my surfboard and we'd put the boards in the car, and we'd get out on the road. And there were three or four guys in the car and me, I'd sit in the back. We'd go up to Trestles, like an hour drive. And getting out of the car at sunrise, and sneaking through the marshes at Trestles, because sometimes the marines didn't want you to be there.'

All that time in the water, and early trips to Hawaii, paid off with a string of impressive contest results and a solid reputation in the big waves of Sunset, Waimea and Pipeline. Rusty won the US Surfing Championship in 1965, and was a finalist in the prestigious Duke Kahanamoku Invitational in 1967 and '68.

He was one of the few top surfers of the day to combine competitive surfing with academia, and received a BA in History from San Diego State College. Matt Warshaw's *Encyclopedia of Surfing* notes, in a slightly mocking tone: 'He occasionally attended surfer parties dressed in a tweed jacket and loafers, took to smoking a pipe, and tried with little success to engage other surfers in conversations about art, politics and world affairs.'

Perhaps seeking broader minds, Rusty attended the University of the Seven Seas, sailing with 350 other students through Tahiti, New Zealand, Australia, Japan, the Middle East and the Mediterranean — literally expanding his horizons far beyond the surf-centric culture of California and Hawaii.

In Sydney he was greeted by a welcoming party from the Windansea Surf Club, which had branches in the USA and Australia. 'The first time I came to Sydney was on the ship. We came into Woolloomooloo and there were about twenty guys with a big sign, '"Welcome to Sydney, Rusty Miller, Windansea Surf Club".'

Local surfers like Rob Conneely, Chris Brock and surf movie maker Paul Witzig showed the visiting American champion around Sydney's surf beaches, surely one of the warmest welcomes afforded an American surfer before or since. The relaxed lifestyle, blossoming surf scene and untapped potential of the coast caught his imagination. After another couple of years living on Kauai, part of the hippy/surfer exodus to the outer Hawaiian Islands, Rusty returned to Australia — and this time never left. He worked for the new surfing magazine *Tracks*, selling advertising, and was recruited by one of its founders, Albe Falzon, to star in a surf movie he was making. Their trip to Bali coincided with a big swell and a startling surf discovery: the images of a thirty-year-old Rusty Miller and a fourteen-year-old Steve Cooney carving the huge empty waves of Uluwatu for the first time are among the most celebrated in surf-movie history. The film, *Morning of the Earth*, became the definitive statement on the emerging 'country soul' surf ethos, with its scenes of tree houses, chillums, and the top surfers of the day eagerly 'turning on, tuning in and dropping out'.

Rusty soon migrated north to the country soul epicentre of Byron Bay, and started the region's first alternative newspaper, the *Byron Express*, to coincide with the New Age Aquarius Festival in Nimbin. He has been conducting personal surf lessons in the idyllic north coast surf ever since.

Rusty is now sixty-four, married with two adult daughters. He and his wife Trish have planted every tree on their tropical rainforest hideaway in the Byron hinterland, once a cleared dairy farm. He still surfs every day and exhibits the fitness, physique and easy, relaxed gait of a man thirty years his junior. He rarely goes anywhere without his quiver of harmonicas, ukulele and small jembay drum — forever ready for a bit of spontaneous music making.

On the evening I find my way down the winding gravel driveway through the rainforest, the Miller household is also visited by two vanloads of travelling Italian and French surfers, whom Rusty and his daughter Taylor have befriended in the surf. It seems a common occurrence, and their family home is thrown open, a barbecue lit and a mountain of food hurriedly produced as if by magic. The European surfers exude a kind of childlike, wide-eyed wonder at the splendour of their extended trans-Australian road trip, and at the serendipity of suddenly being the guests of this bona fide surf legend. Rusty reckons he enjoys the company of these travelling surfers from the newer surfing nations precisely because they remind him of an earlier era, 'that excitement and magic of surfing'.

There is not a whole lot of surf in the Mediterranean Sea for these Italian surfers, but it doesn't seem to have affected their enthusiasm. 'I have the sickness worse than anyone in my village. There is snow on the ground and I still go to the beach, I have the sickness so bad,' one of them, Carlo, confides in me, eyes popping out from his sunburnt features as if they might burst.

'I have a dream,' Carlo continues, in hushed tones, 'to go surfing with my son one day.' He looks at me as if for a reaction. 'This is a very big dream for me.' He nods seriously, lips pursed. Carlo is thirty, single, with no children yet, from a culture that still sneers or scratches its head at the frivolous pastime of waveriding. And it occurs to me that what we take for granted now — this generational inheritance of the surfing lifestyle — stands as his most ambitious and far-fetched goal.

Carlo knows nothing of who I am, this book, or the reason for my visit, but he suddenly declares, without prompting: 'I was a wild boy. The ocean gave me humility. The ocean is bigger than me. It can kick my arse.'

I go to bed early, but the impromptu party rages on for hours. I awake in the guest room at dawn to the sound of the ukulele — the gentle strumming harmonising with birdsong and a quiet breeze rustling the forest canopy. It feels like I'm in Hawaii. I find Rusty on the front porch practising a tune, and we chat over coffee. I relate the conversation with Carlo and we marvel at how far surf culture has come in this country in thirty years. These days, Rusty takes troubled teens surfing to get them away from drugs, crime and a directionless life, once the very things surfing was alleged to encourage. 'That's the big thing that's changed now. Parents thank me for getting their kids into surfing,' he says.

In promotional material for his surf lessons, Rusty makes much of the fact that he teaches the traditional Hawaiian style of surfing, complete with philosophy, etiquette, ocean safety — many of the things missing from the masses of beginners swarming to the surf. Rusty doesn't take large groups or employ dozens of barely qualified surf coaches to cash in on the backpacker or corporate market. His approach is summed up in his simple motto: 'You get one surfing lesson, and a lifetime of homework.'

With Rusty as master, it's definitely a course worth taking.

'Let me assure you, my son is a surfer, and I believe I know at least some of their feelings . . . They have a very deep philosophical attitude towards life which comes from experiencing the exhilaration of surfing in powers they cannot control, but they bend and work with those powers to accomplish a feat no one else can do for them . . . You need never be concerned about your safety from these people.

Since your daughter gave you a surfboard it would surely be a wonderful thing if you could find the time to try it. It would be an experience for you that I am sure you would not forget.'

MRS GEORGE LINDSEY, MOTHER OF A LOCAL SURFER, TO PRESIDENT RICHARD NIXON IN 1969, IN PROTEST AT THE LOSS OF ACCESS TO THE CALIFORNIAN SURF BREAK, TRESTLES.

[Surfers were denied access to Trestles during Nixon's presidency for security reasons, because of its proximity to the presidential retreat at Cotton Point. Nixon was unmoved, and marines were deployed to arrest surfers attempting to sneak in to Trestles. It was eventually declared a State Park and access was reinstated in 1973. Trestles is now one of California's best and most popular surf spots and the site of a major international pro tour event.]

SURF LESSON #229
You reap what you sow

Confession time. I may have ruined an idyllic surf town for the entire global stand-up surfing community. It was 1994. I'd somehow wound up on a stretch of the North Chilean desert coast, known as South America's North Shore. Its half-a-dozen or so quality reefbreaks were all within easy walking distance of a charming, bustling harbour town, where comfortable accommodation and food were cheap, the locals friendly, the girls pretty in that dark smouldering Latino way, the waves incredible. So what if they spoke Spanish and the water was freezing and occasionally you found yourself eating things you couldn't identify? They had their own mini-Sunset, mini-Pipe, mini-Velzyland, and other wave varieties too unique to label — all heaving over shallow, sea-urchin-encrusted rock ledges. I scared myself shitless at Chile's Pipeline the afternoon we arrived. It was only six feet, but I could not for the life of me find a way into the abrupt, square, left barrel. No lesser surfers than Brenden 'Margo' Margieson, seven-time Peruvian champion Miguel 'Magoo' De La Rosa, and his young protégé Maki Block, were pitched and slammed time and again trying to take it on, eventually making a few screaming, stand-up barrels through sheer persistence. I paddled back to shore with my tail between my legs. Margo eventually had to swim in after a broken board, with a gaggle of excited school kids following his progress from the rocky shore. Surfing was new enough here for us to still be regarded as a novelty, and crowds were non-existent.

It went on for days, as a booming swell that had neatly coincided with our arrival lit up the town's reefs. Sunset was eight-feet plus, rearing outside and barrelling through the inside like its Hawaiian namesake. Yet a strange lethargy was known to affect surfers after prolonged hours in the water, and a nuclear power station down the coast was often blamed. For whatever reason, the place had the better of me, stumbling straight into a booming swell off a series of flights in a foreign land. But as the swell dropped I began to feel more comfortable, day by day.

With everyone thoroughly surfed out, I could get no takers when I suggested walking a mile north to investigate a break called La Punta Dos (Second Point), a barrelling right that supposedly worked on small swells. La Punta Uno, the little reef out the front of our *pensione*, had been a fun and playful three or four feet at the height of the swell, but was now flat. Bodies lay about in bunks snoring and moaning in response to my inquiry for takers, so I went alone. It proved to be my session of the trip. A drainpipe barrelling three to four feet, looping section over section along a shallow rock shelf — the thing was a non-stop tube from start to finish. There were only a couple of American guys out. I took my time, wary of collecting any more sea-urchin spines in my pincushion feet. Inevitably, I got launched on my first few take-offs. Eventually, I made a few wobbly drops, ducking under lips, blowing a few, making some. Gradually, I started edging further up the reef, looking for longer rides, deeper tubes, but all the time wary of the shallow bottom. The tide looked like getting too low. I still hadn't had a ridiculous one — a full-on deep tube ride worthy of bragging rights — and I was desperate to get one, to go back to the *pensione* triumphant, full of stories of the waves they'd missed. But I was running out of time, the whole deal looking more sketchy the shallower that rock ledge became.

The two Americans had made their most recent waves their last, and were paddling back in over a short gutter to the beach. A set approached. I paddled furiously. It was now or never. The thing lurched, and I leapt to my feet. I somehow stuck the landing and ducked the guillotining lip just in time. Locked in that watery tunnel, I held my line and hoped for the best. Section after section looped over me as I was shunted towards that almond eye of light. The tube accelerated and compressed and, suddenly, I was out again in the sun's naked glare, squinting, gasping, adrenalised. The two paddlers paused in their progress, looking back at me.

I caught up with them on the beach. They had to tell my friends about the tube I'd got, I told them. My friends would never believe me. They'd claimed there were no waves to be had today, that it was flat. The two surfers regarded me strangely, incredulous, screwing up their faces as if I was a little touched, perhaps by radiation poisoning. 'We're not going to tell them,' they scoffed, dismissively.

'Why not?' I flummoxed, dumbly.

They shook their heads, sympathetic to my condition. 'Because then they will all be out there tomorrow.'

And, true to their word, they denied all my claims of stand-up barrels when we bumped into my travelling companions on the short, sunset stroll back into town. I was scandalised — dismissed as a flake, an inventor of tales.

I sulked and took to surfing the little reefbreak out the front by myself while the cameramen and pro surfers staged their theatrics at the big name breaks as the swell nudged back up.

I was content enough at my little reef, except that every day, when school finished, my private reverie in the ocean would be shattered by the arrival of dozens of excited, pubescent, Spanish-babbling bodyboarders. It was extraordinary. It was as if there wasn't a local stand-up surfer in town. Suddenly I was the minority group, to be ignored or hassled and dropped in on. I grew a bit testy with the treatment, jostled for my spot in the line-up as the little Latino, neoprened turtles splashed about, flapping their flippers and barking sharp exclamations which I assumed were urges to vacate the peak to their manic jockeying. I dug in, feeling like Gulliver in Lilliput, more amused than threatened. In retaliation, in my broken Spanish, I managed to cobble together a crude sentence that I think said, 'In my country the bodyboard is for woman.'

They were aghast, their honour wounded. The Spanish babbling leapt in intensity, into angry protests and quickened splashing and paddling. I caught a wave in at this point, loudly calling them off, defiant to the last.

Soon after, we moved on, as the swell eventually disappeared. We produced a magazine spread and a video segment on the place, but made no reference to its whereabouts, keen to keep the secret safe for our eventual return. I often wondered about that surf town, waited to hear some word of its discovery by the surfing masses, its immortalisation in some surf movie or magazine, and its pronouncement as the next great surf mecca. But I heard nothing and kept my silence.

Ten years later, talking to Margo, I discovered he'd just been back there, chasing a mega-swell and serious tow-in waves, as part of the Billabong Odyssey big-wave expedition.

The only problem was that the town was still ruled by bodyboarders, except now they were twenty-six, not sixteen. And they wouldn't let stand-up surfers near the place. They'd dug in and closed ranks, preserving a kind of sponger sanctuary. I theorised that the waves were simply too radical to learn to stand up on, so the locals remained happily prone and pitted to their hearts' content, and had so become the dominant species. They must have known they were on a good thing, and aggressively guarded it. I couldn't help wondering if it might have been that one afternoon of rudeness on my part that helped turn them so militantly against their upright brethren. Here, the surfing food chain had been effectively reversed, and Margo and his big-wave hellmen chose to move on in search of other big-wave reefs to ride, rather than raise the local ire.

If I have fucked this place up for everyone else, I am very sorry, because, believe me, it really is quite something. Perhaps we should invade it with superior force, execute a brutal regime change. A pre-emptive strike, as it were. But things might get out of hand. This country was once run by a ruthless bloody dictator, chased into exile for his crimes. Soldiers still march through town on Sunday afternoons in an impressive show of strength, as locals promenade by in their

Sunday best, kids licking ice creams and young couples holding hands. No, best to let them have it. But it reminds me, ten years down the track, just how important it is to mind our manners in our global surf wanderings. You never know what you might be leaving behind in your wake.

First published in the Surfers Path, *2006.*

'Surfing introduced me to the intimacy of the surf, taught me to read the waves and study the weather and weather maps, and note the tides. Surfers are dependent upon and hence tied to an ever-changing natural environment. On reaching university I found I could study such an environment and have been doing so ever since. The science of the surf became my life choice. I found, with a surfer's background, I had a distinct advantage over the many non-surfing coastal scientists; it provided me with a very pramatic and successful approach to how the coast behaves. Surfers need to be resilient, to learn without a surfing lesson or kind word, to take every wave that hits you in the face, every wipe out, every cold car park and cold drive home, to rise in the dark, to surf alone for one's own enjoyment. It has enabled surfers to be the envy of the world, the lifestyle the masses would like to believe they follow as they slip on the Billabong t-shirt. Yet only surfers know what lies at the core of their sport — them and the waves.'

ANDY SHORT, COASTAL SCIENTIST

[As Director of the Coastal Studies Unit at University of Sydney, Prof. Andy Short has the enviable job of surveying every beach in Australia.]

peter singer

{ the ethicist }

It does remind me of the majesty and timelessness of nature, as compared to the brevity of our own existence . . . I love being out the back when it's sunny and the water is blue and clean and the waves are crashing down and there is foam and spray all around. Especially if I'm alone, or almost alone, and there are miles of breaking waves. Actually catching the waves can be secondary.

It is a slightly daunting prospect asking world-renowned philosopher Peter Singer for his views on surfing, and how surfers might conduct themselves more harmoniously in the water.

He is, after all, one of the modern world's great minds, best known for his landmark book *Animal Liberation* (first published in 1975, and spawning an entire global movement), and author of a string of influential texts since, which all address that fundamental ethical question: 'How are we to live?'

Some of his more controversial ideas include his insistence that animals have the same rights as humans and should be treated accordingly, and that we all should be giving away any income we earn beyond what we need for simple survival. These days, he is Professor of Bioethics in the University Center for Human Values at Princeton University, in the USA, and part-time Laureate Professor at the University of Melbourne, in the Centre for Applied Philosophy and Public Ethics. His numerous books have been translated into more than twenty languages and in 2005 he was one of the Time 100, *Time* magazine's list of the most influential people in the world today. He surely has more pressing issues occupying his prodigious grey matter than we surfers squabbling over a few waves. But it may come as a surprise to many to learn that he is also a surfer.

I first became aware of Singer's interest in surfing during the Byron Bay Writers Festival a few years ago. Peter had been invited to the festival to speak about his latest book, and local surf legend and former US surf champion Rusty Miller had been appointed Peter's chaperone throughout the festival, to help him sneak away for a few quiet surf sessions in Byron's famous waves. Peter, a long-time bodysurfer and bodyboarder, was keen to try stand-up surfing and Rusty, now a professional surf coach, seemed the perfect man for the job. So the philosopher and the salty old surf legend struck up an unlikely friendship — so much so that Peter agreed to pen an article for the next issue of Rusty's humble little *Byron Guide*, a kind of tourism magazine he produces annually. And so the words of the eminent philosopher were squeezed in among the ads for Byron backpacker resorts, stone buddhas and massage therapists.

Peter writes eloquently about the peculiar beach culture of New Jersey, on the east coast of the USA, where you have to pay to go to the beach, swimming is only permitted in designated zones, and the beach is closed entirely on Sunday mornings to encourage church attendance. 'Australians might wonder how you can close an entire beach,' Singer poses. 'The New Jersey coast in this area has a wide, flat strip of sand, and behind that is a continuous boardwalk that stretches for miles down the coast, separating the beach from the roads and houses behind it. Between the boardwalk and the sand itself is a fence, with gates at regular intervals. So to close the beach, all you have to do is shut the gates.'

Singer paints a grim picture of a controlled and constructed environment, a million miles from the pristine golden beaches of Byron Bay, which he is so obviously fond of.

'I love to walk along the beach as the sun is setting, watching the changing light over the mountains,' he writes. 'It's hard to beat the thrill of sliding down the green walls of water that rear up off Watego's. And I'll never forget a moment when I was paddling out on my boogie board. A wave reared up steeply just ahead of me, and as it began to break, a dolphin came leaping down its front, its entire body length clear of the water ahead of the foaming crest. That was when I thought: Byron really is a magical place. And it's a world away from the New Jersey shore.'

When I came to ponder the list of surfers to interview for this book, I had forgotten all about Peter Singer and his mature-age quest to learn to stand-up surf, when I happened upon an interview with him on the ABC's '7.30 Report'. After a long, in-depth discussion about a range of weighty ethical concerns, interviewer Kerry O'Brien asked Singer whether ethicists ever go on holidays — if there is ever a time when they can put down their lofty concerns for right action and ethical living and simply relax? 'It's nice to go and catch a few waves,' was Singer's considered response. How then might the ethicist feel about applying his study of ethics to the behaviour of surfers in the water? With overcrowding and the breakdown of old unwritten rules of surf etiquette threatening to sour the great waveriding adventure, who could be better qualified to suggest a way forward than Peter Singer?

As it happened, the very next year at the Byron Bay Writers Festival, Rusty was appointed my interviewer for a session on surf writing and I was able to inquire after Mr Singer and pass on my contact details, should he be interested in assisting me in my research. To my delight, he was.

Peter Singer is a busy man, but even in a brief email exchange, and as a relative novice, his ideas on surfing are fresh and thought-provoking. I always enjoy the way beginner surfers, and those removed from mainstream surf culture, discuss surfing free from hackneyed surf jargon and still totally in touch with those first childlike responses to ocean waves. As a late starter, what was his first experience of surfing?

'Fear. That is the first emotion I can recall, when I actually got to the top of a serious wave, and looked down. I was bodysurfing, and there I was, about to fall — maybe it was only a metre or two, but it seemed much more — straight down!' Peter writes. 'The first few waves I caught I was in the foam, tumbled around, and it wasn't much fun. Then I got a wave properly, my head and shoulders were clear of the whitewater and I was sliding down the wave's smooth green face, my arms out in front of me. "So this is what it is all about," I thought.'

He is not, however, about to be drawn on any of my promptings about surfing's supposed mystical qualities or metaphorical pointers to the great mysteries of life. 'I guess you could read whatever you want into it, but I don't see it that way. It does remind me, though, of the majesty and timelessness of nature, as compared to the brevity of our own existence. Those waves have been pounding the beaches for millions of years before I existed, and will be pounding them for millions of years after I have gone.'

As one who has spent most of his life in the halls of academia, and who has done most of his surfing on the relatively remote west coast of Victoria, Singer clearly relishes the solitary joys of waveriding. 'I love being out the back when it's sunny and the water is blue and clean and the waves are crashing down and there is foam and spray all around. Especially if I'm alone, or almost alone, and there are miles of breaking waves. Actually catching the waves can be secondary. Sometimes it makes me feel very tired, at the end of the day. But it's good to feel that your body has been working hard. And to know that you are having fun in a sport that uses no fossil fuel, and does not contribute to global warming or air pollution.'

Unfortunately, even a mind as keen as Singer's doesn't have any magic solutions to the problems of overcrowding and disharmony in the surf, but his own tactics of 'crowd avoidance' could be instructive — especially to many learner surfers who insist on swarming to the more well-known and high-quality breaks, when everyone's interests might be better served if they found a small beachbreak to themselves away from the masses.

'Most of my surfing has been in Victoria, and I haven't had much of a problem with crowds,' says Peter. 'I don't need to be where the very best waves are breaking, so I just move along to where it is less crowded but the waves are still good. But recently I surfed in California, at Malibu, where there was only a short break off a point, and everyone was trying to get on it. The atmosphere was notably less pleasant — particularly if you were not one of the regulars at that particular break. It's an old story — the bigger a community gets, the more strangers are part of it, especially people who surf a spot once or twice and then move on, the harder it is to keep a strong community ethic that works for the benefit of all.'

For those surfers so inclined, Singer's well-documented views on a range of topics are edifying, and might even provide some clues for a more sane and harmonious way forward for an increasingly crowded surfing world. As a microcosm of wider society, surfers are facing increasing competition for the finite resource of surfable waves. How we react to this will determine the kind of surfing culture we develop and ultimately pass on to our children. Singer's views on animal rights, for example, may have some unlikely parallels with riders of alternative surf craft, often derided as lower 'species' of surfers.

'Species is, in itself, as irrelevant to moral status as race or sex,' Singer writes in 'A Philosophical Self-Portrait', in *The Penguin Dictionary of Philosophy* (London, 1997). 'Hence all beings with interests are entitled to equal consideration: that is, we should not give their interests any less consideration than we give to the similar interests of members of our own species. Taken seriously, this conclusion requires radical changes in almost every interaction we have with animals, including our diet, our economy, and our relations with the natural environment.'

Singer has created a career, and an impressive body of work, out of addressing that timeless question: 'How are we to live?' A sense of the collective good seems to be at the core of his conclusions. 'I approach each issue by seeking the solution that has the best consequences for all affected,' he writes. 'By "best consequences", I understand that which satisfies the most preferences, weighted in accordance with the strength of the preferences. Thus my ethical position is a form of preference-utilitarianism.'

Applied to surfing, this approach would lead us all to paddle out into the surf wanting the best outcome for everyone in the water — a sense of operating as a communal whole, with happy and harmonious functioning our greatest goal. And this may be precisely the mindset we need to cultivate if we are to preserve the joy of surfing, and our own sanity, in an increasingly crowded surfing world. On any given day, whatever the conditions, there are those surfers in the water capable of experiencing the ride of their lives — and it is surely those surfers who should be given some sort of preference. When it is small, some young beginner or old-timer just returning to the surf, or a wearied parent just out to wash off some fatigue and emotional burnout, could have their whole day redeemed by one good ride. Expert and experienced surfers could afford to pull back and give them some space, and experience some vicarious pleasure from the joy of the beginner. When it is six foot and perfect, the expert surfers are the ones capable of making the most of the conditions, and the learners and less competent could reasonably stay out of the way and learn from the talents of the elite surfer. In this way, Singer's 'preference-utilitarianism' could help bring about the best consequences for all. In economic terms, surfers could seek to make the greatest collective good, or maximum utility, from the available resources and make the sum total pleasure of the surfers in the water the measure of a successful session.

Singer also argues stridently that the accumulation of wealth beyond our material needs is a largely meaningless pursuit, and it is only in giving it away that wealth holds any real meaning. Singer cites the example of American billionaire Warren Buffett, the second wealthiest man in the world behind Bill Gates, with a personal fortune of around US$42 billion. Buffett recently became the greatest philanthropist in US history when he donated US$30 billion to the Bill and Melinda Gates Foundation, for tackling disease in Third World countries, and another US$7 billion to other charitable institutions. 'At a single stroke, Buffett has given purpose to his life,' writes Singer. 'Since he is an agnostic, his gift is not motivated by any belief that it will benefit him in an afterlife. What, then, does Buffett's life tell us about the nature of happiness?'

If we regard waves as wealth, then maybe those of us greedily racking up our wave counts, hoarding more than our share of wave resources, are profoundly on the wrong track. And we would experience more of the true joy of surfing, by giving a few waves away.

'I think we need to do a good job of explaining the surfing ethic to newcomers — not abusively, but in a positive, friendly way,' Peter says. 'If we are all patient, and not too eager to get that one perfect wave, there are plenty of waves for all of us.'

'At first it's a peripheral thing. You jump in the ocean and you learn and you do all these things to become a surfer. And when you get to a certain ability then you start to have this inner experience because you're past that point of learning to be a surfer any more. You're actually having the energy exchange between yourself and the wave. And I think when you get to that connection where you have that experience on an energy level then you realise that energy everywhere. So once you actually have that experience that you get as a surfer through riding a wave and being deep in the barrel, then you can have that experience anywhere. You can see it in people, you can see it in mountains, because it's the same energy, so you see it in everyone.'

ALBE FALZON, FILMMAKER, FROM *LIFE LIKE LIQUID*

rob page

{ the nomad }

Surfing is the art of making spontaneous change without any negotiation. When a surfer catches a wave he chooses his approach, a direction, but the wave has a mind of its own. It changes its size, speed, position on the reef. And surfers ride those changes with their lives. And just like a bullfighter, there's no negotiation with a bull — there's no negotiation with our mighty ocean. I call it free-riding life — it breeds versatility, adaptability. I'm honoured to be a surfer in this life.

Fifteen years ago, Rob Page was living the dream, travelling the world as a well-paid professional surfer — his raw ability on a surfboard raising him out of a broken home and a bleak housing-commission estate in Bellambi, on the outskirts of Wollongong. He'd consistently rated in the top thirty in the world, won the world's most prestigious surf contest, the Pipeline Masters in Hawaii, and somehow landed an acting role in cornball Hollywood surf movie *North Shore*. Life was sweet.

He'd just been competing in Spain, where a feverish party atmosphere surrounded the contest, and was flying into Tokyo, when his world abruptly fell apart. Going through customs, he was pulled aside for special attention — hardly surprising given his long, flowing blond hair and colourful clothing. He sat and waited patiently in a small interview room for two hours as the officious Japanese customs staff went through his belongings meticulously.

He remembers them becoming agitated as their search proved fruitless, a superior bawling out his subordinate angrily. And then they got to his wallet, opened it and out fell a small folded square of paper. Rob remembers watching the paper fluttering through the air like a leaf falling in slow motion, and suddenly remembering, with horror, 'The acid!'

These few small squares of blotting paper soaked in lysergic acid diethylamide, LSD, would dramatically alter the course of Rob's life. 'We were all in Europe having a good time after the contest finished,' he explained later. 'They were partying in Spain, you know. People smoke marijuana in Spain — and hash. It's all right. It's legal. And myself and a couple of guys bought a couple of trips off this guy, this Spanish guy, had a big night, got wasted, charged on. And I had a couple of them left in a bit of paper which was lost and it was in my wallet with a lot of receipts and shit and then I went through Japan, six or seven weeks later and, Merry Christmas, someone found it for me. Thanks, you know.'

Rob was locked up for sixty-six days, half of it in solitary confinement, while he awaited trial. Estimates of the likely sentence ranged as high as eight years. The prosecution called for eighteen months.

In ten years on the pro tour he'd barely ever been in one place long enough to take in a change of seasons. 'When I saw the leaves on the trees go from green to yellow to red and fall off . . . I watched that go down for those couple of months and that was just like, holy mother. I'd go down to walk in the dog kennel [the exercise yard] and I'd try to pick up a leaf and hide it in my socks so I could take it into my room and sit down and look at it.'

He recalls one young guard, a surfer from Chiba, quietly approaching him and apologising: 'I am sorry these people are keeping you here.'

He can quote verbatim the notes he wrote to himself: 'Hi Rob, welcome to the school of higher learning. What you have as a professional career or what you did outside is of no importance in here. You're just another person trying to exist. Sit back. Anxiety is a negative at this point in time. And you're at university, you're at a university of higher learning. Start to learn.'

He took odd strength from the fact that he was in the same cell Paul McCartney had been held in for a minor pot bust a few years earlier. 'I was holding on to whatever I could,' he says. 'As sad and fucked up as it was, it was beautiful because I had to deal with life at its fullest. I'd sit down and cry and moan and groan and there was a time when they first took me into this solitary room. After a couple of days I just broke down and I thought, you know, if these fuckers keep trying to fuck with me like this I'm going to punch the glass out of this window and cut my wrist because

I've got to get out of here . . . But when it's all over you can look at them and thank 'em for the education they've given you. Thank 'em for making you sit by yourself for a month and find out who you are and what you're really like and what you're really into in life.'

He was found guilty, and the judge released him on a suspended sentence and ordered his deportation. In typical Page fashion, he flew on his original airline ticket on to Hawaii, hoping US immigration wouldn't notice the 'cancelled' stamp on his Japanese visa. The gods smiled on him: he made it through, and paddled out into the booming North Shore surf, lily white, deliriously relieved, greeting incredulous friends who'd heard of his predicament.

He eventually returned to France to see his French sponsors, clothing label Oxbow, who had stood by him admirably through the inevitable furore, even when surfing's governing body — the Association of Surfing Professionals — slapped an eighteen-month ban from competition on him. This despite the fact, Rob reckons, that many of those who voted for his suspension had been known to ingest the odd prohibited substance. His crime, it seems, was getting caught.

In the wake of the bust, Rob took an uncertain path as a travelling free surfer, chasing quality waves in exotic locations for sponsors' photo shoots rather than following the contest trail. Rob dreamt up the idea of a masters' surfing competition and sold Oxbow on sponsoring it, bringing all the sport's legends back together for an annual event. Oxbow founder Fabrice Valéri once told me, 'Robbie is my wizard. He will be with Oxbow for life.' Unfortunately for Rob, Valéri eventually sold the company, and the new owners felt no such loyalty.

When the sponsor gravy train eventually and inevitably ran dry, Rob found himself living in France, coming to grips with unexpected fatherhood with his Moroccan girlfriend, and no income. But Page, despite the white rasta appearance, is nothing if not resourceful. He'd been smart with his money and in real estate, and bought his young family a small-acreage home in the French countryside. Somehow, he found himself a partner in a successful beachfront bar in Hossegor, the booming surf town in south-west France, visited by the pro tour each October. He joked about it with his old pro tour mate Rod 'Box' Kerr, who once gave David Boon's beer-drinking record between England and Australia a serious nudge. 'I used to tell Box, "All you do is drink beer, you're just going to end up at the pub all day." And he'd say, "What are you going to do, just hang round the beach for the rest of your life?" "Now, I'm running a bar, and he's a lifeguard at Bronte!" Page can scarcely believe life's irony.

Like Forrest Gump, Page is one of those people who always seems to be around when things happen. He landed an acting role in Hollywood surf movie *North Shore*, a comic performance that earned the cheesy B-grade flick a cult following. He once dated the granddaughter of the then French president François Mitterand, and is equally at home among aristocracy and commoners. He came out of competitive retirement to win Europe's premier big-wave contest, and again to win the Australian amateur masters title in 2006. He's working with a German scientist friend to develop a totally new, stringerless, flexible surfboard.

I always knew Rob had to be included in any collection of great surfing characters, but as I embarked on this book I hadn't seen him for years, and had no idea where he was or how the latest chapters of his life had unfolded. Then, early one autumn morning, shortly before I signed the contract for this book, there was a knock on our door. Rob — newly landed in Australia, still driving the kind of crusty old Hi-Ace van he'd owned fifteen years before, with a guitar and a couple of boards in the back. His timing has always been uncanny and, as usual, he was full of stories.

He had two young boys now, eight and six, but the relationship with their mother had ended. He'd given it his best shot, he reckoned, and returned to Australia to lick his wounds and regroup.

He'd recently returned from his first trip to Hawaii in five years, as an invitee to the thirty-fifth anniversary of the Pipeline Masters. Organisers had trouble tracking him down to offer him the free airfare and a week's accommodation they were extending to all the previous Pipeline Masters. Because of his past indiscretions, he had to first return to Australia and apply to the US embassy for a special visa. When he fronted up at the consulate in Sydney without an appointment, they knocked him back. In desperation, he approached the founder of the Pipeline Masters, 1968 world surfing champion and now US senator Fred Hemmings, and received a personal letter from the senator requesting the cooperation of US Immigration so Rob could attend their anniversary dinner. With time running out, Rob simply boarded his flight for Hawaii, letter in hand, and hoped for the best.

'I said to my mum, "I'm going to Hawaii tomorrow — I'm either going to be put in jail when I arrive or I'm going to be an honoured guest at the Pipe dinner and have the time of my life,"' he laughed. On his way to the airport, he learnt his good friend, Tahitian surfer Malik Joyeux, had died surfing Pipeline. A surfer who had ridden some of the biggest tubes in history in his Tahitian homeland had inexplicably drowned on a regulation eight-foot day at Pipe. 'I was tripping. I was nearly in tears, thinking about all this shit,' Rob recalled. 'I had to go back and forth to the bathroom a few times just to let some tears out for Malik . . . I was so nervous, thinking about everything. I didn't want to get in any trouble. How do you get into America without the proper visa, especially these days? It was heavy.'

He fronted the immigration lady at Honolulu Airport, 'fessed up to his prior 'form', and hopefully handed over the letter. 'The lady said, "Listen, I can't just let you in, but I'll let you in on bail." So I was in Hawaii on bail. I got in trouble in '92, thirteen years before, and here I was on bail in Hawaii in 2005. But I was in,' he chuckled. Little short of miraculous, in the post-9/11 world, when new arrivals to the USA are routinely packed off on the next plane home if they make even an honest mistake filling in their arrival cards.

Page headed straight to the North Shore, got changed and just made it to the banquet on time. 'It was so amazing. There was Jeff Crawford, Shaun Tomson, Mike Ho — they were all grabbing me, hugging me — MR, Simon. I was just going, "Mate, this is so beautiful to be a part of this." These guys are the vertebrae of surfing, they are the original backbone that carried the thing.'

When Rob was called up on stage as the 1988 Pipeline Master, eight-time world champ Kelly Slater and his good mate and 2000 Pipe Master Rob Machado led a standing ovation for him. 'I just sat there for a minute looking at these guys, holding back tears, thinking, "This is heavy." Before I got my award, I walked up to Kelly and looked him in the eye and went, "You're unbelievable, brah. I can't believe you guys are giving me this respect. Thanks so much." I looked at Rob and said, "Thanks, mate."'

After twelve years living in France and many years in the surfing wilderness, the recognition from his peers meant a lot. 'I've read interviews with people who won Wimbledon where they said what it meant to them: Pipe was like that to me. So that was the biggest night for me. I told everybody straight how important it was and how honoured I was. And I said, "You know what, we lost an angel, we lost our brother at Pipe the other day, Malik, so it's hard for me to be here. But whatever honour you bestow upon me I'd like to offer up to Malik. Malik is a real Pipe Master. Malik rode one of the biggest tubes anyone's ever ridden. Ever."'

Malik's funeral followed a few days later, with the traditional paddle-out and circle of surfers in the ocean. 'Everybody was holding hands in the water, and helicopters came over and started dumping frangipanis,' Rob recalls. 'There we were sitting in the water at Beach Park. I've done twenty-two seasons on the North Shore and I've never seen anything like it. Frangipanis raining down out of the sky into the water, and I managed to catch one. It was so mind blowing. I looked around and laughed, and I turned to Bugs [Rabbit Bartholomew] who was sitting next to me and I said, "How's these Hawaiians, the toughest people ever, hey? Why are they tough? What are they protecting? Look at this, mate. They are protecting the gentlest hearts ever. No one puts on a funeral with that much grace and that much beauty."'

Rob seems to have an affinity with Indigenous, or First Nation cultures. Despite the blond hair and pale skin, he has Aboriginal heritage. 'I got my first surfboard off an Aboriginal man,' says Rob. 'My uncle Ken's full black. His son Robert gave me a 7'9" Terry Fitzgerald single fin with a full mural on the bottom when I was a little kid, and I used to stand on the board on my bed, with surf pictures all over the wall. I only surfed three times a year as a little kid when Mum took me to the beach. I used to sit in my bedroom and there was this photo I had of Gerry Manion at Cronulla Point, this old photo of this huge barrel, and I used to think that I was him in the barrel and I'd be in there and when I could see it closing out I'd click my fingers and I'd be back in my bedroom and he'd take the wipeout. So, if you're reading this, Gerry, you inspired me so much. I could not comprehend how a man could offer his soul and his life to that wave.'

Rob's dad was never around much and he and his mum and sister didn't have it easy. He remembers the 'repo man' coming to their house to take away their Christmas presents because his mum couldn't make the repayments. But when they scored a housing-commission house at Bellambi, close to the beach, his natural surfing ability was allowed to shine. He progressed quickly through the local boardriders and regional contests and soon found himself coming up against the big name, sponsored surfers from Sydney's well-to-do northern beaches in state titles. 'They seemed better educated. I wanted the knowledge they had. I wanted to know what was going on, but it drove me to think for myself. Some of them I thought were pretty lucky and pretty spoilt.'

Page quickly earned a reputation as a strong and graceful goofyfooter, in the mould of his Wollongong mentor Terry Richardson, and an outrageous party clown always up for a good time. He embarked on the pro tour in the mid '80s at a time when it was inhabited by a legion of larger-than-life figures — on the cusp of the change from great pro surfing pioneers Rabbit Bartholomew, Mark Richards and Shaun Tomson, to the new generation of success-hungry pro upstarts Tom Carroll, Martin Potter and Mark Occhilupo.

'I think a lot of strong-minded people find surfing because it's the only thing that can take everything about them and make it go into silence, go into full union, go into full yoga, go into the moment, whatever it may be,' says Rob. 'The greatest surfers in the world have all got stories about what they've grown up with and what they've lived with emotionally and I think surfing was the only thing that was the full yoga, the full meditation, that came naturally to us and captivated us.'

Despite the competitive focus and the party-boy persona, Page has always had a spiritual slant on surfing. 'There's so much raw energy coming out of the ocean. Like it says in the Bible, you can get all the power of God or Jesus, or whatever — the cosmos, the universe — but use it in the right sense. All grommets, when we get all that power we don't know what to do with it. We're pumped, our ego's pumped, we're walking around in a sexy young sixteen-year-old body. We've got all the young girls. We don't even realise we've already got a spiritual growth taking place inside of us that's bigger than all of us. It's taking shape. Surfing starts like an aerobic thing but surfing big waves is spiritual. When I see guys riding big waves, I believe the purest monks, the purest priests, the highest yogis, the highest Zen masters come out of the sea, because we practise it with our lives. We don't sit in a cave for twelve years. We don't sit and meditate in the silence. We let the ocean take us under the sea 'til we have no breath. We can't fight the power of the ocean, and we let nature and the ocean and its power do what it wants with us. In the Bible it says, come to me naked, come to me pure, come to me prepared to lose yourself to find me. And if that ain't what those guys are doing . . . Malik is those scriptures in motion. If he ain't saying to God, you do what you want with me, this is my honest trip, I've come here, so pure with no clothes on, standing here, then there ain't no godly or Christian man left on the planet.'

Without a hint of irony, Page shares his own theory about the story of Jesus. 'I've been all over the world, to different places checking out different so-called gurus and spiritual people and I've never met anyone higher than the people I've met in the sea,' he says. 'I had this vision one day that just came to me . . . There's a lot of waves in the Mediterranean. I imagined that these people in the Mediterranean walked over the hill one day and they looked over the beach and there were perfect five-foot waves, and they watched this guy ride a wave to the shore, and it was John the Baptist. And they went down the beach and went, "You're the Messiah, you're the Messiah." And he goes, "No way, mate, I'm not the main act out here at all. Check out the point." And they looked out to the point and this five-foot barrel spat, and Jesus came out of the barrel. And he materialised himself on the water, and he was walking on the water. So that's my theory on Jesus. I think the people who surf today are holy people, and that's why I say, why do we surf? Because we can't yet walk on water.'

As if to strengthen his case, he shares the story of his visit to India with the Mitterand family, when he was dating the French President's granddaughter Pascale. François Mitterand adored his granddaughter's plain-talking Australian surfer boyfriend and welcomed him into the family fold. 'I went to India with the Mitterand family when François Mitterand was President of France, one of the top five most powerful men on the planet,' says Rob. 'One of the high monks was in a cave for twelve years, like a breatharian or something, didn't have water or anything for twelve years. When he came out people were walking from up to 500 km away because they knew the man was coming out.' The Mitterand entourage were invited to have an audience with the monk and were ushered to the head of the queue to meet him. 'So we went through the monastery and all these people who'd been walking for weeks, months — eighty, 100, the oldest people I've ever seen — were in the courtyard. We went into this hall where only the distinguished guests and a few of the higher people were allowed to be, about 100 people sitting legs crossed, and over the back was the guru, looking like the Cat in the Hat, with a one-metre-long dreadlock wrapped up in a coil on top of his melon.' For some reason, Page was chosen to receive a blessing from the monk. 'I said no, no, because I wasn't devoted like the other people there. But eventually they sent me up and I took a gift. A lot of people put their money on the floor and he pushed it to one side, as a gift for the monastery. I just put my gift on the floor and I meditated on it and said it was my gift to him, and he picked it up and put it in the pocket of his jacket.' For dramatic effect, Page hasn't yet told me what the gift was. He fixes me with an earnest gaze. 'I took him a conch shell from the sea, and I was saying in my soul, "This is my cross, I come from this church," and I think he could hear me because he picked it up and he could relate to it.'

These days, Pagey roams the coast in his old van, chasing swells, calling on old surfing friends and spreading good cheer, doing a bit of surf coaching to pay the bills, planning his own surf label, developing alternative surfboard materials, pursuing a million far-fetched schemes. When his boys come to visit from France for months at a time, he balances all that with single parenthood.

At the core of what sometimes seems a formless, nomadic existence is a simple determination to follow the surfing lifestyle — to be free to wake up each day and hunt down the best waves and continue to push his surfing. He recently took out the Australian Masters title in his first competitive foray in nearly ten years, and remains adamant that pursuing surfing mastery is a valid lifelong vocation, despite the lack of sponsors, recognition or material reward.

'I always remind myself, you just fall in love with your own surfing. If someone else thinks its filth, unreal. If not, I'm still stoked in it. You know, if I'm on a wave and I care what someone else thinks then I'm up and down like a yoyo. But if I can keep it personal and just fall in love with my surfing and keep it like that . . .'

He leaves the sentence unfinished, perhaps aware that there is no established road ahead for this kind of single-minded pursuit of the surfing path into middle- and even old age. Plenty of ex-pro surfers have struggled to find their way on the back-end of their competitive careers, retreating to the safe haven of sales and marketing jobs in the surf industry. But Page is holding his line, free-riding life.

I, for one, look forward to watching where it leads.

'I mean the ocean is yesterday — that's where the waves are coming from, from the past. The shore is tomorrow — where the waves are going to, where they die. Where they meet is where it gets rough, but that's where I want to be, riding the now.'

BRIAN WILSON, OF THE BEACH BOYS, IN THE BOOK *LOOK! LISTEN! VIBRATE! SMILE!*

[Brian did not actually surf himself, but did once claim to have seen God on a Californian beach, after ingesting a large dose of LSD.]

SURF LESSON #427
Pull in, pull in, relax

Robbie Page once schooled me in the art of tube riding with a brilliant but simple refrain, bawled at me from the channel as I edged myself deeper into a remote, Peruvian surf break, pitching over a shallow rock ledge studded with sea-urchins.

'PULL IN! PULL IN!' he'd scream like a crazed football coach as I teetered down the face crazily, hanging on for grim life. Once I'd navigated my way under the pitching lip and into the hollow tube of the wave, inside the curl, Robbie's tone instantly changed. 'Reeeeee-laaaaaax,' he urged soothingly, like a yoga teacher. Somehow, I did — sizing up my precarious circumstances, and unsteadily steering myself through the watery tunnel, back onto the safety of the wave's shoulder. At the time, it seemed like the most concise philosophy on life I'd ever encountered: Pull in — jump through those windows of opportunity, take the leaps of faith and answer the call to adventure — then, once you find you've landed on unfamiliar ground, relax and go with it, in the flow. 'Pull in, pull in. Relax,' became something of a mantra to me during the subsequent few months stumbling about the coasts of South America and the South Pacific, and in the years since on the uncertain path of the freelance writer as sole provider for a young family. It never seemed to fail me.

gary blaschke

{ the giver }

What I have learnt from surfing is to have more confidence in the surf and to respect the waves. I have had to learn to let other people help me and to trust them with me in the surf. I have also learnt that no matter who we are or what may be different about people anybody can surf if they want to. I have made many good friends both young and old and I have learnt to have fun in the surf with them and to enjoy myself.

SARAH WALSH, AGE EIGHT, A LEG AMPUTEE
WHO HAS LEARNT TO SURF WITH THE
DISABLED SURFERS ASSOCIATION

'The one thing that joins us together is the love of surfing and I think that's a little bit more spiritual than anyone realises,' says Gary Blaschke, founder and president of the Disabled Surfers Association. 'We've always said, we're surfers first and disabled second.'

Twenty years ago, Gary was in a motorcycle accident that destroyed his kneecap. Told by doctors that he'd never surf again, after eighteen months of physio and rehab, he'd had enough. 'I had a caravan at Lake Conjola [on the New South Wales south coast] and used to surf Green Island,' Gary recalls. 'I told my wife, "I've had enough, I'm going out." She said, "You'll drown," and I said, "I'll drown doing what I love." It was blowing onshore and I got up and fell down, got up and fell down, but I was enjoying myself that much. And then I looked and saw that my leg was bending. Nothing was bending it before that — no amount of physio was bending it, but surfing was bending it.'

Convinced of the therapeutic powers of surfing, Gary wondered how many other injured surfers out there were waging a similar battle to get back in the waves.

'I was thirty-two and most of my mates had given up surfing. I used to surf Green Island by myself midwinter for hours,' he says.

In 1986, Gary started the Disabled Surfers Association, to help other surfers with disabilities to get back in the surf, and then simply to introduce the thrill of surfing to anyone with a disability. The DSA has helped blind people, blind, deaf and mute people, people with cerebral palsy, and a twenty-five stone paraplegic all experience the thrill of surfing.

'Try judging a wave just with your hearing. It will teach you to respect how we should be using all our senses,' says Gary.

'There's never been a disability that we haven't been able to take surfing,' says 1988 world champion Barton Lynch, who's been one of the DSA's biggest supporters. The DSA's Hands On Days have seen Barton and fellow pro surfers like Tom Carroll and Damien Hardman eagerly helping people with all kinds of disabilities enjoy the stoke of surfing. 'Everyone comes off that day just giggling, smiling and full of happiness,' says Barton. 'I pushed this one lady into a wave. She was deaf, mute and blind. Their ways and means of perceiving things are really interesting. I pushed her into one foot of whitewater at Collaroy and she rode it for about twenty-five metres, and through her interpreter she said it felt like flying in an aeroplane. It's such a goodwill thing, the joy of giving. Gary always refers to people getting the bug. People who go to those days always come back.'

Barton and Damien caught the bug so strongly, they donated $15,000 from their testimonial dinner to the DSA when they retired from the pro tour.

But it's been a severe financial struggle to keep the DSA going. Their only sponsorship has come from the Mitchell Surfing Foundation, a philanthropic institution. Gary's ploughed plenty of his own money in to keep it afloat, and his sign-writing business has suffered because of the time he devotes to the DSA. What keeps him going?

'It's just part of my life. I couldn't even get rid of it now if I wanted to,' says Gary. 'This guy stuck a gum leaf on a bit of cardboard and wrote on it, "Thank you for the best day of my life." That to me was worth the seventeen years. You make a difference, and you change a life, and that for me is more important than making money. You will get bitten by the bug if you are meant to be. They only have to go and help someone with a disability and see the smile on their face and they've been bitten.'

But Gary says the DSA is as much about changing attitudes as pushing people into waves. 'It's not a matter of taking disabled people surfing, it's a matter of helping able-bodied people to accept disabled people,' he says.

Gary once blindfolded himself for an entire weekend, and sprinted the length of a footy field with no sight, just so he could understand the experience of blind people. He's been known to jump into a wheelchair and cruise down to his local shopping centre so he can experience first hand the attitudes of others towards the disabled. 'People take a six-foot berth around you because they're afraid they might catch something,' he says.

A DSA Hands On Day is indeed a contagious experience. 'This is the best surfing on the planet, I reckon,' says Jim Norman, one of the founders of the Gold Coast branch, as we survey the scene at Currumbin Beach one summer morning. An army of fifty or more volunteers are merrily assisting four or five DSA surfers into the small waves. Another dozen or so disabled folk wait patiently in wheelchairs on the beach under sun shelters for their turn. 'Imagine only going surfing three or four times a year,' says Jim. 'It's really hard at the end of the day to tell people they can't have another go, that they've got to wait three or four months for their next surf.'

There are plenty of regulars among the DSA surfers. Luke is a Down syndrome bloke in his early twenties. He charges into the surf like a storm trooper, urging on his team of volunteers with a whooping war cry. He needs little assistance to get out through the waves and only a small push to catch one. He clambers up to one foot and one knee, arms straight out by his side like an aeroplane, until he is washed up on the sand. He leaps to his feet, roaring in delight, high-fiving his team, and charges back out through the breakers. Adam is an enormous bloke well over six feet tall with a bushranger beard, who communicates in raw, guttural grunts and groans. It takes a dozen or more people to steer him out through the waves, turn him around and send him shoreward. He clings to the board grimly with clawed hands until he is spat up on the beach. I am waiting at the water's edge to make sure he doesn't come to grief in the shorebreak. He comes to rest at my feet. I crouch down to greet him. He grabs my arm with a vice-like grip, fixes me with a wild stare and releases an animal roar of pure elation. I have never witnessed such naked surf stoke.

You can see the parents and carers standing at the water's edge, some anxious, some clearly delighted, but you can sense all their relief, that their loved ones are experiencing a few moments of flight and freedom, temporarily liberated from their limiting bodies, wheelchairs or institutions.

It has taken quite some persuasion for various local councils to agree to this unlikely assembly on their beaches but the DSA proudly boast they have never had a mishap.

'I run a tight ship. I have to run a tight ship. Seventeen years of never having an accident and running events with 300 people, we've proved to everyone that we're serious,' says Gary. 'None of us are experienced carers, but there's nobody who can say we're not the most experienced people at taking disabled people surfing.'

And Gary reckons he's continually amazed by the courage and determination shown by those he takes surfing.

'I've walked down the beach with a blind person, and he says, "What's surfing? What's a wave?" And I've explained it, and let a wave break on him. I've taken him out, pushed him into a couple of waves at Collaroy.' Gary tells this next bit in near-hysterical tones, as if he can still scarcely believe it himself. 'And he stood up and rode the wall of the wave. He got cleaned up at the end but if you don't know it's going to happen you don't brace yourself and you don't get hurt. He'd never been to the beach before, never felt sand between his toes. There are thousands of stories that are similar. It makes it all worthwhile.'

The following letter to the DSA south coast branch from the family of eight-year-old Sarah Walsh is typical of the heartfelt feedback the DSA receives:

Late last year we received an invitation to bring our then seven-year-old daughter Sarah (a below-knee amputee) to a DSA Hands On Day at Thirroul Beach. Initially we were somewhat apprehensive about the idea of Sarah attempting to surf, but following a conversation with a DSA member we were assured that there was nothing to worry about so we decided to give it a go. It was one of the best decisions we made, not just for Sarah but for all our family. On that day we were immediately accepted into the DSA family. Initially Sarah was lacking water confidence but within a few events, thanks to the dedicated volunteers, Sarah stood up on a surfboard and rode a wave all the way to the beach. As you can imagine that was a day none of us will ever forget. Since that special day in April, Sarah has been to Ireland to visit her grandparents where she showed them her surfing abilities, spending a week surfing on Ireland's west coast. Not only has the DSA improved Sarah's water confidence, her confidence in public speaking has improved. She now likes nothing better than grabbing a microphone and standing up in front of her fellow students and discussing her surfing experiences. We are so grateful for what the DSA has done for our family and in particular Sarah. The committee and all the volunteers have changed a girl who was scared of the surf to riding a surfboard in the space of five months.

For more information, visit the DSA website at www.disabledsurfers.org

'Once again I'll cast myself into the sea like a stone, to be tossed and tumbled, where all my rough edges and wild sides can be worn away, so that one day the sea will cast me back upon some shore . . . Then I'll know that at last I've come home.'

MIKE DAVIS, SURFBOARD SHAPER

'When I first saw the ocean it made me relax. The stress disappeared immediately. I found the waves put you in harmony. When I first stood, I found myself gliding and I was totally in the present moment, I felt nothing else. Everything else falls away. It was very good.'

LAMA KINLEY, BUDDHIST MONK

[Lama Kinley left his home in Bhutan for the first time at thirty-two, and surfed for the first time at thirty-six. From the book The Surfer Spirit, *by Cynthia Derosier and Tim Anderson* www.thesurferspirit.com]

ian cohen

{ the green warrior }

It shaped my life. It was my central passion. I sometimes think it's possibly my only really successful love affair. And it certainly gave me an in to looking at the world around me and the beauty of nature and what it gave me.

It is perhaps the most widely published surfing photo in history: the long-haired, bearded, anti-nuclear campaigner, lying on a surfboard, grimly clinging to the bow of an enormous warship. The image of the tiny, lone protestor dwarfed by the great military machine struck a powerful chord in 1986, when growing public concern led to daring protests against visiting nuclear warships to Sydney Harbour. Ian Cohen, now a NSW Greens member of the Legislative Council, grabbed headlines around the world when he paddled into the path of one of the ships, the USS *Oldendorf*, on his surfboard and managed to hitch a ride down the harbour, in front of the appreciative telephoto lenses of the world's media. It was the first time most people had heard of the daring environmental activist, but in reality the warships protest was one small act in a long and radical career as an eco-warrior. It's a journey that's taken him from the rainforests of northern New South Wales all the way to state parliament, from long-haired feral radical to clean-cut politician.

Ian Cohen grew up in Sydney's western suburbs, a long way from the beach, riding the train to Cronulla for a surf like so many other 'westies'. Then, with the benefit of a car and a licence, it was roaming surf trips to Sydney's eastern suburbs beaches and beyond — the Pacific Highway eventually carrying him north to the idyllic environs of the New South Wales north coast and Queensland's Gold Coast. This was at a time when surfers were few enough in number to still regard each other as kindred souls, when the waves were uncrowded and the Australian coastline largely undeveloped. 'As a young man, one of my central identities — you're always looking for identities — became a surfer and it was that feeling of belonging to a fraternity or a counter-culture group,' says Ian. 'The joy that was derived from the environment was really quite overwhelming and with all your usual youthful neuroses, it gave you a sense of being able to escape, being able to find joy, being able to lift yourself out of depression, problems, whatever it might be . . . It was just an overwhelming pastime, and then lifestyle, so when I went to university, all my holidays I'd just go up the coast surfing and sometimes I didn't come back in time.' As the '70s rolled on, and surfing professionalism, an industry, and media evolved, Ian's surfing was taking him in other directions. 'It shaped my life. It was my central passion. I sometimes think it's possibly my only really successful love affair. And it certainly gave me an in to looking at the world around me and the beauty of nature and what it gave me. And then I got to a point later in life when I wanted to give something back. When I was going through one of my existential crises as to what I wanted to do in life, I stumbled on a sand-mining action at Middle Head [on the NSW mid-north coast]. Doing something for the planet gave a whole opening of expression and understanding of what is my major passion: nature, both marine and terrestrial. There I was able to express a defence of my major passion on a beach. That was an important thing.'

Middle Head was a magnificent stretch of pristine coastline with towering sand dunes plunging steeply into the ocean — as much of the east coast had been before the devastation wrought by sand mining. Somehow Middle Head had been spared, but now it too was threatened. Ian, who had been feasting on this coastline's waves for years, decided this was the time and place to take a stand — little realising the chain of events he was setting in motion. 'It also brought me in confrontation with authority. It got me in jail, arrested, appearing in court — all these things from, really, a love of the ocean, a love of beaches . . . trying to save a piece of beach that I had fallen in love with.'

As his first environmental action, in 1980, Ian still recalls the Middle Head campaign with obvious emotion. 'Bulldozers destroyed the front dunes, the most magnificent original frontal dunes,' he recalls. 'Ninety per cent of the coastline had been destroyed by sand mining and none of these dunes that we see now are in their original state. They're nothing compared to what they were originally. So to see an original dune destroyed in a sand-mining process right there and then was very moving, very poignant, sad to me even to this day. But, again, that's a microcosm of what's happening all over the world. And so I guess just the fact that I was there as a surfer created enough impetus in my mind to actually have a go at stopping it.'

Ian imagined himself in a communications role, already sensing his natural flair for catching the media's attention, but was instead assigned to dig holes for a pit toilet and compost. It was a sobering welcome to the world of environmental activism. A core of protestors camped out at Middle Head for months, co-ordinating a media campaign and direct action to try and save the dunes. A camp kitchen was set up and three dollars a day would buy you three healthy meals. Even if you didn't have the three dollars, you still got fed. The crew camped, surfed and campaigned together, sleeping under the stars and sitting in front of bulldozers.

Ian recalls it as a magical, defining time. In his book *Green Fire*, an account of the Australian environmental protest movement, Ian writes: 'Nights saw hot food, campfires, music and a sense of community new to all. Mornings witnessed friends surfing together, with regular visits from pods of dolphins. It was a far cry from the usual surfing dynamic of competition and aggression that was the hallmark of the Australian surfing culture.'

'That was a wonderful time before the bulldozers hit,' says Ian today. 'We lived there for several months and surfed every day together in the morning and worked every day together. That was a really profound bonding.' Local landowners and the local Aboriginal group were united in their opposition to the sand mining. But despite their best efforts over many months, and great personal danger in their peaceful resistance, they couldn't save Middle Head. But the experience of surfing and defending a beloved stretch of beach awoke something in Ian, and his life's course was set. 'For me, the significance of Middle Head was immense,' writes Ian in *Green Fire*. 'It represented my initiation into a love of land and gave me a sense of community and purpose. I left physically wounded and bereaved, but with a sense of direction never before experienced in my life. From the bitterness of defeat rose a sense of mission that gave me no choice but to fully commit myself as an agent of change. There would be no more dilemmas concerning my life's directions. I had found something more precious than any bounty the establishment could ever offer. I had discovered a world view that for me rang truer than any other doctrine or religion. Inspired, impassioned and freed in the knowledge that the authorities would regret ignoring our actions in defence of that special place, a sense of commitment coursed like a fire through my veins. I give thanks to the spirit that dwells at Middle Head.'

Coastal scientists, many of them surfers, are only just beginning to understand how dune systems help produce quality surf, in an interconnected flow of sand from beach to seabed and back again. Only a handful of beaches on the east coast still feature their original frontal dunes, and most of them have reliable banks for surfing. One can only imagine how many quality beachbreaks were lost to sand mining. And there are plenty of case studies here and overseas where sand mining and insensitive coastal development seems to have had an adverse effect on the surf. 'It changes the whole dynamic. You sand mine a frontal dune and it changes all the way along from the banks out to sea. You lose your frontal dune formation and you lose your quality waves,' says Ian. 'Middle Head,

I've never seen it any good since, and I know before the sand mining with the natural frontal dune, it had a really steep beach and it had great banks.'

But sand mining wasn't the only threat facing the region. Ian soon became aware of logging operations planned for idyllic old-growth forest in the northern New South Wales hinterland. By now firmly enmeshed in the environmental movement, he threw himself into the fray — camping out in remote forest areas, physically barricading access roads, confronting angry loggers in direct actions. Ian says it was his fitness and experience as a surfer that allowed him to thrive in these potentially dangerous forest campaigns. 'Between actions I was always going surfing to recuperate and the surfing kept me, well, fitter than the average hippy, so I was able to survive and deal with pretty intense situations in forests,' he says. 'The excitement, the danger and risk taking inherent in surfing translated itself to any number of those actions, so it was really the same thing. I have to admit, I'm a bit of an adrenaline junkie. I like riding big waves. So they were big waves, and if there's any epitaph to my life it'll be: "I attempted, I had a go at riding big waves." It's a dance with life. You dance your way through as best you can with all the baggage that you carry, which is plenty in my case. I just kept pushing to create change, to satisfy myself that I was actually giving myself purpose, other than just getting a job and a career . . . I suppose surfing for me is a metaphor for life. Everything you do in surfing reflects in your life in other ways.'

Through the '80s, Ian participated in most major environmental campaigns in eastern Australia: Nightcap rainforests in northern New South Wales, the Franklin River, the Daintree, the south-east forests of New South Wales, North Washpool and Chaelundi forests. He also took part in actions against Honeymoon and Roxby Downs uranium mines in Central Australia. 'I remember back in the early '80s surfing and swimming with the dolphins, and then there was this dolphinarium in Warragamba — a shitty little backyard pool with a whole bunch of dolphins which were entertaining people. And a bunch of people got together and we decided to go out there every Sunday and work on closing it down. We had demonstrations and banners and talked to people. I found at a certain point I couldn't get the same enjoyment from surfing with the dolphins up here if I didn't do something for those dolphins in captivity. We got the place closed down. For me, that's the balance and that's about the best I can do.'

Then, in 1986, Ian mounted his most famous campaign, as founder of the Sydney Peace Squadron, protesting at the arrival of US nuclear warships in Sydney Harbour, as part of the Australian Navy's seventy-fifth anniversary celebrations. His tactic of bow riding — latching on to the bow of a warship on his surfboard — generated enormous media coverage, but also great controversy even within the environmental movement. Some saw it as dangerous attention seeking, discrediting the cause, but there is no doubt it got the message out. 'It was building up a theatrical act and getting known for that, so it was very ego stroking in a way, but at the same time just being out there and pushing hard to get maximum coverage and public interest in the issue. It was like soft warfare. There's no guns involved, just using your skills and ingenuity to beat the system. You get to the point where you've got the warship coming at you, and there's nothing they can do. It's a huge, monstrous thing. They can't turn away from you, so you've got 'em. It was that interaction. It's like riding big waves, you're totally focused.'

The authorities warned protestors that they risked being sucked underwater and minced in the ships' giant propellers, but Ian remained undeterred. How dangerous was it? 'You use your judgement. I knew when not to have a go, when the ship was going too fast. I knew when it would be OK. You get to know your medium. It's like becoming familiar with a particular wave. It's something that any reasonably competent surfer with the right board could do. I'll take credit for the mad idea, but it's no more difficult than riding a moderately big wave.'

I have to ask, what sort of board was he riding, and how did it go? 'I was on a 7'8" single fin, Cooper mini-malibu,' says Ian. 'It went pretty well. It's good to have a malibu board that has a really good paddle, get your paddle speed up, hang on to the nose and just keep going.'

In the midst of all that action, with police and media boats buzzing around him, cameras whirring, the warship itself speeding up and slowing down to try to dislodge him, is there a sense of stillness, of being in the moment? 'You're on the wave, flying. There's no chatter. You're there in the moment. It's sort of a Zen moment, and it's very invigorating and centring. Unfortunately it takes those sorts of things for me as a rather defective personality to find that point of balance. I suspect quite a few surfers are the same way, otherwise they wouldn't be surfing.'

In 1991, Ian found himself back defending a beach, when Coffs Harbour Council proposed a controversial sewage outfall at Look At Me Now Headland, Emerald Beach. This protest was a far cry from the radical forest actions manned by feral hippies. The residents of Emerald Beach, united in opposition to the outfall, were respectable middle Australia — retirees, war veterans, working people, families, housewives, children. Ian and his band of activists were warmly welcomed into the fray by the local residents and an unusual alliance was formed. Accusations of heavy-handed police tactics, dawn raids on the protest sites, the use of police dogs and the rough handling of elderly protestors only galvanised the opponents of the outfall. During October 1991, 250 protestors were arrested, representing twenty per cent of the population of Emerald Beach. But, ultimately, the outfall was stopped. Perhaps the highlight of the protest was the construction of the Big Poo out of bamboo, chicken wire, old sheets, concrete sealant and rubberised 'shit-brown' paint. Rivalling those other 'Big' attractions the Australian east coast is renowned for — the Big Pineapple, Gumboot, Merino, Prawn, to name a few — the Big Poo even went on the road. The eight-metre turd once found itself lodged in the entrance to the Ballina Shire Council and became a figurehead for anti-outfall protests up and down the coast. In 1995, the people of New South Wales elected a Labor government, on a promise of no more ocean outfalls. Ian reckons surfers were central to that issue and made a real difference. 'Compared to where the surfing community was twenty years ago, we have made great changes. We beat Emerald Beach, we built the Big Poo, we've demonstrated, surfers got arrested and they stopped them. I just went back on tour down there to the sewage works [at Coffs Harbour]. While not as good as I'd like, nevertheless, they're pumping the effluent up to the farms and there are people there growing bush tucker, organic tomatoes, producing crops off this effluent. That came out of beach protests. Coffs Harbour Council well and truly got its knuckles rapped and is trying hard to do the right thing in terms of sustainability. We are slowly changing the culture.'

In 1995, after a campaign of stunning guerilla tactics, hijacking the policy launches and press conferences of the major parties, Ian found himself elected as a Greens member of the NSW upper house. 'Back when I was forty, the dole office said I was completely unemployable, so I thought I had no other option than to become a politician,' he laughs. While the reality of living in Sydney and sitting in parliament has taken Ian away from his north coast home, he regards his infiltration of the political system as simply the next stage of his journey. 'If you go surfing every day it can burn you out. You've got to go away to appreciate it. You've got to go into the dirty heartland of the city to be able to come back to the ocean and really enjoy the taste of what it offers,' he says. 'I go off to the underworld down in the parliament, after playing with the fairies up here and having a wonderful time — and fighting the battles up here as well — but then I go to parliament and I can actually knock on the minister's door and say, "Hey, you've got it all wrong and I'm going to bring this up in the house." It's like riding a big wave, it's power surfing. I relate to it that way: I surf my way through that institution and I get some wins, I have some losses, but if I wasn't there the culture would be that little bit different. That seems to be my role for the moment in life until I step down and do something different, but it will still be around the theme of surfing.'

I can't help wondering what this north coast hippy surfer makes of parliament, and what parliament makes of him. When parliament is not sitting, Ian resides in an MO [multiple occupancy] community near Broken Head, surrounded by lush rainforest spilling all the way to the beach. He can walk down a winding rainforest track to a pristine beach. It must be a hard home to leave for the sterility and hostility of the political world. 'It's a very alien realm. I sometimes liken it to my ultimate wilderness experience, with all these strange animals living in a weird environment playing games with your head. You must deal with it as best you can. You find friends in the most unlikely places, and you find enemies in the most unlikely places. For me, I want to be dealing with that. I don't want to be hiding out. I can create an environment for myself that would be very beautiful but I would find it fairly boring, quite quickly.

'I like the challenge. It gets the monkey off my back. It's like surfing. When you go surfing and you've got stuff on your mind, surfing just washes it away because you've got to focus. It's meditation. I'm such a neurotic character that sitting with crossed legs doesn't do it for me. I have to do something hard and fast and intense, whether it's mental or physical. That way I'm centred. When everyone else is freaking out I'm centred. In that way I'm reasonably well designed for political activity.'

And what do the mainstream politicians make of him, this tall, shaven-headed, barefoot eco-warrior strutting the corridors of power? 'First they ignore you, then they laugh at you, then they ridicule you, then they get angry with you, then they accept what you're saying,' says Ian. 'I think that's happening right now. We're coming up to a state election [late

2006], and that will be very interesting because there's a real rejection of all the major parties. People are looking for something else and I think we provide that. And it's good this week to have a good news week. [The Republicans had just suffered a crushing defeat in the mid-term US elections, late 2006.] It's not good news for George Bush. It's not good news for Johnny Howard. But for me it's a good news week in terms of the structures breaking down somewhat, and the alternative voice being heard, and that's, I think, a really powerful thing.'

Ian reckons surfers have a real role to play in this emerging political landscape, where people are disillusioned with mainstream politics. The act of surfing itself, he argues, is most fulfilling when we harness the energy we derive from the ocean and channel it into a defence of the natural environment that provides us our kicks. 'From the days of my first environmental issues, I've argued that surfers, by virtue of their independent spirit, by virtue of their risk-taking behaviour and their general bravery and their engagement with a natural environment which is easily crapped on by government bureaucracies, be it physically shit in the water, or ugly highrises in inappropriate places, or surf spots destroyed by developments to cater for the moneyed set, all of those things put an onerous responsibility on the heads of surfers to become planetary surfers. There's been some fantastic stuff done. I really admire the surfing doctors who've gone up to Aceh, Sumatra and Nias, both before and after the tsunami, just giving something back to these societies where we have taken so much because we go and enjoy the waves. To me that's a spiritual endeavour. You look for what is spiritually uplifting, what's going to give you a sense of well-being and satisfaction. Hopefully when you get to the end of your life you'll be able to say, "Well, I achieved something, therefore I can feel satisfied." You can see it in terms of belief in a deity or in terms of the deity within yourself that you've been able to release and exercise, express and fulfil. In that way I think we have a real opportunity to create a wonderful balance where we take a certain amount and then give back because it energises us . . . because it's a very symbiotic environment for well-being, and they say the ocean heals old men's bones. I've always had that healing through the surfing and the swimming and the ocean in general.'

Ian has mixed feelings about the evolution of surf culture from its counter-culture roots to its present status as high-profile professional sport and big business. 'It was part of the counter-cultural reaction, the same as the hippies, the same as the London music scene, the same as Haight-Ashbury and Kent State University and the anti-war moratoriums. We were part of that and now the freedom that we all sought and to some extent found through surfing is getting wiped out by our own people. They go off and make money and all of a sudden you've got houses in Byron that are worth $8 million, and people who can surf can't afford to live here and have to do service work for some rich bastard. It goes through those phases, but out of it at every step there's something to be learnt, something to be had, something to be enjoyed, something to be shared. You can't condemn the point you are at. It's just historical process. But you can do something about making the point that you're at a little better.'

Surfing's journey, he reckons, neatly mirrors the transformations of Byron Bay itself, from sleepy farming and fishing town, to hippy enclave, to its current status as tourism/backpacker hub, New Age epicentre and refuge for moneyed Sydney escapees. 'People hark back to what it was, but it's also got a lot more awareness. It was a very limited place back in those days. It had been assaulted by agriculture for generations, and wasn't a particularly pretty place. Abattoir, whaling station — just a country town that was basically an industrial area. Now, for better or worse, we've evolved with all the baggage and all the silly things that come with it, and we're at a different stage. Personally, I'd rather be living in the Byron of today. There were times along the way that I'd wish, "Let's stop here." But it doesn't work that way because life is dynamic, just like a wave. You can't stay at the peak; you ride the whole wave. Sometimes you wipe out, but if you survive you paddle back out and have a go again, because it's so beautiful. It's the same with society, with culture, with living your life. You ride that wave. You start in the kiddy pool and you hit the big ones and at the end if you're seventy and riding a little wave out at Watego's and having a bit of fun with your mates, but you're still out there, then that's life.'

Ian recently had the opportunity to teach Michael Franti, lead singer of Spearhead, to surf. The experience left a deep impression on both teacher and student. Franti is well known for his political and anti-war lyrics, and Ian takes heart from the idea that the restorative powers of the ocean can now sustain Franti on his crusades. 'It's something I have always wanted to do,' Michael wrote on his website, after the experience. 'After about a ninety-minute surf session I had amassed an accumulated 2.1 seconds of actually standing on the board . . . I was ecstatic.'

Franti is a big man and needed a board that would float him properly, so Ian and a friend shaped him his own board out of an old sailboard they found on the side of the road. 'We didn't take anything off the thickness. We rounded off the rails top and bottom and came out with this 9'6" fat gun, really classic, nice shape, softened all the rails, single fin, really beautiful,' Ian enthuses. 'Got it glassed in Sydney. Michael came out for a concert there. He's got this line, "You can bomb the world to pieces, but you can't bomb it into peace." Right. He's a good man, a top man, and we wanted to give him something back surf-wise, so we put on the logo of the surfboard, "You can bomb the world to pieces or you can surf the world to peace," and he loved it. So, he got his board, and I wanted to ride it. I said, "Michael, we'll keep it for you here," but no, no, no. We've never seen it again. He's taken it with all his musical equipment. He's travelling around the world with this surfboard in his truck. That is another aspect of where it's at with surfing, that you can share the pleasure of this beautiful experience, and we as two old surfer dudes wanted to give something back. We thoroughly enjoyed it and I know I'll see him at the Blues Festival, if not before, and we'll have a great rave about his surfboard. And that's all part of surfing as well. That guy might only ride two-foot waves in his life but that's OK.'

Ian remains a great believer in surfing's potential to make the world a better place, that even one person at a time it can help shed a little light in a sometimes dark age. 'That joy you get can then translate to your whole being to be more generous of spirit,' he says. But we all know surfers for whom that doesn't seem to be the case — who've had more than their share of perfect waves but remain stubbornly grumpy old buggers. 'It doesn't always work, but you have the potential. It's like a key . . . It's like a wonderful additive to life that can translate into a more harmonious society.'

Is he ultimately optimistic about the fate of humankind on planet Earth? 'Last week I was fairly pessimistic, but now things are rolling along quite nicely so, again, it's like the old surfing metaphor. When the surf's up, you go for it and enjoy it because there's plenty of time when it's flat, and other times when it's full of shit or there's sharks in the water . . . you just have to go, "Right, when it's happening, it's happening." It would be nice to be this high all the time, but when you see George Bush getting a caning, Howard really worried, greenhouse getting really good traction, you see Al Gore strutting the world stage with such statesman-like aplomb, then you have to say, "Shit, surf's pumping, and it's offshore," and make the most of it.'

'The ancient yogis of India, they were pretty much focused on life as the evolution of the spirit, and what they learnt was two of the keys to that were intuition and spontaneity. So that was what the ancient yogis practised — any opportunity to use your spontaneity and intuition was an opportunity to evolve your spirit . . . Every time a surfer paddles out and takes off on a wave, that wave is brand new, it's never broken before, it's never been surfed before. By them just taking off and riding that wave they're giving their spirit an opportunity to evolve because they have to tap into their intuition and spontaneity just as the nature of being a surfer. Every surfer, whether he knows it or not, is practising almost a Zen art, where they are tapping into those two things, the key elements of wisdom.'

CHRIS LANE, MUSICIAN, FROM THE FILM *LIFE LIKE LIQUID*

SURF LESSON #643
He who hesitates is lost

Haleiwa has always scared the shit out of me. I am not alone in this. The notorious Hawaiian reefbreak has a malicious streak, wrapping in on the unwary and trapping them on the inside reef before delivering a merciless pounding. I'd always paddle out tentatively, hovering nervously on the shoulder, watching for clean-up sets, only to have the wave sneak up on me and deliver a blind sucker punch.

You'd be watching the peak when somehow the wall seemed to warp and bend in on you from the left and you'd just glimpse it in your peripheral vision before it moved in for the kill. It was maddening. Several professional surfers nearly drowned out there during a huge swell for the Haleiwa World Cup years ago and vowed never to go near the place again.

The thing was, it looked so damn inviting from the beach: a perfect peak that pitched and curled and reeled off in both directions, though the right was by far the superior wave, one of the most seductive and alluring chunks of ocean on the North Shore, like a femme fatale or mermaid luring the unwary to their doom.

That was until the great Australian big wave rider Ian 'Kanga' Cairns shared the key to Haleiwa with me. Hovering on the shoulder, he pointed out in no uncertain terms, was actually the worst place to be, precisely where that bending wall picked you off. No, the wisest and safest strategy was to paddle directly out to the peak and sit on the other side of it. This may sound like something close to madness but, as Kanga explained, the left is a far softer wave than the right. If a clean-up set comes in you can angle for the shoulder of the left and get rolled by white water, but you aren't going to get bounced off the bottom. And when a wave comes in that you want, you are on the inside for the rights and can get in early and easily before the wave heaves and lurches on the inside bowl. I was sceptical, but tried it out and to my astonishment it worked. Time and again I'd paddle to the outside peak, wait for my wave and pick off glorious rides with ease. If a rogue set caught me inside I'd angle for the left and at worst have to duck dive a relatively soft, pillowy mound of white water.

And this alerted me to one of the keys of surfing larger waves: what often looks brave or heroic is simply the smartest and safest option. It proves itself over and over again in larger surf. Paddle strongly for the wave right on the peak and you will get in early and have a much easier time of it than tentatively scratching in on the shoulder, unsure if you even want to take off.

I remember once paddling into a set wave at Haleiwa and finding myself with no other course but to pull straight into the barrel or straighten out. The barrel looked far too big, deep and intimidating, so I straightened out towards the beach. The lip landed on the tail of my board, catapulted me through the air, snapped my legrope and sent me tumbling across the reef underwater. When I eventually surfaced, breathless and seeing stars, I faced a long and arduous swim after my now creased surfboard, with plenty of time to reflect that pulling into the barrel, even if unsuccessful, could hardly have been any worse. It was a swift and emphatic lesson, one not easily forgotten, ensuring that next time I found myself in such a position I'd at least have a go at pulling in.

I should probably mention that the last time I surfed Haleiwa and tried Kanga's approach, I found myself getting carried out to sea in a raging rip pouring out of the harbour mouth and thought I might need rescuing. I eventually managed to paddle myself into the break and get washed to shore, but it was a timely reminder: neat and tidy theories can be swiftly rendered obsolete by the vagaries of the ocean. Just when you think you've got things sorted, nature will shuffle the deck.

'For me it changes every day. That's something I've been coming to terms with as I get older. Having kids, because you're not out there every day like when you were younger, every time I get out there it's something different. It's fresh every time. It's also a little daunting. I feel it now more than ever. I really want to go surf big waves and I love being out in the ocean when it's big but I'm not as confident as I used to be. It's a hard one. I'm definitely struggling with it a little bit because I'm not as fit. I find it really humbling actually. But I just love being around it. I don't have to be in it. I spent a lot of time with Lynchy [Wayne Lynch] when I was younger and I always wanted to be in the ocean and he'd always cruise, just go sit on a cliff somewhere and watch for a while. I'm starting to understand that point of view. It's like you only have to be near it sometimes. I just have to drive out there as quick as I can sometimes just to look at it . . . Every day there's a new lesson from it. You realise how much you know when you start teaching your kids. There're all these things you calculate when you're running across the beach — where to paddle out, where the water's moving, where the waves are breaking. And you don't even realise you know all this stuff until you start teaching it.'

ANDREW KIDMAN,
WRITER/PHOTOGRAPHER/FILMAKER/MUSICIAN

vezen wu

{ the scientist }

It was this instant when I went in the water, that I knew my life would be changed forever. It's kind of shocking. I will have to make sacrifices, but it's something I'm prepared to do. If you get hooked you're ready to give up a lot of things for the waves.

It was during an earnest conference call, when a colleague leaned over and noticed the doodles on his notepad, that Vezen Wu first realised he had a problem.

'I had been drawing waves on my notepad through the whole conference call,' Vezen marvels. 'I was thinking about surfing every five seconds. It's almost like pornography. Surfers can look at pictures of waves and imagine what they'd do. There was something about surfing that just called me back, constantly. It's completely unscientific, it's irrational. I had to go back. It's indescribable.'

This is not how Vezen, an eminent New York scientist, computer programmer and equity trader, was used to conducting his life. As something of a child prodigy, Vezen had stunned the science world by discovering a new type of antibiotic in carnivorous plants when he was just ten. At New York's prestigious Columbia University he'd taught software engineering, designed groundbreaking medical software and continued his studies into natural medicines — all this while holding down a day job as an equity trader. 'The most demanding high-pressure environments you could put yourself in,' he says.

Yet, just when his life's path of overachievement and success seemed assured, Vezen was invited to California for a holiday by a university friend. And there he made perhaps his most life-altering discovery . . . surfing.

'One of my classmates was from Huntington — his father actually grew up with the Beach Boys — and he wanted me to go surfing,' recalls Vezen. 'I went out there, I didn't know what I was doing . . . but I got hooked. It's like a drug. It made me wonder, what's going on? I'd never come across any sport that I absolutely needed to do. I'm the most unlikely athlete, and the most unlikely surfer. I was the most academic kid in high school . . . but I was instantly hooked and spent the next couple of years trying to learn all I could about surfing technique and surfing at the local beach near New York City, where I live. Something really unusual was that I found myself thinking about ocean waves all day.'

After a life of study, academia, hard work and discipline, Vezen was shocked by the pull of the ocean. 'It's an obsession. It's this feeling that I'm at peace in the water. It was calling me back. I just had to have more of it. I'd wonder myself, how can I be in the water for six hours, and as soon as I get out want to go back? And it never changes, it continues to be this crazy. I control myself now. I don't draw waves on my notepads any more,' he laughs.

Not one to do things by half measures, Vezen was determined to learn all he could about surfing. 'My approach is probably different to a lot of surfers. I wanted to understand scientifically what's going on.'

After some research, he discovered the most sophisticated training facility in the surfing world was located in Australia, the so-called High Performance Centre at Casuarina Beach in northern New South Wales, part of the national headquarters of Surfing Australia. He contacted them, signed up for a two-week course and flew out to take tuition under national coach Sasha Stocker. 'I needed to catch up quickly. Just like maths or science, you learn from a teacher, so I signed up to the High Performance Centre in Australia. It's the only institute of its kind, and I was the first non-professional surfer from the USA to use their facilities,' Vezen explains.

The High Performance Centre is a state-of-the-art training facility designed for elite competitive surfers, so they were more than a little surprised when this mature-age beginner from the USA turned up. Yet Vezen and Sasha, a former world amateur surfing champion, hit it off immediately. 'He truly loves the sport and he truly loves to share it with others,' says Vezen.

'He's definitely a full-on Spock. He doesn't half do things,' says Sasha. 'You wouldn't call him a waterman, but his passion for the sport was just amazing. Although things didn't come to him that easily, he really stuck it out and enjoyed himself . . . and achieved some really good goals.'

Sasha got him on some proper equipment for a beginner, replacing his small board with something thicker and wider to float him better, and taught him how to read the surf and position himself in the line-up. 'It was probably one of the best coaching experiences I've had, and also just spending time with him was really intriguing for me,' says Sasha.

In scenes that sound like *The Karate Kid* on waves, Sasha led Vezen into a deeper appreciation of surfing and the ocean. 'Out in Australia surfing with Sasha, they were the biggest waves I'd ever surfed,' says Vezen. 'Up until then I'd never felt the true power of the ocean. Sasha spent a lot of time with me observing the ocean. He showed me how you can map the ocean floor from where the waves break. I've never seen anyone else do that. He told me just to swim and feel the current, understanding the ocean as a living being, developing a respect for the ocean.'

Vezen's two weeks of coaching reached a peak when he successfully caught and rode a long, head-high point wave on the green face at Cabarita. 'By the end of it he was paddling out into the waves and positioning himself really well, swinging round and taking off and coming back out with a smile on his face,' says Sasha. 'It was pretty thrilling just watching something like that.'

Vezen left Australia determined to find a scientific explanation for the feelings of elation he experienced in the surf, and he became convinced that the answer lay in negative ions, generated by breaking waves. 'I discovered through a medical web site that Columbia University had shown the ability of negative ions to improve mood in clinical tests.

The university study used an artificial generator to generate the negative ions, but related publications highlighted that the ocean surf is one of the largest natural sources of negative ions. Now there was a plausible medical explanation: the surfer's stoke could be explained in part by exposure to negative ions, which were elevating mood by affecting brain chemistry. This hypothesis, if proven, would have significant implications for the treatment of depression and other mental disorders.'

Vezen was also convinced this field of research offered benefits to more than just the clinically depressed. 'Indoor work environments are devoid of negative ions, and have an excess of positive ions, from computer and TV screens. This type of lifestyle isn't natural. In traditional lifestyles, people would be outdoors all day. Because I felt so much better in the ocean, I thought, this lack of exposure to negative ions is causing people problems. I have this suspicion that surfing should be required for mental health. Ironically, it's an intense sport, but I felt much calmer in the ocean than anywhere else. My blood pressure and my pulse were lower.'

An ion is an atom with fewer or more electrons than normal as a result of a chemical reaction to its environment. A positive ion is an atom with fewer electrons, and a negative ion is an atom with more electrons. Positive ions attract atmospheric pollutants, dust particles and harmful airborne matter. Negative ions cancel the effect of positive ions and clean the air, increasing the sense of well-being.

'It's believed negative ions are created by the waves breaking. Water molecules are rubbing over each other. It stands to reason bigger waves are bigger ion generators. We had this idea that the barrel itself contains maximum negative ions,' says Vezen, which would neatly explain the ecstatic feelings associated with tube riding.

As a scientist, and with his interest in natural medicine, Vezen saw huge potential in his theory. 'The treatment of depression could become as easy as a day at the beach,' he says. 'I proposed this research idea to

Sasha. He was really supportive and helped me to apply for an American research grant.'

Surfing Australia agreed to sponsor the study but unfortunately his US research grant application wasn't successful. Vezen remains undeterred. 'I plan on one day working with Sasha and Surfing Australia on this,' he says. 'I'm prepared to spend many years working on it.'

In the meantime, Vezen is broadening his surfing experience with occasional trips to exotic surf locations and regular forays into the frigid waters of New York. 'I live in Manhattan. People wouldn't imagine there's waves out here, but I'm only fifteen miles from the beach. I go on weekends, a couple of times a week.'

But the ocean has held other, more sobering lessons too. 'There was another experience: understanding that the ocean can take your life away. Last March [2005] in Puerto Rico, I was out having a surf, and in a matter of minutes four people drowned. Three of them died, one was revived. I brought in one of the women on my surfboard. I never saw myself as a rescuer. It reminded me that the ocean really needs to be respected. The three people that died, I was in the same place that they were. The woman was in her late sixties, people were performing CPR on the beach, but she didn't survive. That really messed me up for a while. I didn't go surfing for four months.'

But over time, Vezen's passion for surfing has only deepened. 'What surfing's done for me, it's shown me true happiness,' he says. 'It's helped me develop a more intimate relationship with nature. Living in New York and spending a lot of time in front of a computer, I got cut off from the natural world. There's something primordial about surfing. It's like you're a fish, going back to your roots.'

Vezen believes surfing has even informed his work with the stock market, where he has helped develop computer software to track share-price fluctuations. 'There are a lot of Wall Street traders who surf. People are reading *Surfline* during the day — they've got *Surfline* on one screen and the stock market on the other. I've been studying natural patterns in the stock market. We have to watch when that wave is coming. I was speaking to the head trader and he was saying the inexperienced traders pick the wrong points in the wave. It's still reading wave patterns, and many of those waves patterns are deceiving.'

Vezen's curriculum vitae makes fascinating reading: scientist, computer programmer and equity trader, with major breakthroughs in all these divergent fields. One gets the impression that Vezen's will be a life played out in two halves — before surfing and after surfing.

'When I was five years old,' he wrote to me, 'I became interested in carnivorous plants thanks to a PBS Nova documentary. I was intrigued by their ability to trap prey, and studied them religiously. At ten years of age, I became aware of a special group of tropical pitcher plants that ate rats and birds. Native tribes used extracts from these plants to treat infections, which hinted at their drug potential. My mother brought me to the local university where I met Dr Hellmuth, the microbiology professor who would become my mentor. For two years, he schooled me in laboratory techniques to study bacteria. During this time I discovered an antibiotic, derived from a Himalayan pitcher plant, that was highly effective against the drug-resistant strain of staph called MRSA, a leading cause of hospital-acquired infections.

'It took five more years of research to produce the antibiotic in sufficient quantities to elucidate its chemical structure. The results of my experiments showed that I had discovered a new entity: a novel, broad-spectrum antibiotic with the potential to revolutionise medicine and save countless lives. I was awarded the Westinghouse prize for my discovery, and this recognition presented me with myriad opportunities. Ultimately, I accepted a scholarship to study Molecular Biology at New York University. In addition, the university provided a grant that allowed me to continue my drug research.'

'During the summer vacations of my freshman and sophomore years, I went abroad to Germany and Taiwan, respectively, where I collaborated with medical scientists on my antibiotic breakthrough. It was in Taiwan that I made an unexpected discovery. While searching through the local market, I detected a provocative odour emanating from fermented tofu, a traditional Taiwanese delicacy. Back in the lab, I isolated the bacteria responsible for the fermentation and found that one of them produced an antibiotic. The Taiwanese researchers were astonished to learn that their food, in fact, was a medicine.

'In my final year of college, Merck, the pharmaceutical giant, invited me to develop my antibiotics for clinical use. While at their laboratories, I was exposed to database technology and its power to accelerate drug discovery. Hoping to apply this technology to my own drug research, I enrolled in an advanced database engineering program at Columbia University. During this time, my team and I at Morgan Stanley (the global financial services firm I joined after completing my Merck fellowship) engineered a system that improved investors' abilities to monitor stock markets in real time. Soon thereafter, I joined the Columbia faculty and became the chief architect of an ongoing research project to design a bioinformatics system, known as MedfoLink, that will enable us to monitor global health in real time.

'I believe that the age is now upon us when computer technology and medicine will work in synchrony. To this end, I plan to apply my interdisciplinary background in medicine, computing and business to create the leading biotech firm for drug discovery. Furthermore, following in the footsteps of early mentors like Dr Hellmuth, I created a program to introduce scientific research to middle school students in New York City.'

It must be hoped that Vezen's surfing obsession won't mean he is lost to the worlds of science, business, computing and education — and that those who dish out research grants might one day deem surfing's therapeutic powers a credible field for scientific research. Because it doesn't sound like Vezen's likely to give up surfing any time soon.

'It was this instant when I went in the water, that I knew my life would be changed forever,' he says. 'It's kind of shocking. I will have to make sacrifices, but it's something I'm prepared to do. If you get hooked you're ready to give up a lot of things for the waves.'

Still, his surfing research may yet yield his greatest contribution to humanity. 'Part of my approach to life is finding explanations for amazing phenomena. I think that's why I started researching the possible role of negative ions in surfing's allure. Perhaps surfing gives us something that most of us are missing in our modern, distant-from-nature lives. If I want to get spiritual about it, the negative ions could be the "ether" or life-force that the ocean provides. But in the end, I think one of the most powerful outcomes of surfing is how it creates community and shared experiences across all sections of society. Surfing is a *lingua franca* of nature. Even dolphins and other sea creatures surf.'

'There is a need in all of us for controlled danger, that is, a need for an activity that puts us — however briefly — on the edge of life. Civilisation is breeding it out of us, or breeding it down in us, this go-to-hell trait . . . The answer is surfing.'

PHIL EDWARDS

[From his 1967 *autobiography*, You Should Have Been Here an Hour Ago, *sub-titled* The Stoked Side of Surfing or How to Hang Ten through Life and Stay Happy]

captain paul watson

{ the sea shepherd }

I think reverence for the ocean is your best guarantee for protection from the ocean. I almost feel through my life that I've been protected in the ocean. I don't know why, I don't know how . . . I've been extremely fortunate. I've never injured anyone, I've never had any crew members injured, I've never been injured, and we go through these horrific situations. I think that respect actually is repaid. I don't know how, I don't pretend to understand why things are the way they are. I never fear the ocean, I always feel like it's a protective force.

Paul Watson was in a small Zodiac in the path of a Russian whaler, when the captain of the whaler walked from the bridge down to the bow and spoke to the harpoon operator. The Russian skipper barked a sharp command at his harpooner, then looked up at Paul and his companion in their Zodiac, doing their best to protect a pod of whales, and drew his finger menacingly across his throat.

'We'd been reading a lot of Gandhi and we were all very big on the idea of non-violent resistance,' says Paul, 'but I realised Gandhi wasn't going to cut it this time.' A moment later the harpoon streaked over their heads and struck a female whale behind them, its trailing rope slapping down between them on their Zodiac like a clap of thunder.

'That whale screamed, she screamed as a woman would scream,' Paul recalls. Moments later, an adult male whale leapt out of the water in front of the whaler, attempting to protect its pod. The harpoon fired again straight into the whale's head from pointblank range. Paul and his companion were splattered with blood and gore and feared the stricken whale would fall on the boat as its final act of revenge against its human tormentors. But as the whale sank back into the ocean and their eyes met for a protracted moment, Paul says he saw something that changed his life forever. 'I saw understanding. The whale understood what we were trying to do.' He says the whale managed to change its course as it fell and miss their Zodiac. 'The whale chose to spare our lives . . . and I also saw pity, not for the whales but for us, that humans could act this way.' In the thirty years since, Captain Paul Watson has dedicated his life to saving as many whales as possible from the whalers' harpoons, as co-founder of

Greenpeace, and these days as the head of an organisation called Sea Shepherd.

Paul and his supporters have attracted controversy around the world for their radical direct actions, ramming whaling boats, sinking boats in port, using helicopters, Zodiacs, stink bombs and whatever else they can think of to thwart the efforts of whalers. Paul says they are simply enforcing international law in what is supposed to be a whale sanctuary in the Southern Ocean, because no governments will police it.

It's his background as a surfer, he says, that allows him to place himself and his crew in such radical situations and maintain composure. 'I think what's most important about surfing is it makes you feel comfortable with the ocean,' he says. 'Just being able to get entangled with a big wave and being wiped out, and not panicking when you don't know top from bottom. It teaches you to let yourself go and not fight it, move with the flow of the water. I think moving with the flow of the water is really a good strategic way of approaching any situation. I've found over the years that I go into situations that have no way out, and miraculously I come out of them . . . Also I think surfing's the most active form of meditation there is.'

His approach seems to work. Despite thirty years of the most confrontational activism imaginable, Paul says he has never caused or suffered a serious injury. 'I think reverence for the ocean is your best guarantee for protection from the ocean. I almost feel through my life that I've been protected in the ocean. I don't know why, I don't know how . . . I've been extremely fortunate. I've never injured anyone, I've never had any crew members injured, I've never been injured, and we go through these horrific situations. I think that respect actually is repaid. I don't know how, I don't pretend to understand why things are the way they are. I never fear the ocean, I always feel like it's a protective force.'

Watson is roundly criticised by his opponents for his radical tactics. A quick scan of web references shows him variously described as a saviour and a visionary on the one hand and a dangerous criminal and eco-terrorist on the other.

'I don't pretend to justify violence. I do not condone the killing of human beings. I've never done that,' he says. 'But I don't view the destruction of property used to take life as an act of violence. People can call it violence, but in my view I've never done anything violent in my life. I think what we take risks for is worth it, the protection of endangered species, the protection of an endangered habitat.'

Sea Shepherd's short video presentation of its latest mission to Antarctica makes riveting viewing. When the Sea Shepherd crew get a whaling boat in their sights, they don black balaclavas and go to work. Captain Paul pulls up alongside or physically rams the boat. Coloured smoke and stink bombs are hurled onboard the whaler to distract and disorient the crew. Zodiacs and helicopters are launched to further hamper the whale hunt. The whalers respond with water cannons and abuse, and banners that declare the killing is all in the name of research. Eventually, the whaler is forced to retreat.

'When I see whaling boats running away from us, that gives me satisfaction. When I see whales escaping from harpoons, that makes it all worthwhile. They're afraid of us. They believe their own propaganda, that we kill people. I don't mind. They can believe whatever they want. I've never injured anyone in my life.'

Paul tells the story of the Buddhist monk who appeared at the wharf shortly before a recent departure and presented them with a small statue of Buddha. He didn't think too much of it but placed it up on the bridge of his ship. Later, he learnt the statue had been sent by the Dalai Lama himself, as a mark of support. Eventually, Paul met the Dalai Lama and asked him about the statue's significance. He told Paul the statue represented the compassionate wrath of Buddha. 'What does that mean?' Paul asked. 'Scare the hell out of them,' the Dalai Lama laughed. 'When

Greenpeace accused me of violence I said, "Well, the Dalai Lama is the ultimate authority on non-violence. I think I'll defer to his judgement on this over yours.'"

Paul resigned from Greenpeace many years ago and doesn't have a lot of time for the mainstream environmental movement these days. 'I think they're a bunch of posers, out there pretending to do things and raising lots of money. The environmental movement has become a feelgood organisation. People join it so they can feel good.'

He is unimpressed by images of dead and dying whales used by other anti-whaling groups. 'We don't have those images because we will not watch a whale die. So people go, "Oh, Greenpeace have all this incredible footage. How come you guys don't have it?" 'Cause we won't sit there and watch them die. I'm not into posting whale snuff flicks on the Internet. This bearing witness thing that Greenpeace has is one of the reasons I left Greenpeace, because I got tired of watching whales die. There was this idea that just the witnessing of an atrocity is enough to change that, and it isn't.'

Whatever you think of his tactics, it's difficult to question his conviction — that humankind is in the midst of creating one of the greatest mass-extinction events in the history of the planet, a path that will inevitably lead to our own extinction.

'The problem is we're on this treadmill out of control, we don't really have control over our own lives. People disagree with things but they carry on living the life they disagree with because they don't see any way out of it,' says Paul. 'One of the things I've learnt over the years is not to care what people think. As Leonard Cohen wrote, we are locked into our suffering and our pleasures are the seal. Everybody's too busy entertaining themselves. The real suffering is, as Henry David Thoreau said, "most men live lives of quiet desperation", and that quiet desperation brings them down so they never really live at all. So I think you have to be prepared to throw it all out.'

This willingness to go for broke, whatever the consequences, was evident in Sea Shepherd's actions from the outset. 'When we rammed the pirate whaler *Sierra* in one of our first actions, we had twenty crew members on board. I said, "Look, I'm going out and I'm going to ram that boat. I can't say you won't get hurt but I'll guarantee you one thing, you'll be going to jail." We were in a Portuguese harbour. Seventeen of them got off and three stayed on. We took the boat out, rammed the whaler, permanently shut it down. We were boarded by the Portuguese Navy, got arrested and were hauled in front of the port captain. He said, "You're going to be charged with gross criminal negligence." I said, "Captain, there wasn't anything negligent about it. I hit the ship exactly where I intended." He looked at me and he said. "You know, I can't find who owns that damn boat so as far as I'm concerned you're free to go." And we walked out the door. One of my crew members who got off said, "If I knew you were going to get away with it I would have been there too." You have to go into these situations knowing there's no way you're going to get away with it, and it's surprising how many times we do get away with it.'

It's an attitude that Paul says makes surfers natural allies in the fight to protect the world's whales and dolphins. Professional surfer Dave Rastovich has been a big supporter of Sea Shepherd, and has started his own organisation, Surfers for Cetaceans, in a bid to rally the world-wide surfing community. Paul says he'd like to see the wealthy and powerful surfing industry do more in defence of the oceans and its creatures.

'There are people who feel that reverence for the ocean. Dave Rastovich is one of them. They understand that it's not a commercial commodity,' says Paul. 'And there are those who just see an opportunity to profit from it and in the end they're the ones that it won't mean anything to. They're the ones that believe it's only money, that's all it ever will be. They'll never get the true treasure of it, the understanding.'

Paul's own surfing had unlikely beginnings in the chilly climes of Vancouver, Canada. 'I grew up in Canada and at fifteen I left for California to be a surfer. I got stopped at the border so I didn't make it until I was eighteen. I knew all about surfing even before I could surf. We didn't have much surf in Canada. I spent quite a few years living in Hawaii and California.' Paul doesn't get as much time to surf these days, but still travels with surfboards and windsurfers aboard his boats. He usually has at least a few surfers among his crews and has discovered waves in remote locations he'd rather not divulge. 'I know people who've devoted their lives to it and I think they're better people for it really,' he says. 'Sea Shepherd goes a long ways back with the surfing community. Yvon Chouinard [founder of Patagonia] is a big supporter of ours. It's really an identification with what the ocean's all about and understanding that the sea is our connection to life and that if we destroy the ocean we destroy the ability of life to support itself. It is our life support system.'

Among Paul's more contentious claims are that whales are the most intelligent life form on earth, and that worms are more important than humans. They're views he doesn't back away from. 'If there were no worms there'd be no humans, but if there were no humans there'd still be worms,' he says. He believes it's absurd to be exploring space for intelligent life forms when there are life forms here on earth whose intelligence we don't yet comprehend. He says a whale or dolphin's brain is both larger and more complex than a human brain and whales and dolphins are capable of forms of communication we can barely imagine.

'I think there's a lot we can learn from them. They're extremely intelligent creatures, but we have to learn to understand a thing called non-manipulative intelligence,' he says. 'We decide who's intelligent and who isn't. A dog could come up here and tell you who sat here yesterday. That's an awareness that we cannot even imagine, so all species are intelligent relative to the environment they live in. The Zulus have incredible stories of how the elephants used to come down to the shores in Africa and spend days bellowing out to sea to the whales, and the whales would be there bellowing back. Who knows what that's all about? We arrogantly assume that we know what's going on. Personally I think ecologically we are one of the most stupid species on the planet.'

For more information go to: www.seashepherd.org

'You must live in the present, launch yourself on every wave, find your eternity in each moment.'

HENRY DAVID THOREAU

SURF LESSON #2362
You have to give it away to keep it

The Twelve-Step community, those brave souls trying to heal their lives and retrieve their sanity through Alcoholics and Narcotics Anonymous, have a saying: 'You've got to give it away to keep it.' By this, they mean that the teachings and spirit of recovery promoted by NA and AA need to be passed on to others to be truly learnt and appreciated. Those in recovery help one another along the way, building up a matrix of mutual support — a kind of pyramid marketing for the soul. I believe a similar principle applies to the joy of surfing — maybe because surfing needs to go through its own period of recovery after an age of greed and selfishness.

When we try to hoard the waveriding experience and guard it from others, we lose the essence of its magic. If it is something that is going to be stolen and defiled by the invading masses, then we must be forever on our guard. It is only in sharing the joy of surfing that we truly come to appreciate it to the full, through the fresh perspective and childlike joy of the beginner.

I became convinced of this when I started taking my own child surfing. Until that moment, surfing was something to be squeezed in among my myriad responsibilities and commitments as a father/husband/provider, a guilty pleasure to sneak off and indulge hurriedly in early mornings or quick breaks from work. To combine child-minding and surfing — it almost seemed too good to be true. Yet I didn't want to be a pushy 'Little-League' parent goading my child to fulfil my own unrealised sporting dreams.

One family holiday, when my daughter was four and a reasonable swimmer, I offered to take her out on the front of a longboard. The waves were tiny. A perfect one-foot right-hander peeled into the corner of an almost deserted beach. She was thrilled. We paddled out and caught a series of zippering rides as she perched on the nose in front of me. Every time we washed up on the sand she'd squeal, 'More, more, more.' Suddenly, this wasn't a purely selfish pursuit, and as she lay trustingly on the front of my board, I did my best to guide her safely through the best and longest rides I could find.

Her nervous mother stood on the beach and waved me in, just as my own mother had thirty years previously, similarly aghast that their tiny vulnerable child was out so far in the vast ocean. When we finally came in my daughter was buzzing. And I felt a strange new hit of surf stoke myself. The waves were tiny but I was as high as if I'd spent the morning riding perfect six-foot Grajagan. A totally new sensation surged through me, the sensation of having passed on my love of surfing to another, my own flesh and blood no less. The surfing experience was moving through me, not simply accumulating in me. Perhaps like water itself, surf stoke is only healthy when it is in motion, not stagnating.

The next morning, I heard those words that every surfing parent craves, 'Come on, Dad, let's go surfing.' So off we went again, my daughter and I, to ride a few waves.

My daughter may or may not choose to become a surfer. But if she does, I hope that it's a welcoming, sharing, compassionate surfing world she enters, where ocean-goers look out for one another, experience some of their surfing pleasure vicariously through the joy of others, and cultivate a harmonious surfing environment. I have been a dickhead in the water enough times myself over the years to know that one act of greed or aggression sets off a chain reaction. Civility in the surf, like democracy and a humane society, is a delicate state easily damaged by thoughtless or selfish acts. It is all ultimately one ocean and all our actions send ripples around the world.

Send out good waves and they'll surely come back to you.

'I'm fifty-four, and just started surfing three years ago, but I surf almost every day. I was diagnosed with cancer seven years ago, and I believe surfing heals me and makes me strong (physically and spiritually) so I can bounce back from all the constant chemo. I believe in the *mana* of the ocean. As many of the beach boys will tell you, it heals. Blue [well-known Waikiki beach boy] often tells me that that is what is keeping me alive: I believe it. Less than twenty per cent with my particular cancer are alive after five years, and I'm still kicking after seven. Many days after chemo, I go surfing weak and with a terrible headache, but I come in clearheaded, refreshed and stronger. I don't know why it works, but I know it works. Physically, surfing keeps my muscles strong so I can bounce back after the treatments. I will never lose 'my fight with cancer'. No matter what happens in the end, every day I go out surfing is a day I have beaten cancer — I have already won.'

JERI EDWARDS, WAIKIKI, HAWAII

mick fanning

{ the contender }

I think the biggest thing is to enjoy it along the way. A lot of people don't enjoy it and if you're not enjoying it, it shows in your results. I think that's a huge thing — just to go and enjoy it and really appreciate why you are where you are. You've got a gift, so enjoy it.

The first time I interviewed Mick Fanning he was a gawky sixteen-year-old who called himself a kook, still in the shadow of his Coolangatta mates Dean Morrison and Joel Parkinson. I shouted the three of them to an all-you-can-eat smorgasbord dinner at the Kirra Pizza Hut to discuss their already impressive junior careers and their hopes and dreams for the future. As the hottest trio to come out of the Gold Coast since '70s surf stars Rabbit Bartholomew, Peter Townend and Michael Peterson, the so-called Cooly Kids were already being heralded as future champions. 'I think if one of us made it, we'd all make it . . . We all thrive on each other's goals,' young Deano declared with uncanny prescience. Parko reckoned his most memorable surf session was one rare, rainy morning he and Deano had Kirra to themselves, then found a ten-dollar note on the side of the road and binged at the local bakery. The life of a grommet surely couldn't get much better.

Ten years on, Mick, Joel and Dean are all rated in the top ten in the world and very wealthy young men, with generous sponsors, jetsetting lifestyles, expensive cars and impressive real-estate portfolios. The last time I saw Mick he was being chaired by a cheering crowd out of the Snapper Rocks surf as the first two-time winner of the Quiksilver Pro, and the great Australian hope to wrest the world title from the American Slater–Irons duopoly.

With a tattoo of his dead brother's name on his arm, and a metal grappling hook keeping his hamstring muscle attached to his hip bone, it's been far from an easy ride for Mick. But the cruel losses and daunting setbacks seem to have only strengthened his resolve to pursue those outlandish teenage dreams to their ultimate conclusion. What hasn't killed him, as they say, has only made him stronger.

Mick was just seventeen, walking home from a party with a pretty girl by his side, when an unmarked police car pulled up alongside him.

'Around that time our mum would get really worried about us, and she'd always be like, "If you're not coming home ring me",' Mick recalls. 'This car pulled up. I was just thinking, "Ah, it's the cops. We're just walking home, we haven't got any drinks in our hands or anything. We'll just keep walking." And then two of our family friends stepped out of the car. They're like, "Mick, get in the car" . . . and they just told me and I just totally freaked out.'

What they told Mick was that his older brother Sean had just been killed in a car accident on the way home from the same party. The brothers, both young, promising, aspiring pro surfers, had their future dreams inseparably mapped out together — travelling and surfing on the world pro tour. They'd already begun competing successfully as juniors, had sponsors giving them free boards and clothes, and helping out with the cost of travel and contest entry fees. Life was sweet. In one awful moment it all unravelled.

'Afterwards I wasn't allowed to go down and see the crash site. I tried to sneak out. No one would let me go down and see the tree until the car had gone. I didn't surf either. I just sat in my room. I think I stayed there for about four days, and then I finally went surfing. I remember the first surf I went for. Everyone knew I hadn't been out of the house. I had all my mates there, every single one of them. D-bah was uncrowded until we paddled out. There were just so many of us. It was epic, everyone screaming and hooting. I was still overwhelmed by the whole thing. I remember I didn't do a turn, I was just going straight along the wave. It was wild to go surfing again.'

There's no doubt the loss of Sean has profoundly shaped who Mick is today, and provided much of the drive for his extraordinary success. 'I think it's made me appreciate life more. I'd known people die before that and I was really rattled by it, but when it hit so close to home . . . it was so different. I thought about what I really wanted to do: "I want to be a pro surfer and that's what I'm going to do."'

Does he feel Sean's presence much? 'Sometimes, I'll be so happy, I'll dream a lot of him for like a week and get super psyched on that,' he says. 'The dreams I do have that he's in seem so vivid and so real it gets me stoked to see him again. Sometimes I feel like I'm with him. Just the feeling that he's around gets me happy and amped. Some people have like a certain person, when they're around they get a gnarly energy. I think it's sort of like that.'

It has certainly worked for Mick, as if he were now surfing and competing for two. He won the second-tier World Qualifying Series in 2001 to make the cut for the elite World Championship Tour. In 2002, he finished fifth in the world at his first attempt, and fourth in 2003. Then, just as the world title predictions were piled upon him and his glorious sweep to pro surfing glory seemed unstoppable, the pressure got the better of him. 'I don't think I'd been home for more than a month in five years. You'd have ten days or maximum three weeks,' says Mick. 'Everything just got to be so stressful. You get all these people in your ear going, "If you don't do it this year," or, "You've got to be world champ this year." I really lost the passion for surfing. I was so over the Gold Coast. I think I got drunk for like a week straight.'

His 2004 season began with an uncharacteristic thirty-third and didn't get much better. By mid-year he was in a definite slump and almost uninterested, when he headed off to Indonesia for a restorative boat trip. 'It was only small, about four to six feet. I came along the wave and went up and did a floater. As I was up on the roof it jacked up, and as I came down I tail-dropped and my back foot came off the board a little bit. When I went to put it back on I missed, so when I landed I did the splits.

My front foot was still on, I was doing the splits, and then the wave hit me in the back and pushed me further through it. I tore my muscle, and all of a sudden I got a sensation that went down my leg, like a cramp, and my whole leg cramped up, and if I moved it was just worse.'

Mick had torn his hamstring muscle clean off the bone. It hung in his thigh, limp and useless, like a deflated football bladder, as his leg bruised and swelled. A ten-hour boat trip and at least a couple of flights from the nearest First World hospital, he was destined for a dizzying twenty-four hours of indescribable pain and valium-induced delirium, and a full five months out of the water, his 2004 season shot to pieces.

'Had to sail for ten hours. Had to bribe the Indo guys to get us on the plane. Flew from Sibolga to Medan, Medan to Singapore, Singapore home. When I got to Singapore I went to see the doctors and hit them up and they pumped me full of valium again.'

Then there was the surgery, an extremely rare procedure in which a metal grappling hook was screwed into his hip bone, and the muscle re-attached with needle and thread. 'What they do, they slice the back of my arse open and peel it back and they drill into your arse bone and put like a grappling hook in there,' Mick explains candidly. 'It's so strong the doctor said he was lifting me off the table just with the grappling hook. That's why you can't do anything for the first six, eight weeks. It's just the stitches holding it together. You've just got wait for the scar tissue to grow over the grappling hook.'

Given the frame of mind he'd been in, it would have been easy to consign the wounded Mick Fanning to a mere footnote in pro surfing history, another crash-and-burn shooting star heaped up with too many expectations and riches, and too little guidance, at too young an age. Mick, to his undying credit, took the injury as a blessing. 'I was telling my mates, it's probably the funnest year I've ever had, even though I couldn't surf. Just hanging with my mates, doing what I wanted to do, it was really, really fun.'

Mick had just built his million-dollar dream home on Kirra Hill, two doors up from his mum, and settled into its refined luxury, with its plush home theatre, wall-sized TV and leather lounges, for the duration of his recovery. After six weeks of almost total immobility, he began tentatively exercising his re-engineered leg, and eventually embarked on a concerted training regime.

'It's gnarly, mate. They concentrate on your core and get that strong and then start building. 'Cause I was lopsided as it was, they just gradually straightened me up. It's just evening out the body, pretty much keeping a good posture through all your movements.'

Eight months after the accident, and after only three months back in the water, Mick turned up at the 2005 Quiksilver Pro at his home break superbly fit and exuding a steely determination to re-prove himself. Astonishingly, he beat all comers to leap to an early ratings lead and a career-best third in the world at season's end. He surprised even himself.

'Coming back at that first event I didn't expect to win it. I wasn't concentrating on the contest, just on getting to a level to compete against those guys, and then once I got to the contest I was that focused it just carried through the event and, man, it all flowed really well.'

Now perhaps the fittest man on tour, happy and settled, engaged to his model girlfriend Karissa, a Porsche 911 in the driveway, and his mum Liz retired from nursing to manage his career full time, all finally seems right in Mick's world.

It's a long way from the tiny reforms under the bridge at Ballina where Mick learnt to surf while his mum struggled to bring up four boys on her own.

Mick's parents split up when he was one and he has only recently got to know his dad.

'I took time out. I wanted to get to know him. I didn't want to have any regrets,' he says. 'He's worked his whole life. I want him to quit one day and get on a farm or something, do something cool like that. Hopefully he'll stop next year.'

Mick has repaid all his mum's years of hard work by convincing her to retire from nursing and look after his affairs. 'She was doing my stuff and also doing her stuff at work and she was so stressed. She was actually going for a new job and I said, "Why don't you work for me full time?" She came home and she said, "Well, I didn't get the job," and I said, "You've got a job already, working for me," and she just seems so much happier. Now she's gone to Africa before me. I try and give her a trip a year.'

Family's important to Mick, perhaps a legacy of his Irish ancestry, and he seems to have only one complaint about his current nomadic existence. 'It gets lonely,' he admits. 'Sometimes it's just like, really, really lonely. And you want someone there just to hang out with the whole time, someone you can talk to and stuff. That'd be pretty cool sometimes. Even though you're all going to the same place, you always check in by yourself.'

Now, with Karissa by his side and a wedding planned for 2008, he seems to have solved that problem, and has only one box left to tick, the world title. Yet he manages to keep even that lofty goal in perspective.

'It's the whole reason for being there,' he declares. 'I don't want to get second. I'm focused on that, but also I think the biggest thing is to enjoy it along the way. A lot of people don't enjoy it and if you're not enjoying it, it shows in your results. I think that's a huge thing — just to go and enjoy it and really appreciate why you are where you are. You've got a gift, so enjoy it.'

It seems more than coincidence that the rise of Mick and his fellow Cooly Kids has come in the age of the Superbank, the unnatural build-up of sand from the Tweed River Sand Bypass System which has created a perfect mile-long wave in their backyard. This happy accident of modern coastal engineering has allowed Mick and his contemporaries to refine their surfing to previously unseen levels, performing thirty top turns on a wave, pushing each one a little harder than the last, learning nuances of timing and positioning that wouldn't otherwise be possible. Despite horrendous overcrowding, Mick manages to pick his path through the pack, to dance through the chaos with a speed and creativity unmatched in the surfing world. As in his unlikely ride through life, Mick seems ready to trust in the flow of events, and hurl himself into each new section with speed, commitment and a readiness to adapt to ever-changing circumstances.

'I can be surfing the exact same wave and then sometimes something will just set off, even if I'm riding the same board the whole time. Something will just set off and it feels like you can push just that extra bit harder ... everything just clicks.' He pauses, groping for the words. 'Sometimes things just happen. Sometimes, surfing this bank from Snapper to Kirra, you don't even think what you're doing but you do it anyway. You get to the end of a wave and go, "What did I do?" Sometimes you go into a totally different state of mind.'

'I think every day brings something new to life when you're surfing and in the ocean. You really get to read the weather and see how the planet changes day to day, year to year, the way different climates produce different waves. Sometimes it feels like you can tell when Mother Nature is angry, happy, calm or quiet. You can see this all in the way the ocean looks at first sight. The flow of the waves seems to sooth even the most agitated people. I like to watch people at the beach and how they react to different situations and the most common is they walk away with a smile and drop their shoulders to relax. Surfing has taught me how

to deal with life's situations —
good or bad, people, money, fights,
whatever people come up with
there has been a lesson in surfing to
deal with all that shit on land.
Because every day in the ocean is
different, it really teaches you how
to deal with your own moods.
There have been times where I have
been totally lost in life and surfing
always brought me back to a sane
level of thinking. Just diving in the
ocean or running your feet through
the water really levels out your
inner self and calms everything
down to where it all runs
smoothly again.'

MICK FANNING

buffalo and brian keaulana

{ surfing's first family }

In the ocean, you're in heaven because you're in God's creation. You feel like you're in the arms of love. It heals us physically and spiritually. Whenever my kids were sick, I'd take them to the ocean.

MOMI KEAULANA

As you drive down Farrington Highway along the Waianae coast, you could be forgiven for thinking there has been some kind of natural disaster here and a state of emergency declared. Everywhere along the beach parks, people are living out of old rusted cars, makeshift camps of tarpaulins strung up among the low bent trees, and tents pitched along the foreshore. Not just a few, but hundreds, along every available stretch of beach.

This is the westside of Oahu, the dry leeward coast, the wrong side of the tracks you never see in the tourist brochures. At last count there were more than 3000 homeless people in the area. As many as thirty per cent of school kids are considered homeless and schools now provide washers and dryers so students can do their laundry as well as receive perhaps their only cooked meal of the day. In a sense, a disaster has occurred here, but it is man-made, not natural — the result of ever-escalating real-estate prices that has left even the most basic housing hopelessly out of reach for Oahu's low-income families.

Rundown homes, derelict shops, abandoned cars and fast-food outlets dot the highway. Crime and drugs are rife, the insidious ice turning once-healthy teenagers into thieving zombies. As you drive on, a mounting sense of apprehension grips you. If you've heard the stories you know not to leave any valuables in your car. Rip-offs are common. Visiting surfers who are too pushy in the waves might look shoreward to see their hire car in flames. You are sternly warned not to hang around after dark.

But resist the urge to turn tail and flee back to the package holiday mecca of Waikiki or the overrun surf ghetto of the North Shore, keep driving long enough, and you'll come round a bend to be greeted by majestic, towering volcanic mountains and the most idyllic sweep of golden beach — a picture-perfect scene with swaying palm trees, blue water, quaint beach shacks and a smart hotel out on the point. If there's surf, a perfectly peeling wave will play host to every kind of surfcraft imaginable in easy harmony. Locals sit on the tailgates of their pick-ups playing the ubiquitous ukuleles, talking story, drinking beer. Someone might have been spear fishing and the aroma of grilled fish will waft over from small hibachi barbecues. Families are gathered under sunshades, kids frolic in a whomping shorebreak, elders cruise on longboards, kids bust air on shortboards, bodyboarders spin 360s off the backwash.

This is Makaha, proud stronghold of traditional Hawaiian surf culture. If you have an in here, a whole world opens up to you. If you happen to stumble on the place during local patriarch Buffalo Keaulana's annual Big Board Surfing Classic you are in for a rare treat. For over thirty years Buffalo, now seventy-two, has been running his traditional Hawaiian surf meet. Conceived originally to get his overweight friends back in the surf, it has grown into a celebration of Hawaiian culture and every form of wave-riding under the sun. There are longboards, tandems, canoes, bodyboards, tandem bodyboards, stand-up paddleboards, traditional paipo boards (flat plywood bodyboards). The unique judging system rewards surfers who can best perform a series of oddly named tricks such as the tiki, the buddha, the scooter boy, the helicopter, the king stance and the dying cockroach.

'It's a kind of forced silliness,' observes local surfboard shaper Dave Parmenter, which prevents anyone taking themselves or the contest too seriously. Watching a procession of enormous, well-muscled Hawaiians perform these theatrical tricks with the grace and dexterity of dancers as the crowd hoots and roars with delight from the beach, you are granted a rare glimpse of surfing's roots. Buffalo's is a surf contest unlike any other, with the emphasis on fun and raising community spirits, providing relief from the day-to-day struggles of westside life.

'We were all getting old and fat, so I have a division that is 250 pounds and over,' says Buffalo. 'That's good, I bring my fat friends back to surf. And I have a fifty and over so that brings the old-timers back. My kind of surfing is longboard, ten-foot and over.'

Proceedings begin with a solemn early morning ceremony to bless the event and generate the necessary vibe for a successful surf meet. 'We're Hawaiians. We believe in God and our parents taught us the word, *aloha*, so we try to keep that in mind so we have respect for each other,' says Buff. 'My meet's different from everyone else's because it's not just blow the horn or shoot the gun and start it. It doesn't go like that. We want to thank the gods, and then to start, me or my son paddle out and give a *hokupu*, an offering in the ocean, and then we start. So you cannot say the meet will start at seven o'clock or eight o'clock. It's not going to start until we have the ceremony. That's the Hawaiian way, so everybody's got a good feeling that it's going to be a nice day, and it happens.'

Sure enough, when I attend the thirty-first anniversary event in February 2007, the winds have been howling onshore for days and huge seas and wild weather have made the waves completely unrideable for a week. One local tells me they sat down at the beach on the Friday night before the event, played some music, said a quiet prayer and, right on cue, the winds swung offshore overnight, the swell dropped and cleaned up and contest morning dawned bright, sunny, offshore, and a clean six to eight feet for the whole weekend.

Makaha was once the centre of the surfing world, home to the unofficial world title, the prestigious Makaha International, which kicked off in 1954, the only gathering of the global surf tribe before an official world championship and eventually a pro world tour evolved.

Buffalo grew up virtually homeless in Makaha, after his father died in a dockside accident before he was born, and a violent stepfather forced him to seek the shelter of friends and neighbours. He'd wait in the shorebreak for stray boards and quickly catch waves before their owners retrieved them, and became an expert bodysurfer before his great talent on a surfboard emerged. He placed highly in the Makaha International throughout the late '50s and early '60s, winning it in 1960. He was park keeper and then lifeguard at Makaha for over thirty-four years, ushering several of his sons into the profession before finally retiring at the age of sixty. He remains a kind of unofficial mayor, or king, of Makaha, with royal ancestry stretching back to the great King Kamehameha.

Buffalo was at the forefront of the renaissance of Hawaiian culture in the '70s, a crew member of the *Hokule'a*, a replica of the ancient Hawaiian double-hulled canoes that retraced the journey of the Polynesians between Tahiti and Hawaii using traditional navigation by the stars.

'It all started because I went on the *Hokule'a*. When we reached Tahiti and I came back I was kinda like a hero with the island and everyone kinda looked up to me,' says Buff. 'Because I came back a hero everybody was happy, and it made me realise this is our culture and we should share what we have.'

Buff decided to hold an old-style Hawaiian surf meet, but knew the westside's heavy reputation would deter people from coming. 'A lot of young boys would rip off cars, like thirty, forty of them from here to Nanakuli [a distance of some 15 km]. The whole Waianae coast only had four policemen, from Nanakuli to Makaha. Now there's 400.'

Buffalo called a meeting of the troublesome young men of the westside. He told them of his plans for a surf meet and forbade any acts of thievery for the weekend of the contest. Like a royal decree, it was observed by even the most wayward youth. 'I would talk to all the boys and say, "We have to cater to the *haoles* so they can come surf with us," and they'd say, "Nah, not with those *haoles*," and I'd say, "No, let 'em come. We give them two good days here. While they stay here, thou shalt not steal, or you're going to get a licking. I'll find out and you'll get a licking." So what we did was, we don't let the cars park just anywhere they want to. They park in the parking lot where we can watch them. The rest of the year they're going to rip off your cars, I can't stop them, but little by little we can make two days and pretty soon they will start respecting each other. And more people will come. Great entertainers from Honolulu have come out here. Don Ho was one of our first sponsors.'

Part of Buff's concept was to end the isolation that the Waianae's fearsome reputation had created. Makaha is almost the end of the road and few outsiders venture there since the end of the old Makaha International days. Buff recognised that embracing the outside world, setting aside the resentment of a displaced people in an occupied land, was vital to improving the lot of the Waianae people.

'Then we had a lot of white people come and a lot of good feeling was happening,' says Buff.

Even so, there is good reason to approach Makaha with a degree of caution. 'We always warn people, when the sun sets: "Go home. Do not stay here. You can sleep here Saturday because we all here, but Sunday go home. Don't hang around, because we cannot control everyone. Everybody go back to their old ways."'

The Saturday night, when all the locals camp out at the beach, is a rare glimpse of what Hawaii might once have been like before the devastation wrought by European settlement. Freshly caught fish sizzle on barbecues, the ukuleles, songs and stories come out. Kids play on the beach late into the night. Whole families sleep under the stars.

A film crew from the Discovery Channel are on hand to document this year's event, as a window into Hawaiian culture. They are shown royal hospitality but are not above being the butt of local jokes. When one of the cameramen comes to grief on an oversized bodyboard, known as a bullyboard, in the tricky Makaha shorebreak, the contest commentator is straight onto him. 'There's our man from the Discovery Channel, discovering how hard it is to ride a bullyboard,' he quips over the loudspeakers, to uproarious laughter from the beach gallery.

The Keaulanas are giving the Discovery crew the full gamut of traditional Hawaiian practices. 'My son Brian went out canoeing and stand-up paddling, and then my son Jimmy went net fishing, and Rusty took them up the mountain to hunt pigs,' reports Buff.

The result should be a fascinating portrait of a family who live as close as possible to a traditional Hawaiian lifestyle in the twenty-first century. 'The Discovery Channel is doing pretty well and we're only charging them $200,' says Buff dryly. 'But we let that go for now because I tell the boys, "You gotta give your time." They say, "I should get paid for what I do." You should but you're nobody until they find out who you are, then they'll pay you. But you're nobody now, you gotta give your time.'

Despite the laidback Hawaiian surfer image, Buffalo is not one to preach an idle, surf-for-today short-sightedness. Surfing is just one part of a holistic ocean-based existence that makes up the Hawaiian lifestyle — more a means to become better acquainted with the ocean than an end in itself. 'You cannot say, well, I'll just go surfing. If you just go surfing and go home, don't expect to eat because you didn't bring anything. The first thing you got to do is go fish, catch something, put it away, and then you can play, and when you go home you've got something. Like a hunter — they don't go, "Oh, let's go hiking," know what I mean? They hunt to get something — a bird or a pig.'

It's a lesson Buffalo's oldest son, Brian, appears to have learnt particularly well. Buffalo's sons are all accomplished watermen. Rusty is a three-time world longboard champion and Jimmy is a lifeguard, but it is

Brian who appears set to inherit the mantle from his father as community leader. Brian has used his lifeguarding and ocean skills to launch a multi-layered career as a professional surfer, businessman, stuntman and, more recently, film director. He says the ocean has taught him everything he's needed for these varied vocations.

'It's everything. It's my grade school, my high school, my college. It's a full education,' says Brian. 'And the ocean is a harsh educator — you have to learn really fast. My father was like my guide my whole life. He'd take me out as a bag boy when we go out fishing. He took me out when I was three months old surfing. We used to have a double-storey house right on the beach here and my dad was park keeper and he used to make rescues all the time. My mum remembers, it was right about this time when the sun is in your eyes and she was upstairs, and she goes, "Wow, look at that dark man with that white baby surfing the big waves." The waves were eight feet, and no leashes back then. She looked outside to the silhouette of this guy, and was yelling downstairs to my dad, "Look, there's this dummy out there with his kid in big surf." Then she looked downstairs and saw his board was gone, and she looked again at his silhouette, and she looked at me and started freaking. She ran to the beach yelling and swearing. Dad caught two waves and came in. She was hitting him with one hand and grabbing me with the other.'

But that early schooling in the ocean helped make Brian one of the greatest all round watermen in the world today, skilled on any kind of surfcraft: longboard or shortboard, canoe, or jet ski or stand-up paddleboard.

'I was born and raised on this beach here. This is my backyard. My father taught me not just about surfing but how to play, how to work. We would surf on anything and it didn't really matter if it was a McDonald's tray or a piece of driftwood,' says Brian. 'One thing about the ocean, that's my biggest teacher, water is fluid. Mould yourself like water and adapt. The ocean is always adapting. It can be calm or it can be fierce, and it's all about respecting the ocean and respect is another word for educate.'

Brian was the first to recognise the potential to use jet skis in surf rescue, after one particularly nasty wipeout at Waimea Bay, and he invented the rescue sled which is now standard equipment behind jet skis. It's no exaggeration to say there are probably hundreds, if not thousands, of people alive today because of Brian's innovation.

'I was in the first Eddie Aikau [big wave contest] at Waimea. I wiped out on one huge wave and I was underwater for a long time. I struggled up to the surface and the next behemoth was right there, right? At that time, if something happened, you could only help the guy after he comes out of the impact zone. Squiddy Sanchez [lifeguard] had a stand-up ski and he came over to me right as I came up from the first wave. He looked down and said, "Brian, are you all right?" I looked up at him and went, "Yeah." He couldn't grab me with the stand-up ski so he got out of there. I got hit by the next wave and driven under, and the whole time I was freaking out because, as a lifeguard, I've literally seen people drown and die in front of my eyes, looking into the impact zone and trying to get them to come out. I remember this one guy who died actually out here [Makaha]. We never found his body. It was a long time ago and I was just out of high school. I never forgot that . . .

'So when I survived that two-wave wipeout thing, I went home and got every single magazine to do with jet skis and started researching and found the first Waverunners that came out. So I made a loan for five grand, went down to the airport where they sell the jet skis and bought one that very next day.'

He practised rescue drills with fellow lifeguard Terry Ahue, but found it was difficult to pull someone out of the water onto the ski. 'So I went home, thought about it, got one boogie board and started braiding up the bodyboard with a bit of rubber hose and ropes. I hooked it up to the ski and it was all trial and error from that day on.' Thus, the rescue sled was born.

But others were not so enthusiastic about the presence of jet skis in the surf. 'I went through so much grief. I remember one time going to Sunset and rescuing seven people: going out, pulling people in, and back out. And when I came in to the beach one of the officers there — I can't mention what division — wrote me one ticket. And I told him, "Ay, those people would have drowned," and he said, "It's illegal, that's the law." So, if that's the law I'm going to fight it in court. I went to court and I called every single doctor, police, every single person I rescued, everyone, and showed up in force and went there, told the judge what I was doing and the judge freaked out. He looked at the officer and said, "The law is there to protect people." The judge was so mad he wanted to throw him in jail, so they threw it out of court.'

To convince local councils of the value of jet skis, Brian invited them to sit in a lifeguard tower and consider the everyday scenarios lifeguards face, when they might have to make life and death decisions about who to rescue first. 'When we sit down and look at the water, sometimes you almost feel like God because you've got to choose: if you've got a double drowning there and another guy knocked out here, and you're only one, who do you run to? Who do you save? So we took the city council people down to Pipeline and we put them in our place and gave them the scenario! OK, you choose. And they freaked out. It's a heavy emotional decision, like triage.'

It's been a long battle, but jet skis and rescue sleds are now accepted as standard equipment in surf rescues, and Brian and his colleagues have travelled the world training other lifeguards in their use.

'That's been our culture, to share, and we wanted to share everything with everyone in the whole world. We could have patented the sled but we felt it's better to just let it explode. More people make sleds — that means more people get rescued. My greatest success is sharing my knowledge, creating people like me that can be better than me.'

He proved the value of the jet ski again and was awarded the United States Lifesaving Association medal of honour in 1993 for the daring rescue of a tourist trapped in an ocean cave at the notorious Kaena Point, on the north-west top of Oahu.

'He went to the Moi Hole to take pictures with his girl and got washed over the side,' Brian recalls. 'Humungous waves. They've got pictures of Kaena Point, 100-foot faces, not a place to play with. And the guy was trapped in a cave for two and a half hours. It was lucky on his part as well as ours that we got him out.'

How did they get him out? 'With the ski, and luck and timing. Pretty much everything you learn you put to use,' he says. 'I had maybe five lifeguards standing there so I run up, now I've got to choose between these five lifeguards. In choosing I'm thinking to myself, I'm risking my life to go in there and now I've got to choose who and they might die. It was pretty heavy. Everybody there was like, "Don't pick me," but between all five guys, no matter what, they would have gone.' In a break between the sets exploding over the cave entrance, Brian reversed the ski into the cave, and his partner Earl Bungo swam into the inky darkness with a flotation tube, following the stricken tourist's cries for help. With only seconds to work with, they got him onto the ski and accelerated out of danger before the next set inundated the cave.

Not content with ocean-based training, Brian has seized any opportunities to educate himself in the science of what he calls 'risk management'. He even undertook a military training course, finding unlikely parallels there between bombs and enemy fire on one hand and rogue sets exploding on an outer reef on the other. 'I walked into my officer in command's main office, and I saw this paper crumpled up in the waste basket, and I saw "risk" and something else. I reached in and pulled it out and saw this risk management class that the military was offering . . . and inviting any emergency government entities that wanted to participate. I said I wouldn't mind checking it out. Everybody was saying, "Ah, that's military, it's got nothing to do with water." It wasn't about water, but I wanted to learn and I ended up signing up, went and did this risk management course and learnt a whole bunch. What we'd been doing was the right thing, but there's a process, step by step. It makes everything so much smoother, so much more efficient. I learnt so much in that one week. When I came back I applied that, and then I went back for an instructor's course with the US Army Safety Center. They're talking range and bombs and explosions and guns and planes and calibres and all kinds of stuff. And when I was writing notes I would write down, impact zone, shorebreak, strong current, reef, you know, just all the different things that applied to us, but they were all similar things.'

Brian's unique range of skills has kept him in demand in a diverse array of roles. When Kevin Costner embarked on his mega-budget Hollywood epic, *Waterworld*, it was Brian he employed to oversee ocean safety. When surfwear brand Billabong announced a million-dollar bounty for the first person to ride a 100-foot wave, it was Brian they asked to train the world's top big wave riders in safety and jet ski rescues. He even trains Hawaii's other emergency services. 'I recently trained our own people here with the Hawaii fire department, and then just a couple of weeks ago I trained the Hawaiian SWAT team.'

His calm under pressure and ability to adapt, ocean-like, to any situation, has seen Brian's film career expand far beyond ocean stunts. His film and TV credits as stuntman, actor or stunt director include: *50 First Dates*, *The Big Bounce*, *Blue Crush*, *Baywatch*, *In God's Hands*, *Memoirs of a Geisha*, *North Shore*, *Pearl Harbor*, *Waterworld* and *Rescue 911*.

'I've done film work since I was seventeen, just little gigs. I learnt to work smarter, not harder. I saw other guys doing the same thing but they were getting more pay than me. I was doing lifeguarding work and I'd look at one guy doing stunt work and go, "Wow, how come I'm risking myself and not getting the cash or the credit?" And trying to understand the process — like there's union issues, and pecking orders and all that kind of stuff. I got into the Screen Actor's Guild and I recently joined the Director's Guild, which is hard to do. You have to get endorsed by, like, three directors to get in and then you've got to pay your dues. I've been directing a lot of action for years in the water, and finally I got credited in cash. It's good, and eventually I'll probably do my own movie. We're working towards that.'

At the 2004 Hawaii International Film Festival, Brian received the Film in Hawaii Award, in recognition of his contribution to the film industry. 'In my mind, Brian is a modern-day Duke Kahanamoku,' says film commissioner Donne Dawson. 'He has become an ambassador for Hawaii and our film industry.'

The morning after Buffalo's event, the scene down at Makaha Beach could not be more different to the down-home scenes of the weekend. The locals are mildly outraged that the entire beach car park is taken over by enormous film trucks. Actors, extras, crew, cameramen and directors swarm all over the beach, barking directions. The latest cheesy Hollywood interpretation of the surfing lifestyle is under way, with its skinny Californian white boys awkwardly clutching tiny surfboards, and bikini girls preening themselves on beach towels. There is no way the Makaha community would tolerate it if Brian wasn't involved. But they are employing a few locals, and involving Waianae High School media students in the production so they can learn about the film industry first-hand.

Brian turns up at the beach around midday, clearly drained from the weekend's event, having competed in half a dozen different divisions, and made the finals of most of them. He's shielding bleary eyes behind sunglasses but looks every inch the Hollywood player, cleanshaven and smartly dressed, smoothing over local concerns about the beach parking and tending to his Hollywood connections. He seems to have inherited his father's role of looking after the local community and creating opportunities for their youth. 'The best thing is I get to employ a lot of my family and friends,' he grins, while keeping all his plates spinning.

'I had the greatest teachers in the world for what not to do. I was surrounded by drugs and violence,' says Brian, of his westside upbringing. 'My dad always said, "Spend more time in the water. I know you're safe."'

Yet, amid the many perils and challenges of westside life, the Keaulanas and the Makaha surf community have managed to maintain their own little bubble of *aloha*, a side of Hawaii you won't find in the tourist traps of Waikiki or the snarling surf colosseums of the North Shore.

'That's the thing with my mum and dad: everybody becomes part of our family, and that's always been our way. It doesn't matter if you're Hawaiian blood. Anyone who's involved in the water becomes part of our family,' says Brian.

Buffalo concurs: 'If you were born in Hawaii and raised in Hawaii you're a Hawaiian, but if you've been here and you understand what we're doing then you're Hawaiian in heart. It's good. If you're white, yellow, red, black, we're all Hawaiian. We learn how to share. Hawaiians, we love to share.'

tom blake

{ voice of the waves }

Waikiki has been kind to me. The native Hawaiians have been kind. I have had the honour of riding the big surfs with these Hawaiians — I have sat at their luaus — watched their most beautiful women dance the hulas. I have been invited into their exclusive Hui Nalu surfriding club, a club for natives only. I have held the honour position [bow seat] riding waves in their outrigger canoe, the honour position [holding down the rigging] on the sailing canoe. I have been initiated into the secrets of spear fishing far out on the coral reefs.

Tom Blake was one of the first mainland American surfers to spend prolonged periods in the Hawaiian Islands, and experience the traditional Hawaiian surfing lifestyle up close and personal. As such, he is seen as the pivotal link between the ancient origins of waveriding and modern surf culture.

Blake was a champion swimmer in the 1920s and '30s, who became a top lifeguard and surfer, then moved from California to Hawaii and studied at the feet of the great Hawaiian surfers of the day such as Duke Kahanamoku.

Blake is revered by US surf historians as the originator of many elements of modern surf culture: lifestyle, board design, fashion, attitude. 'If Duke Kahanamoku is rightfully known as the father of modern surfing, then Tom Blake was its midwife,' writes Drew Kampion, veteran surf writer, in the foreword to *Tom Blake: The Uncommon Journey of a Pioneer Waterman*, a biography written by Blake's friend Gary Lynch with Malcom Gault-Williams and William K. Hoopes.

Blake's many achievements and innovations include setting the world ten-mile open swimming record in 1922, being the first to surf Malibu Point in 1926, inventing the hollow surfboard and paddleboard, inventing the waterproof camera housing, inventing the sailboard, patenting and manufacturing the first production surfboard, inventing the surfboard fin or skeg, publishing the first book solely devoted to surfing, *Hawaiian Surfboard*, in 1935, producing and patenting the first torpedo tube and rescue ring for lifesaving, and helping to pioneer the physical fitness and natural diet movement.

He also developed a sophisticated philosophy around the lifestyle and lessons of surfing, best summed up by his famous equation, 'Nature = God', and an informal religion he termed the Church of the Open Sky.

His essay 'Voice of the Waves', written in 1968, is perhaps the most complete articulation of a philosophy of surfing in existence. This edited extract is reprinted with the kind permission of Spencer Croul and the Croul Family Foundation, keepers of the Blake archives. Blake passed away in May 1994, in Ashland, Wisconsin, at the age of ninety-two.

Voice of the Waves

There is more than meets the eye to the deep water swells as they march majestically across the sea, to the silent drums of the atom. Dedicated sailors of all times knew this. So do surf riders who have spent years of their lives viewing these waves at close range, as the locked-in power is released upon the reefs and shores in a symphony of sound and shapes of strange dimensions.

All of this the surf rider has going for him, and he experiences a peculiar joy and inner satisfaction in putting this force to work under a board. This may be because that force is a spiritual, a divine force that has been in production by nature or God for a long time. Why say nature or God? Just this: over the years, the close association with waves of all kinds, coupled with a religious background, has convinced this old surf rider that nature is synonymous with God. So the word nature, for all practical purposes may usefully be used as an alternative to the word God, to better understand life, living and the ocean waves as part of the Almighty and thus give due credit and respect for its mysterious hidden energy. The same formula applies to all things; each has a bit of the divine power to sustain it, be it an atom, a wave, or man . . .

Each water atom, and there are billions in the smallest wave, is a model of order, harmony and rhythm. Thus, the atom becomes a key point of reference to logic, to right action, in judging the wave as well as all problems in life. Is it any wonder then that the surf rider gets such satisfaction from riding a wave? For the period of the ride, he has this God-given energy going for him, instead of passing by him. One might rightly say surf riding is prayer of a high order, that the sea is a beautiful church, the wave a silent sermon . . .

From the standpoint of health, surf riding is constructive, if pursued correctly. To the mind it teaches one the wisdom of patience, the art of waiting for the right moment to act; for you cannot ride a wave until it comes along. So it is with life: there is a right time and place for everything; nothing good or right occurs contrary to this rule. This, in turn tells one to accept the vicissitudes of life as just and well, as being the inevitable reaction of mass and energy, to the law of compulsion in nature, God or the wave.

Physically, the strenuous paddling and swimming associated with surfing is obviously beneficial and appealing to young growing bodies, especially teenage boys and girls, judging by the popularity of the pastime during the last two decades in Hawaii, Australia, South Africa, South America, France, England and Japan. Surf riding also carries enough built-in danger to give one a healthy respect for those beautiful waves. They can strike back, sometimes with death dealing force, if the rider commits too great an error, becomes careless in judgement of their hidden power. So it is in dealing with our fellow men; that same principle also applies to our life: respect the rules and guidelines and enjoy the ride, disrespect the inner natural or godly power of anything, and reap sorrow and pain, in like measure.

While on a board, either surf riding or paddling, one is truly free from land-bound restrictions. For that hour, he is captain of his fate, of his miniature ship. The burden of city, school, job, as well as the cares and worries of the subconscious mind are erased and forgotten, until the tensions of living build up again. The remedy again is obvious; go surfing. Next time you leave the shore for some fun, look and listen for the muted voice of the atom, the voice of the wave, the voice of the good earth, and you, too, may hear the drum beat. Those who have, say it goes like this:

'All is well.'

'Surfing has taught me balance, in the ocean and on a board, but it also translates to life and how you live it. The ocean tells us we have to let life happen and fit into it the right way for us but also that a lot more things are possible when you look at it from different perspectives.'

KELLY SLATER

'One day,
the whole world
will surf.'

BERNARD 'MIDGET' FARRELLY,
1964 WORLD SURFING CHAMPION

afterword

{ a slightly indulgent and esoteric ramble from the author }

I've been writing about surfing — for a living — for twenty years. Seriously. I know, I know, the taxation department finds it far-fetched too. And maybe claiming depreciation on surfboards is a bit rich.

But there have got to be some pay-offs for this precarious existence, right? Or maybe the sheer thrill of the ride should be enough.

Surf writing has taken me all over the world, through a pretty radical couple of decades in surfing's evolution. Twenty years ago who could've imagined billionaire surfwear moguls and stock market floats, Internet web cams and global swell maps, surfboard super-factories in Thailand, China and Slovakia, Gucci's own designer surfboards, an eight-time world champ in Kelly Slater and a forty-year-old Mark Occhilupo still on tour, the quest for 100-foot waves and aerial loops assisted by jet skis, luxury surf charters to the four corners of the globe and pro contests at remote tropical reefs beamed around the world via satellite on something called the world wide web?

There's been plenty to write about. Yet, having reached forty myself, with a young family, a dog, two cars and a mortgage, some days I sit at my computer, attempting to find new ways to describe people riding waves, and wonder what the hell I'm doing.

Sure, all kinds of people write about all manner of human activity — sport, the arts, politics, sex, business, religion — for their entire working lives, and might never be troubled by concerns that it is juvenile or repetitive or just a wee bit, well, stunted. So why is it that as the big 4-0 sailed by I experienced an unsettling feeling that I had failed to grow up, that the adult world of career goals and respectability had passed me by? Why do I feel the need to defend surfing, or at least the vocation of writing about it?

Surfing has transformed my life — from a be-suited city newspaper reporter to a barefoot, work-at-home freelance surf scribe. It's an existence which, while sometimes financially precarious, is rich in lifestyle, with an office at the beach and the best excuse in the world for lots of indulgent field research. It has introduced me to characters, carried me to places, delivered experiences I could never have dreamt up back in that newspaper office. This journey and the lessons contained therein have opened my mind to a different way of approaching the world from the conservative career-climbing grind that may have been my genetic and cultural inheritance. That is, that life is there to be lived, paddled into with relish and joy, that true free expression in each moment is life's great goal.

I'd been a dour maths–science student at high school, swatting relentlessly, coating my bedroom walls and ceiling and toilet door with mathematical equations and the periodic table of elements, sitting one practice exam after another all through my study leave — in pursuit of what lofty goal I still have no idea. I can still quote the first twenty elements of the periodic table, though the ability has never come in particularly handy. All the hard work paid off with impressive exam results but no clear career direction. 'You could have been anything,' old school chums would taunt me, as if I'd wasted my supposed potential with this frivolous business of surfing magazines.

So, I'd become possessed with a desire, a need, to explain surfing to people — the wonder, the magic, the absolute, intoxicating bliss of it all — to justify my apparent forfeiting of serious career goals. Don't they know what it is to speed along inside a watery, cascading tunnel, chasing an almond eye of sunlight? To be held underwater to the limits of your lungs' endurance? To suck that first, lifesaving gulp of oxygen milliseconds before the next wave erupts on top of you? To travel to remote and exotic lands on the mere whisper of a quality wave? To have gangs of Third World village kids scream and cheer on your every ride and mob you on the beach?

Still, even I harboured a sense that I was somehow cheating, pulling off an elaborate ruse or scam that would catch up with me one day, when I'd have to give up the fun and games, grow up and get a real job. It hasn't happened yet, though parenthood and provider instincts have tested the ruse to its limits. So far, with some small wobbles, it has held firm.

With a young family, I do not travel nearly as much as I once did — giving rise to reflection on the journey thus far, and a simple desire to share it. I'm sure all kinds of people have led far more exciting, adventurous and productive lives than mine. It is not really my story I wish to tell, but surfing's: its strange passage from renegade counter-culture to multi-billion-dollar global industry, and the extraordinary parade of maniacs, misfits and uncanny amphibians who have fed its rich folklore. Or maybe it's both our stories. I sometimes feel like surfing and I have passed each other going in opposite directions. I ditched my suit and tie, quit my job, my established city life and career security to chase the magic and adventure surfing held. Meanwhile, sometimes it seems surfing has relinquished the magic and adventure in its quest for mainstream acceptance and industry growth. While I grew drunk on the thrill of the ride, many surfers around me grew canny, ambitious, rich and materialistic.

What keeps us all coming back to the same path are the simple, timeless, life lessons the ocean carries, even as surfing morphs and evolves almost beyond recognition.

Veteran surf writer Drew Kampion says, 'Life is a wave and your attitude is your surfboard.' Someone famous (I can't for the life of me remember who) once said something like, 'Make your life a masterpiece, every thought and action a brush stroke.' The same principle applies to the surfer of life, except the waverider is also instructed by a powerful imperative of self-preservation, an immediate awareness of the consequences of miscalculation. Ride too high and you can be lip launched. Push too hard and you'll spin out. Get too deep and you might not come back out again. But hesitate, and you're almost certainly going to get pitched. Surfers often say the safest place is in the tube, in the vortex of the breaking wave, holding your line steady even as chaos erupts all round you. Keeping this focus and clarity in the midst of turbulent and intense situations is a great ability to develop, especially in the times we live in.

There is a vibration we feel in peak moments — sex, art and music-making, great surf sessions, intense interactions with the natural world, even using some prohibited substances — a buzz we get that makes us feel like our very being is humming. I believe this vibration is with us at all times. It's what yogis know as *om*, the eternal, universal sound. These intense experiences simply still the intellectual mind, the chattering monkey, long enough for us to feel our core state, this vibration. If we are not used to it, we might almost feel unwell, simply through unfamiliarity with the sensation. This is where meditation takes us, after many hours of often painful sitting, and much practice. Surfing seems to take us there instantly: it absolutely requires us to be present in the moment, or else we will fall off. It is the ultimate flow experience. 'I think it goes beyond flow,' says surfing scientist Vezen Wu. 'I think it's more like nirvana.'

A few years ago, I went on a Vipassana meditation retreat, as my preparation for fatherhood: ten days of silent sitting, up to twelve hours a day, with only short breaks to stretch one's legs. By the end of this often painful process, I felt like I was truly humming. It was a profound, wonderful, life-changing experience. Surfing delivers a very potent dose of this same feeling, in incredibly short and intense bursts, so that one surf session, one ride, one moment, can rival the effects of ten days of sitting. If we lived our lives in the same state of consciousness necessary to ride waves, we'd all be enlightened masters. Doing it on land is the hard part. Surfing history is littered with wave-riding geniuses who came to grief in their landlocked lives. Attempting to live in that realm of the peak experience seems to be what brings so many great surfers undone — instead of accepting the peaks and troughs, the ebb and flow, of life on land.

'It's a strange thing to say but I actually feel more at home in the water than I do on land,' says Mark Richards, four-time world champion. 'I wander around on land sometimes feeling awkward and dorky, and then when I get in the water it all comes together.'

Somewhere around day eight of that meditation retreat I had an experience that put me suddenly, deeply in touch with the ocean within me. We are, after all, seventy per cent water. Waves rose and fell through my body. 'Everything arises to pass away,' we were coached. 'Just observe, and notice how everything arises and passes away, without naming or judging. Nothing to hold on to. Nothing to identify with.' Waves of energy were released from my aching hips and lower back, and long-tight muscles spontaneously relaxed. I could go on and on, but I'll spare you. Afterwards, I felt totally renewed, ecstatic.

The only state I know that comes close to it is tube riding.

Like a lot of surfers, I have always craved great tubes as the peak of the waveriding experience. As I came to surfing relatively late in life, and grew up in the landlocked eastern suburbs of Melbourne, memorable tubes were few and far between. I seemed to develop the knack of avoiding great tubes, rather than skilfully weaving through them, even in the land of the long right points, the Gold Coast, my home for the past fifteen years.

My peak experience came after years of frustration with the wondrous Superbank — a mile-long wave inadvertently created by the Tweed River Sand Bypass System. This marvel of modern coastal engineering was designed to keep the Tweed River mouth clear for boats, and replenish beach sand to the Gold Coast beaches to the north. Almost by accident, the regular flow of sand created the longest wave in the country, perhaps the world. Yet the manifestation of such perfection seemed to bring out the worst in human nature. We had been blessed with a mile-long wave, but it became almost impossible to ride it for more than fifty metres without being dropped in on. Like the pearl in Steinbeck's novel of the same name, the riches of the Superbank were a mixed blessing. Local surfers began to curse the place for the crowds and aggression it inspired. We surfers seemed to prove ourselves unworthy of such perfection. I'd limp away from the place time and again defeated and disillusioned, ending up in dumb, pointless hassles, coming in more stressed than when I paddled out.

Then, one day, I just seemed to click in to the place. I paddled out at Snapper with no expectations, floated down the point enjoying the spectacle, scrounged for a few scraps through Rainbow Bay, then found myself drifting off beautiful Greenmount headland, the sun sparkling and the waves spinning, in the perfect position as a set wave loomed. I knew I was in the spot, knew too the way the wave would lurch and drop in to that shallow inside section, the whole thing going down a level, like

Rabbit at Sanur in *Free Ride*. You have to go with that dropping sensation, as the once pristine blue peak turns into a frothy brown dredging machine over the shallow sandbank and you find yourself suddenly squatting, trying to absorb the speed, simply hanging on and letting the wave do the work. I crouched lower, flying through the wave as the lip pitched and curled over me. I ran one hand along the face. Water droplets sparked off my finger tips, the spray almost blinding me, but I didn't care, didn't even feel like I needed to be able to see where I was going. When my vision cleared I could see people looking in at me with a look I knew well — envy, mixed with joy. It remains one of my two best Superbank moments. The other was a looping, triple-barrel mind-melt of stupendous proportions — within my own surfing frame of reference, of course. I know, if I were ever to see an edited video highlights package of my greatest surfing moments, I'd be disappointed. The tube rides weren't as long, the waves not quite as big, the turns not nearly as graceful, as I would like to believe. It doesn't ultimately matter — and no one is making a video of my surfing life. But as humble as my peak experiences have been, there is something in them, some primordial essence that tells me there is stuff of real value in all of that. A way of approaching life — senses heightened, reacting spontaneously in the moment, feeling the shifting terrain under our feet, the subtle pulses and lurches of energy that we have to ride and go with lest they pitch us head first into the drink.

Parenthood has only convinced me of all this anew. As I've dragged myself to the ocean sleep-deprived and overwhelmed by my new responsibilities, I've only had to hurl myself into the waves for it all to be washed away. Even bodysurfing one foot of whitewater for twenty metres seemed enough to somehow re-align my cellular structure and leave me renewed and ready to carry on. A good tube ride, a few brief seconds squatted inside the vortex of the breaking wave, equalled the detoxifying effects of a week at the most upmarket health retreat. Surely these are among the most potent moments a human can experience. I suspect there's something about vortex energy, the swirling spiral of energy found in tubes, the weather systems that create them, water going down our plug holes, and similar phenomena, that may help explain this potency, but all the references I can find on the subject are a little too New Age and esoteric even for my tastes. I await the appearance of a broad-minded, surfing, quantum physicist who will provide the final piece in this metaphysical puzzle.

There remains in me this curious desire for surfing to be understood, not dismissed as a frivolous, trivial diversion or sneered at for the shameless commercialisation it has endured. I'm on no quest to expunge the old surfie, druggie, dropout stigma, mainly because I find that quaint old anachronism wholly more appealing than the current dumbed down, active youth lifestyle marketing vehicle surfing has become. No, rather, I harbour this weird desire for surfing to be seen as somehow noble; in a crazy mixed up world, this simple regard for the cycles of the planet, this observance of nature's laws, should be recognised as profoundly sensible and, even more than that, needed on this tortured orb of ours right now. To sniff the wind, scan the ocean, observe how the dynamic coastal zones are in a constant state of flux, how nature's magical blessings arise oblivious to any timetable of man's making.

I remember interviewing a young Coolangatta surfer one onshore afternoon, as he and his mates lolled about in front of computer games and porn videos — a portrait of precisely the kind of surfer/slacker youth that conservative elements love to condemn. Yet, in an instant, someone detected a change in the wind and the troops were suddenly mobilised. The wind had swung offshore and there were waves to be ridden, as they grabbed boards and towels and wetsuits in a flurry. When I stepped outside, jumped in my car and drove to the beach I noticed scores of similarly mobilised younger surfers on bikes, in cars and on foot, heeding nature's call, like rats scurrying out of their holes at the smell of cheese. How many of us instantly notice a change in the wind as we go about our daily business? I recall checking the surf at Snapper one early morning with an older local when a cool sou'wester sprung up. 'Ah, there's autumn,' he noted, as if that one puff of breeze heralded the change of season. This attunement to nature's elements might yet prove ultimately more valuable than the shrewdest reading of the day's share-market fluctuations, as our planet's thermostat goes increasingly haywire.

We are all going to have to learn to ride the changes that lie ahead. There are peaks and troughs, swells and flat spells, rips and currents, spinning vortices of energy circling our planet with inexhaustible intensity, and sometimes, no matter how obstinately you struggle to paddle through the maelstrom, it is only when you collapse exhausted, surrender to the greater power, that you are carried safely back out in the channel.

The more strung out things become on land, out there in the so-called real world, the more nerve it seems to take to just keep on surfing, instead of obsessing over the stock market or working fourteen-hour days, salting away your super and scrambling up some slippery corporate ladder. Surfing produces nothing but a temporary sense of well-being, leaves behind it only a fleeting wake and fan of sea spray. Yet somehow it seems more important than ever to keep on doing it — as if this blinkered observation of tides and weather patterns and ocean swells might just provide a map through the maze of modern life.

That said, I still marvel at surfers infinitely more dedicated, or obsessive, than I, who seem to chase their surfing dreams almost to their doom, to the point of chaos in their personal and professional lives, dashing relationships, sacrificing careers, cultivating melanoma, racking their bodies, ruining their eyes and ears, estranging loved ones. The image of the surfer, romanticised or exploited or sensationalised in youth, is rarely re-visited in middle or old age. There is no road map to how a lifelong dance with the ocean might end up. Yet I remain convinced we are onto something, and that it is something worth sharing.

Tibetan Buddhist scholar Sogyal Rinpoche provides an insightful commentary on modern surfing culture in his classic text, *The Tibetan Book of Living and Dying*:

'Six realms of existence are identified in Buddhism: gods, demigods, humans, animals, hungry ghosts and hells . . . The main feature of the realm of the gods, for example, is that it is devoid of suffering, a realm of changeless beauty and sensual ecstasy. Imagine the gods: tall, blond surfers, lounging on beaches and in gardens flooded by brilliant sunshine, listening to any kind of music they choose, intoxicated by every kind of stimulant, high on meditation, yoga, bodywork, and ways of improving themselves, but never taxing their brains, never confronting any complex or painful situation, never conscious of their true nature, and so anaesthetised that they are never aware of what their condition really is . . . Some parts of California and Australia spring to mind as the realm of the gods.'

I'd argue this unflattering description reflects surfing simply gorged on and indulged in as a narcotic, an addiction, an avoidance, a numbing and ultimately limiting escape from life. Perhaps surfing's higher virtues become apparent only when we tap into it as an energy to be harnessed and applied to other areas of our lives: art, activism, entrepreneurship, the quality of our human interactions, parenting, care for the planet.

Many surfers decry the growing popularity of surfing, the floundering surf-school flotsam and jetsam at their local beach, the surf billboards and fashion boutiques. While I wince at surfing's cynical misrepresentation, I find it hard to share in the terror and contempt for growing crowds. Perhaps it is because I came late to surfing myself, never lived at the beach until early adulthood, never regarded it as a birthright but, rather, a precious gift. The more of us who taste this sublime ride atop a natural pulse of energy, harnessing yet surrendering to the ocean and the planet's might, the better off we all will be.

Of course, this going with the flow, riding the waves of life, is all very well and certainly sounds alluring enough, but it must be said — if only as a consumer warning to free me from any legal liability for the consequences of its application — that you take your chances out in the ocean, as in life. You could get the ride of your life or be swatted onto bare reef like a fly. But the alternative is not paddling out at all, cowering on the beach or safe and cocooned in front of the TV. There may well be times when that is the wisest option, but it's hardly going to put you in touch with the grandeur of existence. As the great Hawaiian waterman Buffalo Keaulana says: 'It teach you how to respect the ocean. It teach you about God . . . Because if you don't understand about God, if I take you out and drop you out there when the waves are twenty feet, and the wave's going to break on you, pretty quick you're going to say, "Oh my God." See how quick you learn about God.'

Throw our demented world leaders into the shorebreak and let the ocean sort them out, I say. Let them ride like giddy children clutching their foam bodyboards, bounced and buffeted by the breakers until they are washed up wide-eyed and wheezing onto the sand, and see if they still want to send young men and women off to war.

We might not save the world by surfing, but we may yet help keep it a world worth saving.

Acknowledgments

To all the surfers featured in this book, thank you for sharing your stories and time so generously and for considering this humble little venture worthy of your involvement. After twenty years of surf writing, and a little burnt out on reporting pro-surfer utterances, I went looking for wise elders, and thankfully found them in abundance.

To all the photographers — Ted Grambeau, Jon Frank, Sean Davey, the Colonel, Simon Wood, Bob Barker and Mark Metcalf — thanks for your artistry and for making your great surfing images available. All efforts have been made to track copyright of uncredited photos.

Thanks also to all the surfers and others whose thoughts on surfing and wave energy are included here — again, all efforts have been made to track down these people, and seek their permission. In the case of any ommission please contct me via the publisher.

For all kinds of help in many different ways, thanks to Cynthia Y.H. Derosier, Patricia and Sarah Walsh, Steve Pezman, Jenny Darling, Donica Bettanin, Alice Winton, Jack Finlay, Andrew Kidman, Kirk Willcox, Bob Johnson, Dave and Claudia Parmenter, the Keaulana family, Midget Farrelly, Lama Kinley, John Bilderback, Jeri Edwards,

John Peck, George Downing, Sean Doherty, and the magazines that regularly print my work — *Surfing World*, *Surfing Life*, *the Surfers Path* and *the Surfers Journal*.

Thanks to Spencer Croul and the Croul Family Foundation (keepers of the Blake archive) for permission to use the extract from Tom Blake's seminal essay, 'Voice of the Waves'. The Go-Betweens lyric was written by Robert Forster and Grant McLennan and printed courtesy of Complete Music Publishing Ltd.

Thanks also to Alison Urquhart at Harper Collins for listening to my garbled and nervous explanations of this whacky idea, for being prepared to pitch it to management, and for somehow getting it over the line. Enormous gratitude to Jennifer Blau and Jonathan Shaw for sensitive and patient editing, Graeme Murdoch for the brilliant cover design and Matt Stanton for his inspired internal design.

And, ultimately, all due recognition and devotion to the exquisite Kirsten and our astounding children, Vivi and Alex, for patiently and graciously indulging me, creating the space and time for me to pursue another far-fetched means of supporting us. And for not even blinking when I announced I had to go to Hawaii for a week to finish the book, while our little boy was teething and our big girl started school. And for understanding that I'm much more use to all of us after an hour or two in the ocean.

also by Tim Baker . . .

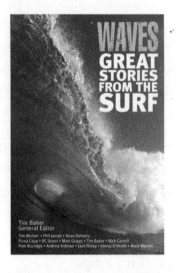

Waves: Great Stories from the Surf

This collection of great Australian surf stories sheds new light on the 'moveable feast' that is modern surfing, and gives an intimate insider's view of the mad compulsion to ride waves — whatever the costs.

If you've never surfed, these stories will make you want to start. If you already surf, they'll remind you why you're never going to stop . . .